Miguel Fernandes
91 969 99 19
maestro@netc.pt

PRESCRIPTIONS FOR CHORAL EXCELLENCE

PRESCRIPTIONS FOR CHORAL EXCELLENCE

Tone, Text, Dynamic Leadership

Shirlee Emmons
Constance Chase

OXFORD
UNIVERSITY PRESS
2006

OXFORD
UNIVERSITY PRESS

Oxford University Press, Inc., publishes works that further
Oxford University's objective of excellence
in research, scholarship, and education.

Oxford   New York
Auckland   Cape Town   Dar es Salaam   Hong Kong   Karachi
Kuala Lumpur   Madrid   Melbourne   Mexico City   Nairobi
New Delhi   Shanghai   Taipei   Toronto

With offices in
Argentina   Austria   Brazil   Chile   Czech Republic   France   Greece
Guatemala   Hungary   Italy   Japan   Poland   Portugal   Singapore
South Korea   Switzerland   Thailand   Turkey   Ukraine   Vietnam

Copyright © 2006 by Oxford University Press, Inc.

Published by Oxford University Press, Inc.
198 Madison Avenue, New York, New York 10016

www.oup.com

Oxford is a registered trademark of Oxford University Press

Library of Congress Cataloging-in-Publication Data
Emmons, Shirlee.
Prescriptions for choral excellence : tone, text, dynamic leadership /
Shirlee Emmons and Constance Chase.
p. cm.
Includes bibliographical references (p.).
ISBN-13 978-0-19-518242-2
ISBN 0-19-518242-1
1. Choral conducting.   2. Choral singing—Instruction and study.
3. Voice culture.   I. Chase, Constance.   II. Title.
MT875.E46 2005
782.5'145—dc22   2005010623

1 3 5 7 9 8 6 4 2

Printed in the United States of America
on acid-free paper

PREFACE

Prescriptions for Choral Excellence has a prevailing idea: Knowing the voice and doing what is good for voices serves everyone—the singers, the audience, the conductor, and the music. We intend to inform our readers of some facts they may not fully understand in the realms of breath management, tonal beauty, intelligible diction, the vocal instrument, legato, agility, and so on. Further, our purpose is to inform in a way that can be understood by those who have not spent their days in a vocal studio and do not intend to.

Even so, understanding the vocal needs of choral singers does not itself fulfill all your directorial needs. What good is a fund of technical vocal knowledge unless accompanied by an ability to communicate and to persuade singers to do what you want? Knowing how to lead requires skill and information; *Prescriptions for Choral Excellence* includes a survey of current leadership theory—covering group, individual, and leader psychology—as well as the most up-to-date information on the nature of practice, mental skills, and performance psychology, structuring both subjects in ways that apply directly to the choral setting.

How to Use This Book

Each chapter opens with a table of contents for that chapter, showing the major sections. Each chapter section commences with a short overview of the subject. We have borrowed terms from the medical profession to address the vocal skills and leadership issues.

> The **Complaint** contains the initial question(s), as a person suffering from some medical complaint would tell a doctor what is troubling him or her.
>
> **Dx, the Diagnosis** contains a brief discussion of the state of the disease and the possible remedies available to the patient.
>
> **Rx, the Treatment Plan** contains the remedy/solution (without a digression to medical/scientific jargon) that spells out the course of treatment.

The rationale behind the suggested treatment is presented in a section that follows the Treatment Plan, through a Discussion of the problem. The

Science boxes contain the scientific background for each assertion. Occasionally, principles are illustrated with true anecdotes, called Science in Application, also set apart in boxes.

Part I deals with technical vocal skills: what the skills are and why, and how to teach choral singers to execute them. Part II addresses the director's self-development: common leadership problems and solutions, mental performance skills, and imagery, as well as rehearsal and practice theory and techniques.

Using the index, the reader will find broad subjects, such as vowel modification. Under the vowel modification index entry, the reader will see an array of individual topics, as in the sample listing below:

Vowel modification
    blend and,
    chart for,
    clarity of diction and,
    the complete vowel modification charts,
    "corners,"
    exercises,
    forte singing and,
    frequency of vowels,
    intonation and,
    methods for teaching of,
    the passaggio and,

The appendixes contain material of peripheral import such as vocal health recommendations, both restorative and preventative.

The reader should expect to encounter some repetition in the text. Directors will refer to different questions at various times, and the information does overlap to a degree. Because we have made no effort to avoid repetitions of salient facts, directors will have before them all the pertinent information related to one subject. Faced with that which is already familiar, they can opt either to pass over it or to reconsider its relation to the topic.

The basic organization and some material of chapter 7 have been extracted from Hughes et al., 1996, and adapted to serve the needs of choral directors and choral singers. Additional material has been extracted from notes taken during several long conferences (March 2000) with Alma Thomas, British performance psychologist and coauthor with Shirlee Emmons of *Power Performance for Singers* (New York: Oxford University Press, 1998).

The material in chapter 9 has also been extracted from *Power Performance for Singers*, as has other material, as noted where it appears. All this material is used by permission.

ACKNOWLEDGMENTS

First, our thanks to the scores of directors, singers, accompanists, and voice teachers whose enthusiasm for the concept of this text encouraged us during the years of its development.

We thank the voice students who brought to us their choral/vocal challenges, as well as directors John Motley, Christopher Reynolds, and David Anderson, who contributed their ideas about what directors want and need to know. Our grateful appreciation to the singers in the choirs of Constance Chase, with whom joyful and productive hours were and are spent in rehearsal and performance.

We are obliged to the forty-two choral directors who responded to our survey, "The Choral Voice," in January 1998. Chief among those who shared their noteworthy convictions were Peter Bagley, Richard Cox, the late Bruce G. Lunkley, Edward Matthiessen, and the late William McIver. We were enlightened by all who responded and are beholden to them for their input.

Our gratitude to three choral directors whose expertise and artistry always inspire: Richard Cox, Patrick Gardner, and Robert Page. We are doubly indebted to Pat for his generous gift of time and his sage, constructively critical eye.

Maribeth Anderson Payne provided generous initial editorial support and guided us directly to Oxford University Press; we also owe thanks to John Finney for an early reading, John Motley for a continual reading, and to all three for cheerful support.

Our colleague, friend, and mentor, Alma Thomas, has gifted us with a supplementary education on mental preparation and performance skills, and, in addition, shared with us her extraordinary knowledge about group dynamics. What we continue to learn from her makes us better performers and more sensitive teachers.

Our sincere thanks to Kim Robinson, our editor at Oxford, and to assistant editor Eve Bachrach, both of whom edited with kindness and expertise and guided us with discernment and with unwavering patience and support. Assistant editor Norman Hirschy earned our gratitude by guiding us through the terrain of preproduction with enthusiasm and kindness.

We are gratified by the technical assistance and input of fellow musicians Janelle Penn, Jackie Jones, Troy Messner, Erik Johanson, Mark Rehnstrom, Emily Faxon, Lisa Bressler, Marka Young, and Joshua Fein.

To our husbands, Rollin Baldwin and Randall Chase, deep appreciation for unfailing sustenance and support of every kind. To our children— Hilary Baldwin and Joseph Guagliardo, and Alexander and Gregory

Chase—our love and appreciation for their very real assistance and for matching our enthusiasm so genuinely with their own.

We are under deep obligation to the voice scientists and pedagogues of recent decades. Owing to the work of the following twentieth- and twenty-first-century voice scientists, we may now equip ourselves with fact where supposition and intuition once governed:

- Master flutist and renowned pedagogue Keith Underwood, whose long dedication to discovering the essence of performance breathing has expanded the technical skills of singers everywhere.

- Berton Coffin, singer and voice teacher, and Pierre Delattre, acoustical phoneticist, who worked together in the Sound Laboratory at the University of Colorado–Boulder and the Phonetics Laboratory at the University of California–Santa Barbara in the late 1950s. Dr. Coffin's curiosity about how his knowledge of aerodynamics—gained during military service in World War II—related to the physical and acoustical events of singing spurred his interest, as did his observation that not only register events but also vowel colors on certain notes informed voice classification. Over time, Dr. Coffin catalogued acoustic phonetics as related to pitch, aligning the optimal relationship between vibrator and resonator, resulting in therapeutic and resonant singing. His findings are the foundation of the vowel modification material in this text. The Coffin techniques are widely and successfully employed in voice studios and rehearsal halls throughout the country, and are with increasing frequency hinted at in professional journals. If this text clarifies the precepts for choral directors, and teaches their application to choral singers, the authors will be very gratified.

- William Vennard, who set down the complete mechanics of the singing voice, first in 1949, and in four later editions. We esteem his work and share the opinion expressed in his preface that "the knowledge of literal fact is the only justifiable basis for the use of imagery and other indirect methods."

- Ralph Appelman, whose utterly thorough interdisciplinary *The Science of Vocal Pedagogy* is a landmark publication in that it integrates the physiological with the artistic events of singing.

- The late James C. McKinney, whose excellent handbook, *The Diagnosis and Correction of Vocal Faults*, guided us in our belief that our chosen material would indeed be relevant to choral directors and could be presented in ways both practical and applicable to them.

- The ongoing work of scientists and pedagogues such as Richard Miller, Johan Sundberg, and Ingo Titze, which continues to educate us and to illuminate all.

And, finally, a toast to the spirit of Robert Shaw, whose passion was ever to attain that place "where song becomes spirit."

CONTENTS

PRESCRIPTIONS FOR CHORAL EXCELLENCE

INTRODUCTION

From the viewpoint of an untutored bystander, the choral director's art constitutes a director in place before a group of singers, baton in hand (or not), leading the coordinated singing effort of the chorus. End of story? Clearly not. The director's art is far more complex. It requires skills in the intellectual, physical, and social arenas. It entails expertise in matters musical, historical, linguistic, and vocal. Further knowledge in the areas of leadership, performance psychology, and the mental processes that enhance rehearsal and performance add immeasurably to the director's success.

To inform and enrich their interpretive choices, choral directors draw upon their knowledge of music history—periods, styles, performance practice—and their training in music theory: how elements of pitch, rhythm, harmony, and form create meaningful structure. Beyond these, choral music embodies the added element of language. Choral directors are sensitive to the literary intent of text and to the subtext of the music. Recognizing and understanding literary devices—homily, irony, metaphor—deepens the artistic level of interpretation.

In addition, choral directors are acquainted with the foreign languages of their repertoire in two important respects. The first is diction, which involves correct pronunciation for singing as well as vocal techniques for rendering the words intelligible as they are being sung. The second is the basic syntax and grammar of the various singing languages. Important interpretive cues are found in literal word-by-word translations. The implications of a change in verb tense (from past to subjunctive) or a shift from the formal, polite pronoun of address (*Sie/Ihre, vous/votre*) to the personal, intimate form (*du/deine, tu/ton*) can be great. Recognizing subtleties of text is a companion skill to recognizing subtleties of harmony, rhythm, or voicing.

Regarding the mechanics of conducting, choral conductors express their intent through physical movement. The character of the beat, the movement of hands, arms, trunk, and the expression on the face are the fingers on the keyboard. Each motion elicits response, and when the choir's response proves unsatisfactory, directors examine first whether their own conducting technique could be more reflective of the sound they desire to hear. The purposes of this book assume the director's command of the rudiments and advanced techniques of conducting.

Conversely, a well-chosen word evokes powerful emotion or a dramatic image. A strong command of spoken language facilitates communication via word choice and inflection. Once directors determine what they want to hear, they ensure that choir members understand what that means.

Articulate, evocative language and the imagery that inspires it, in concert with expressive conducting technique, are powerfully efficient tools.

In the sections that follow we will enlarge upon the choral director's aforementioned areas of expertise. We will also introduce readers to

- the daunting collection of roles played by the choral director
- the quandary that faces directors who must transmute sounds present only in their imaginations into beautiful and musical singing
- the problems linked to their instrument—the human voice
- the misunderstandings that commonly tax the relationship between choral directors and voice teachers
- an expanded view of the importance of leadership and imagery knowledge
- the procedures needed to solve vocal problems
- the advantages of continued learning

The Diverse Roles of a Choral Director

Consider this list of the myriad and diverse roles required of choral directors, some essential, others ancillary to the art of choral conducting:

Performing Arts	Behavioral Sciences	Business
Group voice teacher	Leader	Fund-raiser
Linguist	Psychologist	Publicist
Instrumentalist	Sociologist	CEO
Singer	Diplomat	Financial planner
Actor	Politician	
Dancer	Group facilitator	
Mime	Motivational speaker	
Stage director		

It is these many and varied labors that generate those moments of choral beauty and expressivity that all directors work for.

The Sound the Director Wants to Hear

In the 1940s Arturo Toscanini and the NBC Symphony Orchestra engaged the Robert Shaw professional Chorale to take part in their performance of Verdi's *Aida*. In the midst of one rehearsal the Italian conductor suddenly threw down his baton and walked off the stage to his dressing room. Shaw followed him, believing that the maestro was frustrated with the chorus. "Is there something the singers can do better?" Shaw asked, very perturbed. "No," said Toscanini, sadly and wearily, "it's not your fault. It's just that I hear this sound in my head of how I want it to be, but it never comes out that way. Sometimes it's me; sometimes it's the soloists; sometimes it's the orchestra. It just never sounds exactly the way I hear it in my head."

Like Toscanini, thoughtful directors already know the sound they want to hear. Achieving the sound may present a problem. At least part of the key is understanding how best to accomplish responsive singing. Directors of professional choruses enjoy the luxury of making musical requests and leaving the technical execution in the capable hands of their trained singers (that is, unless the conductors do not clearly communicate their requests). A potentially more serious problem arises if their requirements run counter to what is healthy or practical for the voice. Thus the importance of knowing what is and what isn't possible for each voice category applies to all directors, even those who conduct professional choirs.

Choral directors of singers with some, little, or no vocal training have still more to gain from a solid understanding of the vocal process. At the very least, a comprehension of how the singing voice functions will prevent directors from asking for that which will be unattractive, difficult, tension-inducing, or harmful. At best, vocal knowledge will enable directors to realize the sounds that their artistic imaginations conceive.

Vocal Knowledge of the Director

Choral directors are in the business of shaping and building vocal instruments by the very way in which they give instruction. For this reason, it is imperative that choral directors understand the vocal techniques that underlie the sound they wish their choirs to produce. Directors may wisely choose an affect or an appropriate piece of imagery, but they should first understand the process that leads that choice to musical fruition. Otherwise, no matter how specific the instruction, how colorful or eloquent the image, it may be ineffective.

An unfortunate situation that often occurs will serve as an example:

A choral director is unhappy with the corporate sound of the choir in a particular section of the piece. She identifies the sound somewhat nonspecifically as disjointed and ragged, rather than unified and

> expressive. Instinctively she instructs the singers, "Shhhhhh! You must blend. One voice, not individual voices. Not so loud, some of you! BLEND!"

At face value, this approach may seem valid. However, it may also actually prevent the best version of the sound desired.

That instruction may hinder the realization of the tonal ideal in several ways. First, singers—especially amateur singers—often fall back on unsupported singing, a vocal tone that lacks core or focus, in their effort to blend. Although a short-term blend problem is solved, expressive capabilities are eliminated. Without support, it is difficult to execute a legato line, to deliver dynamic contrasts, register shifts, or melismas, among other vocal skills. Second, there may be diligent singers—particularly those with larger voices—who, in their conscientious efforts to hold back the sound, will introduce vocal tension. The companions of vocal tension are fatigue, discomfort, tightness of tone quality, and sometimes poor intonation.

None of the above was intended by the director who said, "Shhhh! Blend!" She might have congratulated the chorus on achieving a better blend so quickly. But at what cost? At the cost of limiting the choir vocally. Are there other courses of remedial action? There are many, depending upon the demands of the piece. These will be presented in part I. The focus here is not on a specific question but rather on the process.

The Choral Director's Instrument

The choral director's instrument is the chorus.

And what is the chorus? A group of human voices.

Vocal sound is the raw material with which choral directors work. Directors should understand the functioning, capabilities, and frailties of the human voice in order to shape the raw material into something of beauty. If not, disappointment and frustration ensue for both directors and singers—directors, because they lack the requisite knowledge and skills to bring about the results they seek; singers, because they cannot meet the aspirations of the director.

Choral directors have come to each of the authors' voice studios saying, "I need to know more about singing and more about the voice." A public school choral director of some twenty years' experience said, "For too long now I have been teaching music, not singing." Each of these directors had reached the limit of what their choruses could achieve through musical instruction alone. It is our belief that neither musical nor vocal considerations may be excluded.

Misunderstandings between Choral Directors and Voice Teachers

When applied music departments became parts of institutions of higher learning, a tense situation developed between voice teachers and choral directors. The teachers found that a lack of vocal knowledge on the part of some choral directors created some physical problems for their students, especially those with unformed vocal technique. Choral directors, for their part, understandably resented the active interference. After some years of subtle and not-so-subtle strife, a solution was reached: Directors would stay strictly away from vocal instruction of any kind, limiting themselves to musical and inspirational help. This is generally the situation today, with choral directors justifiably concerned about avoiding conflict with the voice faculty. Those directors not working in an educational institution do not, of course, have such worries. The underlying cause of strife between voice teachers and choral directors is this: Although orchestra conductors may have to cope with diminished returns when the players are fatigued, they never have to concern themselves with causing damage to the actual instruments. Not so for choral directors. Fatigue, overuse, tension, and efforts to meet impractical demands may each cause damage to vocal instruments. Hence the great concern on the part of voice teachers.

Clearly, if teachers knew that choral directors were using accurate voice science, they would not object to vocal solutions for the problems of singing in a group, which add another dimension to the singers' skills. Voice teachers would also not be likely to object to their students singing in choirs where the director, armed with knowledge of accurate and timely voice science, consistently nurtures and protects the voices under his or her stewardship.

The Legitimate Role of Imagery in the Choral Director's Work

Should the choral director be using imagery in rehearsal? Yes. Imagery is and has always been a major component of the language of teaching and learning music. In fact, where singing is concerned, imagery has often substituted for, rather than enhanced, the teaching of vocal/choral technique. The issue for choral directors is not whether to use imagery but how to use it more effectively.

The field of performance psychology has introduced myriad ways in which the proficient use of imagery stimulates the human mind to its best thinking, best learning, and best performing.[1]

The possibilities afforded choral directors through the deliberate and skilled use of imagery are limitless. Employing imagery increases efficiency, improves consistency, and reinforces performance levels. It does not serve as a substitute for the mastery of a technical skill, however. The physical processes of the singing act must be as correct as possible. Half-hearted attempts to get good results by subtle brow-beating or inept imagery will not work. An important step in the development of performance skills is to learn to trust the technique at whatever level it exists, and then, through the use of imagery and other mental skills, to transcend preoccupation with the technical and proceed to the realm of real performance—a vital and expressive place, Robert Shaw's "realm of the spirit."

Conductors will find imagery an effective tool for teaching specific skills, and for guiding choirs to the best performances they are capable of giving. Imagery cannot, however, create skill of its own accord. To restate the case, if the technical skill is not yet in hand, the use of imagery alone will not bring it to pass. Therefore, it is incumbent upon directors to know whether their choristers have the technical skills necessary to produce the intended result. It is also directors' responsibility to understand clearly the technical skills needed. To be less adequately prepared is to render the use of imagery ineffective.

The power of imagery for good or ill and the power of effective performance skills are illustrated by the following true story of a rehearsal.

> A world-class conductor was rehearsing his equally world-class orchestra and professional chorus for an upcoming performance. Interrupting the rehearsal at one point to express his dissatisfaction with the chorus, he instructed them to make it "more holy." Two subsequent efforts pleased him no better, as he continued repeating his exhortations to make it "more holy," adding to his own and the choir's mounting frustration. The perplexed choristers simply had no idea what he meant. Should they sing more softly? Should the phrasing be more sustained? What exactly did he mean by "more holy?" Finally, the *sotto voce* words of a quick-thinking baritone were heard in a low mutter, "Everybody, paste a holy look on your faces." The conductor was enthralled. "Yes! You've finally got it." The singers agreed that they had not changed anything about their vocalism. They had simply adopted the holiest countenance each could muster.

What is the meaning of this story? To the choristers, it signified that the conductor lacked either the technical skill to know exactly what vocal result he wanted, or the verbal skill to communicate what he desired. What then accounts for his pleasure when the singers adopted a "holy" facial expression? It is possible that he simply gave up gracefully, perhaps concluding that the choristers were incapable of meeting his demand. It is also possible that the expressive extravocal performing skills of the choristers were enough to convince him that he had indeed heard a "more holy" sound. Whatever meaning is taken from the anecdote, it clearly illustrates a common frustration in the choral rehearsal:

> *Conductor to himself*: "Why aren't they doing what I want?"
> *Singers to themselves*: "What on earth does he want?"

When Imagery and Musical Solutions Are Not Sufficient

The musical and linguistic problems are solved. Ideas about the text have been clearly communicated. The imaginations of the singers have been inspired verbally and by the director's expressive conducting technique. Yet the director is still dissatisfied with the results. Clearly, the use of musical solutions and imagery are not enough. Now is the time to think vocally.

What is it about the sound that displeases me?

This is the first question to ask. Specific answers could include the following:

The *forte* is too harsh.
The *piano* section lacks character.
The quality of sound is too relaxed for the energetic mood of this piece.

What prompts me to make this judgment?

Try to pinpoint how you arrived at your opinion. Specific answers could include the following:

The tenors often sound strident when they sing *forte*.
The emotion should be one of great resolve even though the line is marked *p*.
The section seems to drag even though it is rhythmically accurate.

Which part(s) of the problem is (are) technical?

Since you have already exhausted any possible musical, conducting, or interpretive solutions, you may assume that there is indeed a technical problem, such as,

The tenor part in the *forte* sections happens to lie within their passaggio;

> The unfocused tone produced as a *piano* evokes the wrong emotion; or,
>
> The many consonants of the text are interrupting the forward motion of the line.

What shall I do about the technical problems?

Here is where the choral director's knowledge of vocal solutions is essential. Directors of young or amateur singers must think *for* their singers. Directors of professional singers must have the vocal knowledge to think *of* their singers' vocal well-being. To neglect this important responsibility is to accept less than the best of which the chorus is capable. Such neglect also reflects prodigal misuse of a treasured resource, the human voice.

Using this kind of procedure for thinking vocally can open up many new possibilities for leading the choir closer to achieving that ideal sound that resides in the director's imagination.

The Role of Leadership Skills

Some would say that the traits of a leader are inherent, not acquired. Or that leadership is purely a matter of exercising common sense, which one either possesses or does not. Indeed, leadership is rooted in common sense. Yet, just as gifted singers of innate ability may further develop their skills and just as average, less naturally talented singers may improve theirs, leaders can develop and expand leadership skills through practice and increased knowledge.

By any criterion, directors and their choirs must be defined as leaders and followers, whose relationship is subject to the psychological principles of leadership excellence. Fortunate are those choral directors who are taught early that musical expertise is not the sole measure of their professional skills. Trained to be highly sensitive to their responsibilities as leaders, they take their positions of leadership seriously. The goal of part II is to dispel the notion that such matters depend solely upon existing common sense—although that ought never be discounted.

Part II further seeks to acquaint readers with tested solutions for leadership problems. The selected leadership issues (chapter 6) present material culled from the ever-continuing research into human interaction, human thought/work processes, and human potential. The insights offered include practical devices, which stem from the practical tools and empirical knowledge that have been adopted by choral directors everywhere. It also uses newer techniques for leadership excellence offered by the cutting edge of today's psychological research into leadership and group dynamics.

The Choral Director's Continued Learning

The reasoning set forth in the sections above prompts the authors to add another item to the already daunting list of requisite areas of expertise for the choral director: continued learning. Voice scientists have made and continue to make huge strides in understanding the physical act of singing. The days are over when choral directors and voice teachers could emerge from music school with a neat package of ideas to see them through a career. Cherished notions about vocal pedagogy must give way to scientifically established truths.

Increasingly, the results of scientific research disprove many of the old chestnuts of vocalism. The eminent vocal scientist, singer, voice teacher, and author Richard Miller enumerates some of the most prevalent in an aptly titled article, "The Flat-Earth School of Vocal Pedagogy." Here is a short selection taken from his lengthier list:

> Some theories of voice production which are dependent upon what *appears* to be logical do not have a basis in actual physical fact. Many of them are familiar concepts, often deeply ingrained in the language of vocal pedagogy.
>
> 1. To open the throat, open wide the mouth by dropping the jaw.
> 2. Pull *in* on the abdominal wall so that the diaphragm will stay longer in one place.
> 3. Push *out* on the abdominal wall in order to keep the diaphragm low.
> 4. Push *down* on the diaphragm for high notes and pull it *up* for low notes.
> 5. Pull *in* on the diaphragm to give extra support for high notes. . . .
> 6. Pull down the upper lip to "focus" the tone.
> 7. Cover the bottom teeth with the lower lip to "focus" the tone. . . .
> 8. Make a spacious cavity at the back of the mouth and in the throat by pulling the velum upward.[2]

To continue to rely on these old chestnuts is limiting at best, harmful and nonproductive at worst.

It is the goal of this book to demystify the three large encompassing subjects that comprise many of the roles of the choral director:

vocal technique

the eliciting of good singing and reliable musicianship in rehearsal and
   performance

leadership

If we have done our job well, not only will you benefit by reading and
re-reading its pages, but you will seek out new opportunities to learn, grow,
and bring new knowledge to your professional life as a choral director.

Part I

PRESCRIPTIONS FOR CHORAL SINGING

Technical Vocal Skills

CHAPTER 1
Breath Management

It is often said that with good breath management all vocal technicalities are possible, and without it, nothing vocally satisfactory can happen. This statement is not altogether true, but is close enough to make breath management extremely important. Any number of breathing methods for singers have always been touted. In the twentieth century it was common for the voice-teaching profession to accept some five or six different breathing methods as equally valid. Dr. Wilbur Gould, founder of the Voice Foundation, once stated that he had collected, by discussing breath control with every professional singer who consulted him, 226 breathing methods. Clearly the singers were describing their perceptions of what they did. Indeed, researchers have concluded that singers seldom describe their own breathing methods, however successful, with anatomical accuracy.

With the increase in vocal research, however, and the newest ten-year study on breathing for singers (1983–1993),[1] the science of body mechanics has isolated what might be termed the "appoggio method" as most reliable and effective. The felicitous study of breathing for singing published in 1993 completed the work pioneered by Proctor (1980) and Hixon (1987). It put to rest the many fanciful versions of how singers breathe efficiently that resulted from personal perceptions of kinesthetic feedback handed down from teacher to student through the years. With this publication it became clear that the maintenance of the posture known as the appoggio is the most important aspect of breathing for singing. It also made clear that it is not a natural event, but must be trained. Thus the modern study has validated the accuracy of the old singing masters' observations about breath support requiring a "noble posture," which were made in the absence of scientific information.

Understandably, it might seem preferable that this text codify the various vocal skills separately for organizational clarity, but it is literally impossible to do so. Because technical singing skills are inextricably interrelated, to foster correct, healthy singing technique we consider in this chapter how breath relates to legato, onset, melisma singing, upper- and lower-range pitches, tension, dynamics, vibrato, diction, and so on. Some repetition of related material is inevitable and unavoidable.

1.1   Breathing

THE COMPLAINT

Because breathing is a natural function, why must breathing to sing be taught?

Dx, The Diagnosis

Contrary to some prevalent beliefs, singing is not just speaking on pitch. The requirements of breath for singing exceed those for speaking. Problems of pitch, tone quality, legato, onset, melisma, extreme ranges, and dynamics are each helped in varying amounts by good breath management. Choral singers generally have no resource for improving their breathing skills other than the director's teaching during rehearsals. Given training by the director, they can achieve a technique that delivers a longer breath, a more stable vibrato, better pitch, improved legato, and the capacity to blend even at varied dynamic levels.

Rx, The Treatment Plan

1. Some part of rehearsal time should be reserved for teaching the singers to manage their breath for singing. Once they learn the appoggio technique, many problems are resolved.
2. Brief verbal or visual cues aimed at maintaining or redeploying the appoggio, along with an occasional review of the technique, ensure its habitual use.

Discussion

Breathing to Sing

A baby takes his or her first breath with no tutoring; humans breathe for the needs of life with no particular or conscious effort. We inhale when the brain says that the body needs oxygen. We breathe while we sleep. The system prefers to work automatically and needs no conscious controls.

Why then the mystery and the need for scientific research? Because breathing for singing is another matter entirely. It requires conscious control that diminishes the spontaneity with which one breathes, a control that must be learned. Although the efficacy of various theories about breathing are difficult to test because of the complex interactions between the thoracic and abdominal muscles, the recent advances in voice science have clarified the issue.

Most requirements for "singing air" do not apply to air used for day-to-day living. Ordinary persons have no particular need for a "long" breath; they just breathe again when it runs out. Ordinary persons do not need to have pressure behind the air; if they must shout, the abdominals kick in automatically. Ordinary persons do not need to time the inhalation; they just breathe when it is time to talk or when the air supply needs replenishment. Not so for singers.

The body's motor program, designed to provide life support, results in a problem for singers: They must manage breath pressure that, left to its own devices, will always be too high at the beginning of long phrases and too low at the end. They must balance the amount of flowing air against the pressure under which that air is moving. Singers must maintain constant beauty of tone, while inflecting that tone with colors appropriate to the text. In the Western hemisphere, the tone that is regarded as beautiful is a supported tone. This translates to the singer's need for muscular control of air supply and pressure.

Although skillful singing does not require gargantuan amounts of energy, most amateur choristers and beginning singers tend to use too little energy, more like that suitable for folksinging with a guitar. The quantity of breath that suffices for speaking is not at all the level required for singing; singing requires more breath energy than does speaking. Its breath supply must last longer and be stronger than that of speech.

Diaphragmatic Breathing and Other Flawed Concepts

Because the lungs are nonmuscular, they depend on the diaphragm and the muscular movements of the chest, back, and abdomen during the act of respiration. Thus, all breathing is indeed diaphragmatic, although conscious direct control cannot be exerted over the diaphragm.[2] It is basically a passive muscle during singing.

If efforts to teach your singers a diaphragmatic method of support brought less than the desired result, it was probably not your pedagogical skills that were at fault. Singers do not know where the diaphragm is at any given moment, because they cannot feel the diaphragm. Neither can they exert any direct influence over it. Furthermore, the diaphragmatic approach to breathing attempts to employ the diaphragm as a high-pressure piston, which often results in vocal distortion of some sort, such as the infamous vocal "pushing," or the "squeezing out" of air by the end of the phrase. If you added imaging, a tried-and-true system, into the pedagogical mix in order to help them find their way, it probably did not change things appreciably.

Many singers believe wrongly that when they inhale, the bulge that appears in the upper abdomen is the diaphragm. In reality, the bulge is caused by the diaphragm, but it is not the diaphragm itself. Inhaling is an active process that requires muscular contraction, but exhaling is passive, due to relaxation of the diaphragm. This, too, is confusing to some singers: To think that the diaphragm is passive during singing is the converse of a diaphragmatic image that many singers have, that of a pump tirelessly driving air upward toward the larynx. In fact, a better image is that of a blown-up balloon when the neck is released. There is no need to squeeze the balloon; air will just issue forth when nothing holds it back.

Learning to breathe efficiently for sustaining sound requires an integrated effort of at least thirty-six postural, inspiratory, and expiratory muscles. Furthermore, the breathing activity of each individual singer will be idiosyncratic and will depend on many factors, including the basic shape of the rib cage and the manner in which it is held while singing.

The most efficient way to make the diaphragm do what is needed is by secondary means. The means recommended by today's vocal scientists is the appoggio. The appoggio will deliver the long breath, stability, and evenness of tone. Asking your singers to push the abdomen in or out will not. The appoggio position will actually dictate that the diaphragm and abdominal muscles do the right thing voluntarily.

How to Do It: What Is an Appoggio?

Defined in basic terms, an appoggio consists of a raised sternum and expanded ribs (shoulders remaining low), maintained from beginning to end of the phrase. While the breath is being replenished for the next phrase, nothing should change—shoulders should stay relaxed and down, sternum should maintain easy height, and ribs stay extended. This maintenance is perhaps the most difficult part of the skill to learn. Yet, unlike other vocal skills, an appoggio is visible to the director, which makes the training easier. The director can see whether or not the effort is correct.

Like the grace note called an appoggiatura, *appoggiare* in Italian means to lean. The appoggiatura, a nonchord tone, leans on the next note, the chord tone. To the old Italian voice teachers, a breath appoggio signified a feeling of leaning the air against the sternum from the inside, accompanied by expanded ribs. Actually, when a singer keeps a high sternum, expanded ribs will come along as part of the package. Or, when the ribs are expanded, the sternum usually rises. It is the appoggio that allows your singers to decide what musical effect they want (in obedience to their conductor's instructions) and gives them the power to deliver it.

THE SCIENCE

1. The appoggio technique answers the physical facts of breathing. Human beings live in a pressured atmosphere.
2. When the subglottic pressure falls lower than the atmospheric pressure, reflexive physiological response causes one to inhale, and the diaphragm descends.

3. During inhalation, the lung volume is increased by the downward contraction of the diaphragm and an expansion of the intercostals.
4. When the subglottic pressure is above the level of atmospheric pressure, one reflexively exhales. As one exhales (sings), the diaphragm ascends, and lung pressure and subglottal pressure decrease until below the level of atmospheric pressure, when one again reflexively inhales.

   The appoggio technique avoids the rapid collapse of normal speech by retarding the ascent of the diaphragm. This allows subglottal pressure to remain steady during phonation and creates a stabilizing effect that leads to fewer intonation problems and a seemingly longer air supply.

How to Do It: Training Your Singers to Use the Appoggio

Teach the ideal position of the shoulders, ribs, and sternum using one or more of these three methods:

1. Raise arms above the head. Lower the arms and shoulders, leaving as is the ribs (expanded) and sternum (high). This is the appoggio that should be kept at all times.
2. Pretend that the underside of each shoulder blade is fitted with a magnet. Imagine the two magnets straining to touch each other. The sternum then is high; the shoulders low, and the ribs out. This is the ideal appoggio that should be maintained.
3. Vigorously "slurp" the air in, allowing the effort to make a loud vulgar noise. This effort forces the ribs to make the requisite sideways movement to full expansion, with no concomitant raising of the shoulders and no concern about the abdominals. It will seem much like forcibly pulling liquid in through a straw. The noisy slurp facilitates singers' recognition of the correct rib action. Shortly after learning the technique, the noise can be abandoned.

Some muscular fatigue may be experienced for about two weeks, just as in learning a new athletic skill. You may wish to warn your singers about this, but be sure to motivate them by reminding them that, once the skill is under command, singing is actually less fatiguing. Remember that the advantages of your singers learning to maintain an appoggio include virtually every skill on a director's wish list.

It is helpful to augment the appoggio training with imagery. Two useful visual images accompanying appoggio breath management are (1) leaning the air against the sternum, and (2) vigorously sucking liquid through a straw. Before asking the singers to assign a personal image to this execution, be sure to let them experience the leaning and hear the sound made possible by the use of the appoggio.

When the appoggio is correctly maintained, the abdominals will do exactly the right thing and the diaphragm will rise slowly, thus giving true "support" without further effort from the singer. Some choral musicians, it has been reported, believe that the abdomen must be pushed out or tucked in as part of the appoggio. Such pushing or pulling movements are contraindicated. Not only are they useless but they also constitute a hindrance. On the other hand, if the abdomen happens to move out or in while maintaining the appoggio, which it naturally will do, it should be permitted to do so. It need not be micromanaged. This method simplifies singers' performance thinking, already crowded and busy, and renders some physical acts automatic. Accustom your choristers to hearing your command "Up!" to request the appoggio position and the (silent) sucking in of air. When used consistently during rehearsal, this word is short enough to be easily deployed by the director, and will eventually create the habit of maintaining an appoggio. At other times, a visual cue such as tapping his or her own high sternum with the index finger will serve to remind.

As for the inhalation, the air is taken in with what might be called a sideways, rather than an up-and-down, movement. This command will be "Sideways!" To train your singers for this inhalation, have them do the following:

1. Put the index fingers under the bottom ribs, thumbs on the back.
2. Place the little fingers on the hip bones.
3. Pull in the air forcefully.
4. Feel the sideways movement in the area now spanned by the fingers.

At first the singers may fear they have insufficient air supply, until they see how very long the air lasts. At that time, the worry will disappear.

To use imaging in your teaching of breath management, you should attend to the principles involved in this skill. Images do not take on a special meaning until singers have executed the skill successfully and experienced more than once the sensation described by the imagery. Then they can settle on a three-part image for what was just done:

1. The feedback muscular sensations from the ribs, back, abdomen, and so on
2. A visual image of what is actually taking place
3. An auditory image of the sound produced by that procedure

When the visual and auditory images are theirs, not yours, their execution will be more efficient. You can guide them to find an appropriate image, but it is best that you not invent it for them.

Another aid to feeling how the muscles work during inhalation: Have your singers sit bent over their separated legs with elbows resting on the knees, then breathe. The expansion of the ribs and back is unmistakable and not too difficult to recall when the loud slurping of air shows the way.

THE SCIENCE

The eminent Richard Miller clarifies the function of the appoggio thus: "Breath management is the essential foundation for all skillful vocalism. . . . Breath management for singing is best achieved by preserving a 'noble' position that permits interplay among the muscles of the upper chest, muscles of the ribcage area, and the muscles of the anterolateral abdominal wall. . . . The internationally recognized appoggio (from *appoggiare*, [It.], to lean against, to be in contact with) is a breath-management coordination that must be learned if the singer is to unite energy and freedom. . . ."[3]

There are other long-lived breath management schemes that have been discredited by the research of today. Among them are the following:

1. A method built on sighing with a high air flow
2. A method based on damming the breath with a strong glottal closure
3. A method based on breathing with the belly
4. A method based on high-chest breathing while keeping the sternum low
5. A method based on inhaling and expelling the largest volume of air during a phrase

"Those who advise thrusting the stomach out are trying to achieve a kind of strength, which objective is better served by the appoggio that forces the abdominals to do the required movement." Those who advise starting the tone with a "spritz" of air manage to "remove upper harmonic partials from the spectrum reducing all voices to one dimension of non-vibrant timbre."[4]

THE COMPLAINT

If the singer has good posture already, is the appoggio necessary?

DX, THE DIAGNOSIS

When you teach the importance of posture and provide prompts during rehearsal, the tone probably improves as the singers stand or sit straighter. This is because better posture often comes along with a raised chest and expanded ribs. Yet the appoggio is more than good posture; it is the maintenance of a sternum raised farther and ribs expanded beyond that usually described as good posture.

RX, THE TREATMENT PLAN

1. Train the maintenance of the appoggio position as part of correct posture for singing. Maintaining the appoggio provides the greatest challenge. Draw attention to the ensuing improvements to provide encouragement and incentive.
2. Train habitual use of the skill via short verbal prompts such as "Up!" and "Sideways!" or the visual cue of your own expanded ribs and raised sternum.
3. In a mirror have your singers observe themselves in profile, standing erect with good posture. Then have them consciously take the appoggio posture position. Point out the visibly higher position of the sternum and the greater expansion of the ribs.
4. Attend to maintenance of the appoggio in both standing and seated positions.

DISCUSSION

Posture and What the Appoggio Does for Singers

A great vocal pedagogue, Ralph Appelman, once said that the singer who seems to be doing absolutely nothing is, in reality, the one who is totally aware of what each muscle in his body is doing at any moment, while the one who seems to be adjusting his musculature constantly, does not. This is particularly true of posture.

Choral directors may, with reason, be confused by the many basic ways they have encountered that purport to train singers in good posture. It may seem that, regardless of which method is employed, the singers abandon their good posture within minutes. Years of study, thought, and research have sought a fail-proof, truly superior way to teach this attribute. Because most singing skills depend in large part on breath support, because the most effective and dependable breath support includes good posture, and because good posture is an integral part of the recommended appoggio position, your singers will profit greatly from the maintenance of an appoggio. It is your best choice for long-term memory of the physical position for supported breath, easy vocal production, and generally effective vocal results.

A choral director's wish list for his or her choristers would include the same elements that professional singers strive for:

a vibrant and on-pitch tone
a long air supply
easy access to high and low ranges
unproblematic vibratos
carrying power, loud or soft
easy access to pianissimo
control of fast singing
long-term vocal health
good articulation without diminished tone quality
sufficient vocal skill to permit concentration on musical values

This entire list is dependent upon good breath management, which is in large part contingent upon posture.

The Science

Voice scientist Johan Sundberg gives us some facts about pitch and loudness as they relate to the appoggio:

"In singing, variation of subglottal pressure is required not only when loudness but also when pitch is changed. When we increase pitch, we stretch the vocal folds. It seems that stretched vocal folds require a higher driving pressure than laxer vocal folds. Thus, higher subglottal pressures are needed for high pitches than for low pitches. [Singers] have to tailor the subglottal pressure for every note, taking into consideration both its loudness and its pitch. Thus, each new pitch has to be welcomed by its own pressure in the respiratory apparatus. Given the fact that pitches tend to change constantly and rather frequently in music, we can imagine that the breathing system keeps its owner busy during singing. . . .

"As if this were not enough, there is a musically highly relevant complicating effect of subglottal pressure. It affects the pitch: other things being equal, a raised subglottal pressure raises the pitch. This means that an error in the subglottal pressure is manifested not only as an error in loudness . . . but also as an error in pitch, which . . . may be a disaster for a singer."[5]

The last word on the appoggio as a means to breath support comes from another research study: "rib cage activity was greater than abdominal activity during the singing tasks *for all but the unsupported voice* at medium pitch" (emphasis added).[6]

Perhaps choir directors, frustrated in their endeavors, have wondered at times whether they routinely make the request for good posture simply out of habit. Its importance cannot be overstated. The bodies of athletes, dancers, and singers are their instruments. For this reason, any position of their skeleton or any particular deployment of the musculature has a pronounced effect on the body's ability to deliver the technical requirements of their various arts, and certainly of singing. Posture, including head, neck, torso, and leg stance, is crucial. All physical controls function less well when the posture, standing or seated, is faulty.

The subject of seated posture is compelling. Opera singers, who must often sing while seated, treat this as an important skill to be acquired. Although choral singers spend very little time seated while performing, they spend a great deal of time in that position while rehearsing. Singing for several hours in a seated position has the potential of solidifying a bad posture, and a bad sitting posture that accompanies singing is capable of destroying good vocal habits.

A possible answer lies in the type of chair provided for rehearsal periods. Most folding or meeting-room chairs slant upward from the back of the seat toward the bent knees—exactly the wrong angle for best results. Fortunately, musical equipment manufacturers such as Wenger, among others, offer mass-produced musicians' chairs that slant downward toward the front of the seat. A less expensive option is foam rubber seat cushions shaped in a very shallow triangle, with the highest part, generally about two inches deep, placed at the back of the seat and the thinnest part to the front. Where neither option is practical, singers should sit forward toward the front edge of the seat until the thigh is at least parallel to the floor. To better align the seated body, direct the singers to locate the two *sitz* bones by placing their hands under the buttocks on the chair and shifting until they feel the bones. This angle will make it easier for singers to sit upright and use the appoggio consistently.

Several celebrated voice teachers insist that students sing with the arms held straight down behind the back, hands clasped together, for as much of the nonperforming time as possible. This is another way to make the appoggio position habitual. Certainly such a practice would be possible during the warm-up, if not while holding music. Because singers consistently lose the appoggio at the end of their air, consider using progressively longer musical phrases to train the maintenance of correct postural position under the usual difficulty. Mandating periods of time for standing during rehearsal is also important for training. Asking for the same appoggio posture during both standing and sitting periods is a must.

Science in Application

Four college choirs from different parts of the country combined for a national broadcast performance that required a prerecording. One rehearsal period was allotted for the choirs to meet for the first time, warm up, rehearse, and record. After several run-throughs of the piece, the recording session began.

Loss of pitch was apparent within the first three notes, a descending arpeggio, and painfully obvious three-fourths of the way through, when brass and percussion entered. Repeated attempts showed little improvement. The seasoned arranger/conductor, accustomed to working with professionals in the television and film industry, was at a loss to correct the problem.

One of the four directors suggested a short break from recording. She taught the appoggio posture and energized singing in fifteen minutes, a measure of its efficacy. The pitch problems self-corrected and the recording was successfully completed on schedule.

1.2 Onset

The word onset *is a voice scientist's term for the start of the tone. Its often-used synonym,* attack, *is sometimes an unfortunate choice for singers that tends toward self-fulfillment, particularly in amateurs. The onset, then, is the initial intersection of the processes of breathing and singing.*

In choral singing, certain breath management issues that will adversely affect tone quality may reveal themselves in the choral entrances, or onsets. Setting aside consonants and their incumbent problems for purposes of this discussion, cues indicating that poor breath-voice coordination is present may include entrances on vowels marred by such imprecisions as delay, blurting, inaccurate pitch, and instability of tone.

THE COMPLAINT

Why do singers need a balanced onset?

Dx, THE DIAGNOSIS

Any sung pitch is the product of a complex interaction between brain, nerves, and muscles. Similar interactive processes occur throughout the body in the performance of all physical tasks. The simple act of crossing one leg over the other, for example—a seemingly spontaneous action—is not so at all; rather, it is the result of an intricately coordinated process. The more complex act of typing without looking at the keyboard is a skill that an accomplished typist may take somewhat for granted. A beginner, however, recognizes that, although the skill does not occur spontaneously, it may indeed be improved through regular practice. So it is with the functional efficiency of the vocal folds. Vocal fold efficiency can be improved through the use of onset exercises. The companions of increased vocal fold efficiency are improved breath management and tonal focus.

Balanced resistance of the vocal folds to the airflow is achieved when the proper flow of breath occurs in conjunction with well-coordinated vocal fold action. Its achievement results in the most efficient use of air and better tonal focus. Under balanced resistance, air is expelled at a slower rate, resulting in a longer-lasting breath. Balanced resistance also ensures the effective coordination of the breathing and singing processes. The proper coordination of these processes constitutes the "hooked in" or "connected," or "on-the-breath" singing to which many voice teachers refer. Balanced onset addresses both the proper use of the breath and the efficient function of the vocal folds.

Rx, THE TREATMENT PLAN

Train the coordination of the breathing mechanism with singing by incorporating a few moments of onset exercise (see the Discussion below) early in the warm-up period at every rehearsal. Developing a balanced onset trains the vocal folds to function most efficiently, thereby facilitating optimal breath management.

DISCUSSION

An often overlooked component of breath management is the efficiency of the vocal folds themselves. During singing, the vocal folds regulate the flow of the breath. In well-coordinated vocal fold action, the folds provide a balanced resistance to sub-glottal pressure (the air pressure beneath the vocal folds). This results in the most efficient use of air, which slows the expulsion rate, with the further result that the breath simply lasts longer. When the regulating action of the folds is too tense, the result is an abrupt glottal stroke, as in the spoken "uh-oh." When the action of the folds is too lax, the result is an imprecise onset, as in a spoken "hhhhuh." In the cases of both hyperfunction (too much tension) and hypofunction (not enough tension) breath management suffers, as do tone quality and, frequently, intonation.

The goal of the onset exercises is to achieve a flexible muscle balance between the vocal folds and the muscles of respiration: *balance*, because too tense or too lax is inefficient and produces unsatisfactory results; *flexible*, because the requirements of varying pitch and dynamic level cannot be met by a fixed effort. Neither the "grunt" of a glottal stroke nor the long "h" of a soft onset uses breath efficiently. A balanced and coordinated action of the vocal folds is required to regulate the breath flow optimally. Underscoring the fact that no single component of singing can be addressed without exerting some effect on the others is the fact that efficient vocal fold use results not only in better breath management but also in more stable, better-focused tone quality and, often, improved intonation.

Common choral antidotes to onset problems are admonitions to imagine an "h" at the start of the tone, or to blow a bit of air across the cords before starting the tone. Neither course of action develops the skill of healthy onset. The exercises below, adapted for the choral rehearsal from the work of preeminent vocal scientists/ pedagogues, will do exactly that.

EXERCISE 1.1
Suspending the Breath (James McKinney)

Modeling a good appoggio posture yourself, cue a relaxed sideways inhalation from your singers. Check that the singers are aware of a feeling of expansion around the middle as they inhale. Instruct them to suspend the breath when they are comfortably full of air. Demonstrate the difference between suspending the air (keeping the glottis open while stopping the intake of air) and stopping the intake of air by shutting the glottis (the familiar sensation that occurs when lifting a heavy object or when holding the breath, both of which make the cords hold together). With the singers' breath suspended and the cords open (think "empty throat"), cue them to start the tone by simply thinking to do so, on a comfortable pitch for all ranges. Use a pattern of scale degrees 1–2–3–1. Prepare the vowel first, on as many as three repetitions of the pattern: [o], [u], and [i].[7]

EXERCISE 1.2
Strengthening the Onset (Richard Miller)

Build a chord that provides a pitch in comfortable range for each section of the choir, such as basses on scale degree 1, tenors on 5, altos on 3, and sopranos on 8. Have the choir sing a pattern of four quarter notes followed by a whole note, taking a breath between each note. Demonstrate again the difference between healthy onset (start air only; do not let the throat aid in the effort) and unhealthy onset (a glottal stroke or [h]). Alternating between front and back vowels, ascend and descend by half-steps, staying within a comfortable range for all sections.[8]

EXERCISE 1.3
Pulsating a Tone (Ralph Appelman)

As in Figure 1.1, on a comfortable unison pitch, have the chorus sing five pulsated sounds on the neutral vowel [ʌ] (as in *up*). Ensure that tonguetips are at "home base" (at the top of the lower teeth) and that mouths are about half open (an opening of 7 or 8, numbering the widest-open mouth as 15). Repeat the pattern, cuing a relaxed breath sideways between repetitions. Singing should be at a *mezzo piano* to *mezzo forte* with no suggestion from you as to timbre. The goal is to develop and maintain balance without introducing undue physical effort. When the singers consistently demonstrate increased speed coupled with reduced effort, have them practice the pulsing [ʌ] vowel on a five-note scale, singing five pulses on the top note before descending. Vowels: [ʌ], [I], and [u], mouth preparing vowel position during inhalation.[9]

EXERCISE 1.4
Introducing Staccato (Johan Sundberg)

Increase the technical demands of the onset exercises when your singers are ready for it. The example (Figure 1.2) takes the Appelman five-note scale (now eliminating the repeated top note) and adds the element of staccato. Teach the choir to sing a five-note scale, alternating between a front and back vowel, ascending and descending, followed by a descending full-octave staccato arpeggio. According to Sundberg, the element of staccato is useful, if employed appropriately, for training muscle memory.[10]

For exercises that strengthen the laryngeal muscles themselves, see Stemple's Vocal Function Exercises in appendix 2.

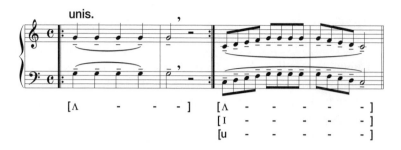

Figure 1.1

Figure 1.2

1.3 Legato and Breath

The achievement of beauty and line are dependent upon legato, and the achievement of legato is fully dependent upon proper breath management. Extrapolating from the publications of today's vocal researchers, proper breath management can be said to be dependent upon the appoggio. Indeed, legato is air, with a secondary respectful salute to the felicitous input of nondisruptive consonants.

At least 75 percent of the time, singers are performing music that depends on legato mode. Staccato, marcato, martellato, and so on are outside the normal, are not the mainstream effort. Although the positive results of singing a legato line are many, that skill depends principally on two vocal factors: air and consonants. The air must move at all times, and the consonants must not stop it from moving. In principle this is simple, but in practice it is more complex.

The Complaint

If the notes are connected and the phrase uninterrupted by a breath, isn't that legato?

Dx, The Diagnosis

Maintaining a legato line is the basic way to produce a healthy and beautiful tone. Other modes of singing—regardless of their musical effectiveness—are fundamentally exceptions. Singing in a non-legato style inevitably causes fatigue and, when it supplants legato singing as the primary mode of singing, vocal health problems as well. The first qualitative result to show itself is unevenness of tone, the second is undue vocal fatigue, and the third is incipient vocal damage. Teaching singers to execute legato well and to regard it as the basic skill of their singing is a challenging but vital task.

A precise definition of legato for singing is important to this discussion. The literal meaning is "bound together." Music educators often define it as "connected," making legato a simple opposite of staccato. The most useful definition, however, is "a constant forward movement of air and tone." Used by singers and wind players alike, it implies movement through the consonants, through the large melodic skips, through the tempo and register changes, a movement that never ceases to forge ahead.

Rx, The Treatment Plan

1. Remind your singers that the normal mode of singing is legato. The exceptions to the legato rule—staccato, marcato, and so on—are only used sporadically.
2. Train the singers to execute legato, their primary vocal skill. Demonstrate the stark musical contrast between a phrase sung with legato and one in which legato is abandoned.

Discussion

The Importance of Legato

Voice teachers' insistence upon legato singing is not just a whim or a caprice. It is a fundamental principle of beautiful and healthy singing. In the history of the art of teaching singing, there has literally never been a knowledgeable vocal musician who disagreed with this principle. In vocal pedagogy every effort is made to instill the habit of legato connections from the first lesson. Basically, one cannot sing well or effectively without legato.

The enthusiasm with which teachers and singers embrace this philosophy of a legato singing mode must reflect an anticipation of great results. What are they? First, legato singing produces beauty and continued vocal health through firmer control of the vocal musculature. Second, because it serves as the basic mode of singing, legato singing affords the opportunity to achieve musical variety through the use of other contrasting vocal modes such as staccato, marcato, martellato, and portamento. Third, legato singing produces that most desired musical element: line. For all practical purposes legato *is* line, and breath management *is* legato.

Vocal Connections between Notes: Legato and Non-Legato

Manuel Garcia II, one of the most skillful voice teachers in history, set down five possible types of vocal connections between notes:

> *Slurred*: connected by means of a portamento that glides swiftly but audibly through all intermediate sounds
>
> *Legato*: connected in a neat, smooth manner without interrupting the flow of the vocal sound, yet without openly and audibly slurring over the intermediate pitches
>
> *Marcato*: laying particular stress on each note, without detaching one from the other, by giving pressure to the lungs and dilating the pharynx as if repeating the same vowel for every note of the passage
>
> *Staccato*: uttering each note individually, separating the notes by a slight pause
>
> *Aspirated*: Allowing breath to escape between notes

Of these five modes of connection, legato is fundamental. It is a basic tenet of healthy, beautiful singing, inextricably entwined with the concept of "moving the air" forward at all times. It is virtually impossible to achieve a legato line without keeping the air moving. In addition, the image of constantly moving air is an easy one to impart to singers. Other advantages accrue from employing this image: pitch stabilizes; access to high notes is easier; vibratos should even out.

THE COMPLAINT

Won't sliding or a lack of rhythmic precision result from too much legato?

DX, THE DIAGNOSIS

Even developing professional singers tend to confuse legato with portamentos and sliding. It should be made clear what the differences are. Furthermore, although nonprofessional singers have been exhorted to sing with legato as their basic mode, they should be taught to execute it, first by imparting a correct understanding of what constitutes legato. It is the thinking that must be uniform in order that the execution be precise. This requires that your singers know the difference between sliding and singing legato.

Rx, The Treatment Plan

1. To avoid a lack of rhythmic precision, your singers must have an understanding of the differences between legato, portamento, and sliding. Make a very clear demarcation among the three techniques, perhaps having them practice legato alongside other non-legato modes. See the Discussion below.
2. In teaching the continuous air flow required of legato singing, utilize physical and visual cues. During the rehearsal, encourage the singers to use physical gestures of continually flowing movement as an image. Adapt your beat to include flowing gesture. A fluent, forward-moving rebound is especially helpful, but do not neglect rhythmic precision that indicates when and how swiftly to move to the next note.
3. The skill of making energized but swift consonants is also a part of singing with legato. Legato depends to a large degree on these short, sharp consonants while preserving the movement of the breath. See Demystifying Consonants, p. 75, for helpful details.
4. Achieving a successful combination of the suggestions above depends upon rhythmic skills as well as a command of air and consonants. See the following Discussion for details.
5. An appoggio position is a must for legato.

Discussion

How to Do It: Legato, Portamento, and Sliding

Connecting between scale notes is generally not difficult. Skips, on the other hand, need a clear-cut method. The three modes of connecting notes—legato, slides, and portamentos—are almost exactly the same. The only difference among them lies in the amount of time taken when going from one note to the other. Thus the skill is primarily rhythmic.

A *slide* is the slowest and most overt connection; it openly passes through every pitch that lies between the top and bottom notes of the interval and at a slowish rate of speed.

A *portamento* is a slide that moves to the second note of the interval swiftly, but starts moving at almost the last moment of the first note, allowing just enough time for the connecting pitches to be heard fleetingly.

A *legato connection* is the least overt connection. It moves so rapidly to the second note of the interval at the very last millisecond that a listener hears only the two pitches and no interruption. The effect is that of the air alone moving through, connecting the two tones.

Whereas a slide is generally considered to be a careless and unmusical connection, a portamento is deemed legitimate, often mandated by the composer with a clear slur mark, equally often not marked but obligatory according to performance practice of the composer and/or historical period. Observe the examples of the same interval executed as a slide, portamento, and legato connection in Figures 1.3, 1.4, and 1.5.

Slide: all pitches that lie within the skip between the two Fs are heard equally well during the slide, which occupies the entire quarter note value of the low F.

Portamento: all pitches that lie between the two Fs are heard equally during the durational value of the last sixteen note of the low F.

Legato connection: no individual pitches that lie between the two Fs are heard during the value of the last sixty-fourth note in which the voice travels from the low F to the high F.

How to Do It: Learning to Sing Legato

The appoggio position will equip your singers with stability of tone and all the practical advantages of a greater air supply, although it delivers not more air but rather a less wasteful expenditure of air, thus sidestepping the problems of non-legato singing.

The never-faltering flow of air on which tone rides (legato) is contingent on a strong mental ideal of forward movement. The singer must not conceive of the vocal line (the air) as going up to the consonants, fermatas, or dotted rhythms and out the other side to continue, but rather through the consonants, through the entire duration of fermatas, through every beat of long notes, and through dotted notes. An arm gesture of forward movement is helpful. Any physical demonstration of continuous motion, such as imitating the smooth, constant movement of a string player's bowing arm, may be useful. Singing the lines with lip trills will localize the feeling of constant forward movement of the air.[11] So will singing the

FIGURES 1.3, 1.4, and 1.5

lines on an extended voiced consonant like [z]. "No interruptions to the moving air" is the watchword.

Because teaching legato is a continuing process, many approaches should be employed. Among the fruitful methods of teaching it to a group are these:

1. Pick eight or sixteen bars of representative music needing a legato.

   First, demonstrate the plodding quality of the line when legato is absent.

   Then demonstrate the forward-moving direction of the musical line when legato is present.

2. Have your singers sing this excerpt using only the lip trill. Move the air! Move it purposefully toward the goal, the end of the phrase.

3. Have them sing the section again using one vowel only, [ʌ] for example.

4. Have them sing the excerpt using the vowels as written, no consonants.

5. Have them sing the excerpt using the vowels and one (arbitrarily chosen) consonant only, making every effort to keep the same kind of air movement going. The consonant should be executed swiftly, on the beat.

   Let one section listen to another, noting when consonants are precisely together and when they are not.

   Trade listeners and doers.

   Have singers use physical gestures to mark the beat while executing consonants precisely.

   For a discussion of consonants *on* versus *before* the beat, see pp. 80–81.

6. Have them sing the excerpt again, with all consonants and vowels as written. When one particular consonant causes special difficulties, rehearse the correct way to execute that consonant swiftly and energetically but without interrupting the air flow. Eventually the singers will have a large consonant vocabulary.

7. Have them move the index finger or sweep the arm forward through the air to the end of the phrase as they sing. Restart the motion with each new phrase.

8. Clear the floor of chairs so that there is ample space for movement. Instruct singers in taking baby steps at a small pulse level, for example, the eighth-note pulse. On your command, singers step off in every direction, following individual paths, baby-stepping while singing the phrase, pausing only at a rest or a breath, then stepping off again with the next phrase. That is, if there is airflow (singing), the body is moving in imitation of the flow. After initial fun and chaos, the forward body movement induces continuous, forward-moving breath flow. Other fortunate by-products of this exercise are increased rhythmic awareness, acute listening and watching, and a tighter ensemble.

Directors may conceive endless variations on these approaches, adapting the concept to the situation.

To sum up, train the mental goal of connecting all the notes by moving the air through all obstacles—the consonants being the worst of these—to the end of the phrase, and not slowing the forward motion of the air when the note's duration is exceptionally long. Legato requires a rapid execution of the consonant at the very last millisecond of the first note. Adding a mental image that connotes spinning, forward-moving air helps.

1.4 Melisma/Velocity/Agility/Fioratura and Breath

One of the most difficult tasks facing a choral director is teaching singers—those who do not already have a flair for it—to sing melismatic passages with speed and clarity. The agility problem is twofold: The singers must keep the tempo, but cannot sacrifice accuracy and clarity for speed. Professional singers spend years achieving this ability, but directors have no such amount of time at their disposal. Even so, vocal agility is a skill that can be improved with the right kinds of practice. In this section, you will find explanations of what can be done to achieve speed and articulation in your singers' agility singing and why. For practical specifics, see the How to Do It sections.

The Complaint

Which of the general, basic vocal techniques are most important to fioratura skills?

Dx, The Diagnosis

1. Does a straight tone aid melismas? A vibratoless tone does least vocal damage during a velocity pattern that takes place in the area of the middle voice. Once the notes arrive at the upper passaggio and above, however, a vibratoless tone is a liability. Since removal of vibrato increases the tension in the larynx, it will surely reduce the airflow efficiency, cutting it substantially, causing further difficulties with higher notes, and producing a loss of consistent vocal quality. This may matter less in a choral situation where the sound is an aggregate one. Only experience with the skills of your particular singers will tell you. The science of vibrato allied with rapid tempos may explain directors' intuitive leap to requesting *senza vibrato* tone. See p. 149.

2. Are [h]s between each note helpful? When aspirated articulation or placing [h]s between all pitches is requested for the rapid notes of agility, it often has a disastrous effect on choral tone. [H]s are discouraged because a series of notes with this consonant causes the cords to repeat aspirated articulations, eventually causing fatigue. Sooner or later this inevitable vocal fatigue dictates an involuntary slowing of the tempo.

3. Is it useful to accent the first note of every group of three or four? One of the inadvertent results of accenting the first note of a rhythmic group in melisma is that the notes immediately before and after the accented note will lose clarity, pitch, and character. This happens because the singer is either getting ready to make the accent, thus losing the preceding note, or in the process of recuperating from the accent, thus losing the note directly following. Stressing all first notes of the pattern groups elicits fatigue—when fatigue will strike is the only question. When fatigue does arrive on the scene, articulation becomes close to impossible, and tempo inevitably falters. Accenting first notes of patterns might seem to help initially, but in the end clarity is compromised. See item 3 on p. 40.

4. Does it help to lighten the voice in agility sections? There is no evidence that "lightening" the voice gives greater speed or accuracy in agility. In a good agility singer the velocity of the notes may give the impression that the singer is using a lighter adjustment, but in reality that impression is caused by the fact that a skilled singer of agility does not sing each note for itself, but sings through all the pitches, without favoring individual ones. The notes are literally aerodynamically "streamlined."

5. How important is the breath in velocity singing? Air support of a consistently high energy level is the life blood of agility. Consequently, maintaining the appoggio position is of paramount importance in stabilizing

the agility efforts, and speeding up the tempo. By the same token, vowel modification (see p. 46) maintains for the singer the "place of vocal ease" throughout the passage, thus aiding in all three requirements of fioratura singing: clarity, speed, and reasonable beauty of tone.

Rx, The Treatment Plan

1. Insist on extra care in maintaining the appoggio position during agility work. A well-maintained appoggio in velocity sections even minimizes the bad effects of the [h]s to some extent. Remind your singers that downward scales require no less support—in fact, *more*. Therefore attention to expanded ribs and a raised sternum should be unremitting.

2. Even if the tone quality resulting from inserting [h]s into velocity patterns does meet with your approval, monitor carefully how much vocal fatigue and consequent tempo slowing this produces in your singers.

3. Acquaint your singers with the method of modifying vowels in upper notes, especially through the passaggio. Give them permission to concentrate most of all on the places where the patterns go into, through, and out of the notes of the upper passaggio (see p. 110).

4. Skill in velocity singing does not come easily, even to professional singers. It is a long and involved process. In a choral situation, it is probably true that time constrictions and the amateur status of many singers work against acquiring the speed and clarity that the director might wish to have available. The best answer is for directors to try the types of practice used by professional singers, choosing what works best for their singers, and to exploit their usual creativity to invent methods for teaching it. Building upon that success, the director should devise shorter applications of the successful methods that may be employed as warm-up exercises. Regular attention to vocal flexibility in the warm-up and training portion of rehearsal will ensure that the choristers develop and maintain an agile vocal technique that will serve them well when melismatic passages arise in the literature.

5. Fruitful acceptable methods detailed in the following Discussion are

    making sure that an excellent appoggio is maintained for each entire passage.

    teaching singers to imitate a stifled laughter movement when singing agility passages.

    mentally singing "straight ahead," not note by note.

teaching the choristers to recognize patterns and their repetitions and variations.

practicing alternated sostenuto and fioratura patterns.

singing all notes of the melismas at the imagined pitch level of the highest note in the phrase.

using a body gesture to accent and organize the note groups of the passage rather than a vocal accent.

using a mental accent for the first note of each group rather than a physical one.

using staccato to make sure that the patterns and vowel modifications are learned accurately at a slow tempo before gradually increasing the speed to a fast tempo.

practicing at a fast tempo once the notes and rhythms are learned accurately.

teaching the mental skill of gear shifting when increasing the speed of the fioratura passages.

practicing the extended onset exercise; see Figure 1.2, p. 30.

practicing on front vowels ([i], [e], [ɛ]) before going to back vowels.

learning to shift between [ʊ] and [ʌ] (or less often, [e] and [ɛ]) at rhythmically precise places in the upper passaggio and the notes surrounding it.

6. Questionable quick fixes are

asking for "lighter" singing.

asking for no vibrato.

asking for [h]s between every note of the agility passage.

DISCUSSION

Traditional Study of Agility

Solo singers who wisely spend many years on completing velocity works (such as the Marchesi, Garcia, or Bordogni methods, which include every melody and rhythm known to man) recognize certain truths that escape those who try to acquire agility skills by a shortcut. Here are some of those facts:

1. The constant changes in pitches and registers cause the compression to vary in agility passages unless the singer is vigilant with the appoggio. Keeping a constant, high level of compression and airflow (aided by a focus on singing "straight ahead") makes all types of patterns easier to execute. This requires an appoggio that never flags.

2. Agility is easier to execute in higher ranges than in lower ones because singers automatically give more compression to higher notes. This is as true for altos and basses as it is for the higher voices. In this context, the importance of the appoggio is clear, because one of its functions is to stabilize low pitches.

3. A heavy accent on the first note of a group often means that the second note of the group is lost, as is the fourth note while the singer prepares to accent the first note of the next group. The conductor hears this as unclean. He may not recognize the cause: a rebound effect caused by the accent on the first note of the group, eliciting a less supported second and fourth notes.

4. Untrained larger voices will find it more difficult to execute velocity patterns as rapidly as do lighter voices. Heavier voices can learn to move their voices rapidly; it just takes more study and practice over a longer period of time. Pay special attention to the heavier voices of all sections.

It goes without saying that choral singers cannot be given as detailed and stringent a course in agility singing as can be done in the voice studio. Time considerations make this all but impossible. Shortcuts should be devised that give reasonably good results. They should be based on the methods for solo singers with pragmatic adaptations to the choral setting.

How to Do It: Appoggio

The importance of the appoggio cannot be overemphasized. Because the singers should already be using the appoggio position for their singing, it is a reasonably simple matter to instruct them not to abandon it during agility singing but, in fact, to strengthen it. Evening out the compression for all notes in agility passages gives the stability needed for clarity of pitches high and low. A consistently high level of compression is especially important in those patterns that contain skips. Maintaining the appoggio, which will keep all the notes at one level of compression, is the key. This is why some professional singers consider the machine gun to be their ideal: It has no nuance; it either fires or stops, both at one high energy level. An evocative analogy for reinforcing the importance of maintaining the appoggio during agility singing is this: A plane need not land in Toledo in order to say, "This is Toledo." It is enough to be in Toledo's airspace. Similarly, the agility singer need not stop mentally on each note of a melisma to sing it well. Sailing through the notes at one even level of compression will deliver speed and articulation.

EXERCISE 1.5

Sing up a scale of a ninth, as in Figure 1.6, and then down in a normal fashion using [ʌ]. Then sing up a nine-tone scale with an appoggio, on the way down reiterating the appoggio. Make sure that the choristers feel the difference when the appoggio is added. The lower notes then feel stable.

EXERCISE 1.6

Sing a pattern of 1–2–3–2–1–8————5–3–1, as in Figure 1.7, first singing normally using [ʌ]. Then sing it again, pausing to add an appoggio during beat 1 of bar 2 before going up to the octave. Feel the difference in the support and the consequent easy high note. In effect, extra compression is elicited early rather than on the way to the high note—the unthinking, automatic execution normally employed by most amateur singers.

How to Do It: Starting the Melisma

From *Messiah*:

No. 13. "He led them through the deep," in all parts, as in Figure 1.8. Beginning notes of an agility passage are the most difficult. A short pattern like the one in Figure 1.8 is virtually over before it starts. When the phrase "as thro' a wilderness" appears, it contains a group of four sixteenth notes preceded by an eighth note. The answer to the problem of clear agility here is to make the pickup eighth note strong and legato, leading strongly into the agility, thus putting the energized air in motion before the sixteenth notes start. In addition, if the [z] sound of the written [s] of the word *as* is allowed to create a staccato note, then the singer is concerned with getting the first two notes of the agility pattern going. Often those first notes will not be clear or on time. The phrase should be executed as if the words were *ae zthru wuh wilderness*. Marking a horizontal arrow that leads to the right above the notes reminds singers of where their concentration should be. The director's body language shows the singers that they should lean into the sixteenth notes.

No. 27. "And with the blast," in all parts, as in Figure 1.9. The word *blast* is set with a quarter note followed by a group of four sixteenths, of which the first is tied to the quarter, finishing with

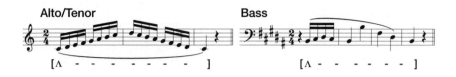

FIGURES 1.6 and 1.7

FIGURES 1.8 and 1.9.   From *Israel in Egypt*

another quarter note. If the singers do not keep the air moving through the quarter note (another arrow), then the second sixteenth is late. Changing from a sostenuto to an agility pattern is a matter of keeping the air moving energetically ahead.

Figure 1.10 is a good beginning exercise that is helpful in acquiring the habit of moving the air ever forward in this rhythmic pattern. Air must move through the quarter note into the sixteenths so as not to be late on the second sixteenth note.

How to Do It: Accenting Groups

As for the accenting of the first note of agility groups composed of three or four notes, singers often end up aspirating the accented note, a very unhealthy vocal practice. To repeat: Because the vocal fatigue is extreme, singers cannot keep this practice up for long without slowing the tempo. Directors then wonder why the insidious slowing down takes place. If an accent is notated, a fast upward stroke of the abdominals does it best. Meanwhile, sing straight ahead (like the machine gun firing), not stopping for single notes that are conspicuously above or below the median pitch, but strengthening the appoggio to give the requisite compression for all the notes.

FIGURE 1.10

How to Do It: Body Movements as an Aid to Velocity Singing

Avoid (unwritten) vocal accents in agility passages altogether by transferring the accent to another part of the body during the learning process. (Written accents are sometimes added in the misguided hope that it will aid the speed.) Substitute a physical gesture for the vocal accent; for example:

> Strike the air with an imaginary timpani mallet.
> Flex the knees, then shift body weight from one foot to the other on the desired pulse.
> Tap the smaller pulse on the sternum.

How to Do It: Practice

Initially, slow practice, either in staccato or legato mode, must be done, not because going slowly eventually enables the singers to go fast—although it does help a bit—but because they must get the patterns in their heads. Where is there a repetition? Where does pattern 1 repeat? What is the tune that concludes the patterns and finishes the line? Securing the musicianship, aided by staccato practice, can only be done slowly. High passages should be sung down the octave for repetitive note-learning practice, gradually increasing the tempo. Generally speaking, when the singer is truly singing with one level of compression for all patterns in a line, a fast tempo is actually easier than a slow one.

In the composer's musical organization of each fioratura passage there is, perforce, a "big tune," the tune formed by the salient notes of each group. As an example, this excerpt from *Messiah* has an easily recognizable big tune:

No. 26. "All we like sheep have gone astray," bars 68–70 in the soprano part, the big tune identified by asterisks above the notes F,
E♭, D, C, B♭, A, D, B♭, G (Figure 1.11)

Once the singer has mentally established the "big tune," the small patterns between notes of the "big tune" are easy to conquer. Marking the
notes of the "big tune" and then singing only that tune enables a quicker
and more precise knowledge of the agility pattern of the smaller notes and
a better sense of the harmonies on which the big tune is based.

There is some conjecture that each singer's optimal agility tempo is
related to his or her heart-beat tempo or mathematical variations on that
tempo. In a chorus, the individual's preferred tempo cannot sway the one
chosen by the director, but fast will eventually be easier than slow. Once
the tempo is so slow that the chorus is singing individual notes, it is no
longer, by definition, agility. It is cantabile or sostenuto—a different thing
altogether.

How to Do It: The Stifled Chuckle Method

One of the useful ploys in teaching the rudiments of agility singing is
imitating a real chuckle or soft laughter, but stifling it. Once the singers
find this trick comfortable and reasonably easy, they are able to teach the
larynx the vocal cords' efficient adductions during fioratura movement
and retain the unconscious kinesthetic memory of what has to be done.
The larynx's agility movements are far more active than most singers
expect, although they are not the focus of their attention. They are usually surprised to find that, although good agility sounds light and effort-
less, a successful fioratura is backed by a higher energy level and higher
mental concentration level (straight ahead!) than expected. Asking for very
light singing at a piano level with gentle, graceful action, and careful attention to the accuracy of each and every note is not productive of speed
or clarity.

EXERCISE 1.7
(borrowing from Richard Miller's brilliant explanation)[12]

1. On one comfortable pitch, exactly as if you were chuckling quietly but rapidly, sing *Hm! hm! hm! HM!* on a triplet and a quarter note with the tongue tip on top of the bottom teeth. There will
   be space between the notes. Be sure that your singers note the involuntary slight movement of the abdominal wall (no conscious

FIGURE I.II

pushing or pulling of the abdominals), and that they not try to initiate conscious throat action.

2. Gradually change the single pitch into a higher range, using the same rhythm and the same chuckled *hm!*

3. Repeat 1 and 2, changing the *hm* into *ha* with a bright [ɑ] and the rhythm into four sixteenth notes and a quarter. Ha, ha, ha, ha, HA!

4. Repeat 1 and 2, deleting the [h], Ah, ah, ah, ah, Ah! unaspirated. (To conquer this element may take more time.)

5. Sing a downward fifth (5–4–3–2–1) with a higher range for all parts, using the laughing *ah!* To change the pitches causes some difficulty. Continue with the same tune, changing keys, singing at a fairly quick tempo until a facility begins to come.

6. Use the tune from #5, singing with a reasonably fast repeated [ɑ].

7. It is probably best to do 1 through 6 at several warmups before going on. At the time when you judge your singers prepared to attempt a real agility passage, choose a short, small range example from the standard repertoire and let them have a go at it. Gradually move to longer and more complicated passages, making sure that the notes are under command before asking the choristers to do the rapid-tempo chuckle.

How to Do It: The Balanced Onset and Fioratura

The approach, as in Figure 1.12, builds on Exercises 1.3 and 1.4 (p. 29) and takes the singers step by step from broken to sostenuto agility singing. Once the singers' skill in the balanced onset technique is extended to repeating notes without an intervening breath, expand the exercise further to the five-note scale. Both the chuckle and the extended onset approaches develop the fine laryngeal motor skills required to execute clear articulation of all notes in a fioratura passage.

FIGURE 1.12

How to Do It: Vowel Modification and Ascending Swiftly to High Tones

Very few melismas avoid the passaggio altogether. Therefore, to ignore the use of vowel modification will rob the breath—the lifeblood of agility—of its power. Those readers unfamiliar with the elements and principles of vowel modification and the passaggios may wish to read pp. 110, 119–21 before proceeding. Vowel modification plays a very important part in agility singing because the vocal cords can best deliver speed and clarity when the tone goes into head voice at the upper passaggio and above. Velocity passages written on the vowels [ɑ], [ɔ], [o], or [u] should use the modification [ʊ] in the upper passaggio and [(ʌ)] on high notes above the passaggio. Passages written on front vowels should use the modification [e] in the passaggio, [ɛ] above, substituting [ø] and [œ] for German and French vowels that include protruding lips. The most efficient procedure when the pitches pass rapidly through the upper passaggio of each part is the use of the [ʊ] or [e], but the high speed of the patterns can cause a problem in remembering where to place the modifications. A fast tempo dictates that the vowel cannot be changed in the space of two sixteenth notes, for example. Therefore, if specific instructions are for when the singer should change the vowel, then it remains only to change the vowel gradually over several notes before arriving at the completed vowel on the appointed note.

In addition, the practice of velocity patterns on front vowels ([i], [e], [ɛ]) only in the beginning often allows their automatically forward vocal position to create an ease and speed, which can then be insinuated into those passages written on the less efficient back vowels. Then, assuming the written vowel to be an [ɑ], proceed to the [ʊ] vowel in the passaggio and the [(ʌ)] with rounded lips for the pitches that rise above the passaggio.

Once your singers have been trained to modify through the passaggio in normal music, doing the same thing while singing rapidly is only a

FIGURE 1.13

FIGURE 1.14

matter of paying attention. One of the elements that always slows down a melisma section is going through the passaggio badly, thus making difficulty on the high notes that lie above the passaggio. See p. 110 for proper modifications for each section. Only the sopranos have the possibility of avoiding the vowel modifications by the use of the "silver [a]," see p. 48.

From *Messiah*

No. 26. "All we like sheep," bars 43–45 for basses (Figure 1.13). The bass line sits quite high and predominantly within the passaggio. The necessary change from the majority of passaggio [ʊ]s to the one instance of the upper E♭ [(ʌ)] vowel is carefully placed on an even division of the four sixteenth notes in order to aid the memory of when to change. The C is also left on the [(ʌ)] vowel for two reasons: (1) on descending pitches correct passaggio notes are less important; (2) the tempo is too fast to attempt to change back to [ʊ] for one note. A line such as this can effectively be practiced down an octave until the maneuver is well routined, then returned to the upper octave.

From *Messiah*

No. 26. "All we like sheep," bars 41–43 for tenors (Figure 1.14). The tenor line lies largely outside the passaggio with occasional forays into passaggio notes, thus requiring an execution exactly the opposite of the basses', but using the same rationale as that applied to the bass melisma for the rhythmic divisions.

FIGURE 1.15

FIGURE 1.16

From *Israel in Egypt*

No. 9. "He smote all the first-born," bars 4–6 in the soprano part (Figure 1.15). The agility is performed on the word *strength*, which means that [ɛ] is already the correct vowel for the E and D♯ as written, but at F♯ and G, which are in the passaggio area, the sopranos should sing [e] with a high forward tongue (more a French *aigu* [é] than an American diphthong [ɛi]). If they are careful not to put the final consonants (ngth) on the G, but to carry them over to the lower B (the word thereby becoming *ngthof*), then the G will not be a cut-off "yelp."

From *Messiah*

No. 21. "His yoke is easy," bars 23–25 in the alto part (Figure 1.16). The first bar of melisma is sung in the midst of the lower passaggio, therefore on the [e] vowel. As the melody descends out of the passaggio, the mouth opens much wider, and the vowel changes to [ɛ], both of which results in more sound in this area where the alto is often inaudible.

How to Do It: Sopranos and the Use of "Silver ah"

Requirements for silver [a]

[æ] or [a] tongue position with tip held on lower lip, not behind it
upper teeth showing
cheeks high

The sopranos' possible escape from vowel modifications in fioratura is the use of the vowel [a], best defined as that front [a] which native Bostonians use to say the well-known phrase "pahk the cah." It is very close to the vowel [æ] but not quite the same. The use of this [a] does away with the need to modify the soprano section's vowels in the passaggio and above, because it accommodates the voice on all pitches, deleting most of the chest voice content, and therefore saving air. For this reason, it sails up to high notes without requiring modification. This tone is probably what directors have in mind when they ask for a "lighter" adjustment for agility. The success of this ploy depends upon the sopranos' ability to find the vowel reliably—not an [æ] but a very forward [a], actually placing the tip of the tongue on the lower lip, showing the upper teeth, and keeping the cheeks high.

EXERCISE 1.8

Using the arpeggiated tune (Figure 1.17) of an octave and a half, singing up on a tonic chord and down on a dominant chord, have the sopranos sing it twice without a breath, the first time phrasing every two notes together, and the second time, singing the notes staccato. Tongue tip is on the lower lip, vowel is the Boston [a], cheeks are held high, and upper teeth are showing. The ease with which high notes are thus sung is immediately apparent.

From Bach's *Mass in B Minor*

No. 4. "Gloria," in the section "et in terra pax," bars 23–27 in the Soprano I part affords a practical example of a melisma that will profit from use of silver [a] (Figure 1.18).

How to Do It: Streamlining the Vocal Line for Speed

Even as a race car driver works at maintaining an efficient speed in order to win the race, mentally straightening out the curves of the racetrack, so must a singer avoid surrendering to the ups and downs of a melisma passage by equalizing the energy on skips versus the straightaway, the high notes versus the low notes, the longer notes versus the shorter notes, and so on. This can be accomplished by an unflagging appoggio and the correct mental set. On the other hand, all these changes, if surrendered to, make inroads on the speed and accuracy of their agility delivery. Change your singers' mental images of agility singing.

The technique of mentally shifting gears is a useful tool. Rather than mentally, and therefore vocally, laboring over each note (equated to many

FIGURE 1.17

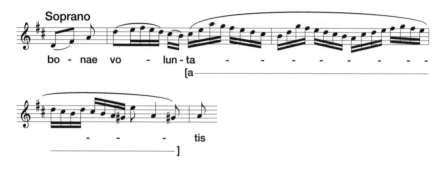

FIGURE 1.18

rapid and energy-draining strokes of the bicycle pedals in low gear), the singer mentally shifts to a larger pulse (the longer, self-propelling stride of a higher gear), powered by unflagging breath support.

Summary

To reiterate, the choral director does well to train the singers using the various principles of fioratura expertise, until he or she sees which are most productive for the chorus in the given situation.

1. Maintain the appoggio position at all times, practicing with arms behind the back when practicable.
2. Conceive of the vocal line as going in a straight line, ever forward, never following the contours of the melody, with high-energy breath at all times, not increasing and decreasing the dynamic level for skips or different pitch ranges, but rather using for all notes the one level of breath energy that is required for the highest or most difficult notes.
3. When the pitches go into the upper passaggio and above, modify vowels on an unmistakable rhythmic spot, arriving there gradually.

4. Try to keep a tone quality that can be described as bright, brilliant, focused and forward, but not "light," using the tongue-tip position (on top of the bottom teeth) to help achieve that tone.

5. Encourage sopranos to use the front [a], (silver [a], Boston [a]), for lengthy high-range fioratura passages.

6. When accenting first notes of the agility groups, do not make the accent with the voice (unless so written, and with care when written) but transfer it to another body part, such as feet, wrists, or hands, eventually to the mind only.

7. Distinguish between the vocal mode of sostenuto and the "chuckle," without adopting [h]s to do so.

8. Sing with a free vocal production, no insistence upon *senza vibrato*, and with a dynamic level of *mezzo forte* at least.

1.5 High/Low Pitches, Range, and Breath

When choral directors hold their initial auditions for purposes of classification, they hear the range that each singer can manage under stress and, sometimes, without the help of technical skills. In most cases, this is not the actual range possessed by each singer; it is the bare minimum. In all probability the singers have never had help in understanding how to open up both high and low ranges.

In this section we consider the basic elements of high and low pitches and how range and its use relate to breath.

THE COMPLAINT

Why is it so difficult for altos and basses to be heard in their low ranges? I can understand tenors and sopranos being inaudible on pitches that are too low for them, but why should the low voices not be audible?

DX, THE DIAGNOSIS

These are basic facts regarding low range pitches:

1. As a rule, lyric sopranos, who compose the majority of choral sopranos, do not have power on low pitches. This is why choral music written by vocally knowledgeable composers does not generally ask them for such pitches at a loud dynamic. If required, the temporary use of chest voice is the only answer for audibility,

unless the singers are too young. No young singers should be asked to sing too loudly (or to sing in chest voice), and the repertoire choices should reflect this fact. Caution demands that female singers of elementary or high-school age should not be asked for pure chest. After that age, they may be taught both chest and chest mix.

2. Carrying power on low pitches is dependent upon the use of chest voice and/or a good deal of compression in the airflow.

3. It is a fact that low notes do not carry as well as high pitches. Therefore, even those real altos (some of the section will be nonaltos who have been placed there because they are good musicians) should ideally be capable of going into chest or not, always excepting those who are too young.

4. Mature male voices naturally sing in chest up to the vicinity of middle C (C4). Mature tenors' lowest note is C 3. When singing that low, they are at an extreme disadvantage.

5. A true bass voice, even in a college-age male, is relatively rare. On extremely low notes, vocal fry is a possibility but should not be made habitual.[13]

6. Evaluating the quantity of sound that the accompanying instruments make and in what range they play compared to the voice ranges helps make the decision as to how much technical aid is necessary for each section. A vocally knowledgeable composer generally does not write low pitches for *forte* singing over heavy orchestration.

Rx, The Treatment Plan

1. Once the choral director has determined that more sound from the low range notes is of importance, then the technical answers must be implemented. The appoggio is an absolute necessity because its greater compression will give more audibility. It is not difficult to invoke; it simply requires an actual lifting of the sternum as the pitches descend. Train your altos, tenors, and basses to raise their sternums whenever they must sing *forte* on low-range notes and/ or when they head downward. Test it out and show them the efficiency of this tactic by asking them to sustain a low note normally and then raise the sternum, without involving the shoulders. The difference is immediately noticeable.

2. Male voices are already singing in chest voice until the pitches arrive at the passaggio; see pp. 107–10 for a discussion of the passaggio. Female voices, notably altos, must decide whether to

go into chest voice or not as they descend in range. The director's task, then, is to train them in two ways: to go into chest at will, or to refrain at will from going into chest. Then the director must designate his or her choice for those passages. Female singers of high-school age should not to be introduced to chest voice unless their voices are very mature. Singers of college age should be taught how to do it without danger. See Falsetto and Chest Voice, pp. 115–16, for suggestions on how to teach it.

DISCUSSION

Basic Requirements for Low-Range Singing

The choice to use chest voice is colored by the accurate observation that true chest notes always sound crass, vulgar, and loud. Nevertheless, when the low notes of the alto section are inaudible, chest voice holds the answer, providing that the appoggio is maintained to keep the intonation correct. Often basses especially, but also altos, harbor a mistaken belief that all they have to do for low pitches is to relax. (It is common to react to low notes by working less hard.) This explains the wobbly and woofy low notes without concomitant carrying power that are sometimes heard from those sections.

When descending to lower notes, almost any singer benefits from determining to keep from collapsing the sternum and ribs. In the end, the director should make the decision as to which mode—chest, or chest mixed with head—presents the best solution, especially for altos. If the director has trained the alto section to do both, it is then his or her prerogative to opt for the one that satisfies the musical demands. When altos must refrain from going into chest, corners on the descending vowels will help to avoid pure chest. Basses need simply raise their sternums and extend their ribs, thereby eliciting more compression and thus more sound.

THE COMPLAINT

How can I improve the high notes that issue from my choir?

Dx, THE DIAGNOSIS

Because of the usual disposition of chordal tones in choral music, sopranos and tenors are most at risk. They carry the high-note duties most of the time. Furthermore, the longer they are asked to stay in the upper regions without respite, the more fatigue and tension set in, thus increasing the difficulty and the shrillness even when they sing well. Note that singing softly most of the time does not alleviate the fatigue and tension. The appoggio position of the chest and sternum will do much to make the high notes easier and less shrill, also contributing to a normal vibrato. The appoggio position will also aid altos and basses.

Vowel modification will also make high notes easier, improving tone quality as well. Deft use of consonants avoids their often deleterious effects upon high pitches. There is no need to question carrying power on high pitches. Even badly sung high pitches carry (sometimes too well). It is the nature of the vocal beast.

Rx, The Treatment Plan

1. Routine your entire choir in the appoggio, which carries with it advantages of every kind. It stabilizes the vocal instrument, thereby providing extended capacity for high notes as well as nonwobbly, audible low notes.
2. Take very seriously the vowel modifications in the passaggio and on the upper notes of each section's range. These modifications are even more effective when accompanied by the unflagging appoggio.
3. The skillful use of consonants helps high notes to be easy. Consonants that precede high notes can be fudged, lengthened, or omitted. Teach your singers these three techniques; see p. 88 for criteria governing the choice of consonant method. Teach them to prepare the mouth for the high note vowel, not the consonant.
4. When the high note occurs on an entrance, have your singers prepare their mouths for the vowel, not the consonant, in the beat preceding the onset. The cords are then ready to produce tone instantly. The consonant must be lightning swift unless it has been deemed necessary to lengthen it, as described on p. 89.

1.6 *Forte/Piano* and Breath

It is understandable that amateur singers often and intuitively simply add air for forte *and subtract it for* piano. *This ignores the necessity for breath support—appoggio being the most efficient form—and inevitably diminishes the tone quality while initiating intonation problems.*

THE COMPLAINT

When I ask for greater dynamic extremes, I often notice a diminution of tonal beauty, some unstable vibratos, and pitch problems.

DX, THE DIAGNOSIS

It is unrealistic to expect young or amateur singers to sing successfully in *pianissimo* or *fortissimo* when a basic technique is wanting, even though their musical responses are of a high level. Singers without training, even those of mature age, are often tempted to remove a certain amount of support or to deliberately sing with a breathy tone in order to achieve a *piano*. Similarly, they sometimes push and compress their necks to increase the dynamic level to *forte*, confusing that with "support."

Maintaining the appoggio is the foundation of singing at extreme dynamic ranges. The softer the sound the director wants to hear, the stronger should be the appoggio, because *pianissimo* demands more compression than *forte*. Breathiness is not the same thing as *pianissimo*. A narrow, focused tone of *piano* is clearer, prettier, and carries better.

RX, THE TREATMENT PLAN

1. A pragmatic method to complement the appoggio will often be to use the vowel modifications in such a way as to convince the listener that a crescendo and decrescendo has taken place, while maintaining a stong appoggio. In simplest terms, *forte* singing requires larger mouth openings and vowels with slightly lower tongue positions. *Piano* singing requires smaller mouth openings and vowels with a very forward tongue. Full information for employing vowel modifications to effect dynamic variety is in chapter 3, pp. 130–34.
2. Exercises for regulating the air flow and maintaining the appoggio while executing a messa di voce are provided in the following Discussion.

DISCUSSION

Dynamic Extremes and the Appoggio

If keeping a strong appoggio and adjusting the jaw opening appropriately took care of all gradations and uses of *forte* and *piano*, it would be very satisfying. That, however, is too much to expect from an extremely complicated vocal issue like control of dynamics. The nature of the vocal instrument is that singing dynamic extremes puts a strain on intonation. Therefore, the director must also request that the singers listen intensely to keep the pitches on track when singing very loudly or very softly. Their sensitivity to, and concentration on, pitch acuity will go a long way toward avoiding intonation problems of this sort.

The Science

Johan Sundberg adds some pertinent facts about how the appoggio relates to pitch and loudness:

"Subglottal pressure is determined by muscular forces, elasticity forces, and gravitation. The phonatory function of the breathing apparatus is to provide a subglottal pressure. Both in singing and speech this pressure is adjusted according to the intended vocal loudness, but in singing it has to be tailored also to pitch; higher pitches need higher pressures than lower pitches. . . .

"In singing, variation of subglottal pressure is required not only when loudness but also pitch is changed. When we increase pitch, we stretch the vocal folds. It seems that stretched vocal folds require a higher driving pressure than laxer vocal folds. Thus, higher subglottal pressures are needed for high pitches than for low pitches."[14]

Professional singers must wait until their basic techniques are solid before they begin to work at the extreme dynamics through the usual intensive training method for learning to do the messa di voce (crescendo, decrescendo on one single note). Even so, one choral director attributes much of her choir's improved tonal focus and expressive capabilities to regular training and practice of the messa di voce.

A standard approach to training choral singers to regulate and expand their dynamic capabilities is found in Exercise 1.9. This exercise balances breath and tone, hones technical capability, and increases responsiveness to the director's expressive requests. At each stage maintain intonation and stay within the limits of the individual voice, that is, neither louder nor softer than can be sung with beauty, the dynamic level relative to the individual voice.

Exercise 1.9

Extending the expressive capabilities of the voice via crescendo/decrescendo, based on breath management.

1. Using 4-part voicing in comfortable range for each section, with singers thinking the numbers in order to crescendo/decrescendo evenly, make up an exercise such as Figure 1.19.

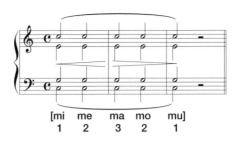

FIGURE 1.19

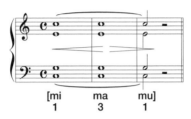

FIGURE 1.20

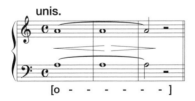

FIGURE 1.21

2. Once the messa di voce is consistently even, eliminate syllables 2 and 4, as in Figure 1.20.
3. Eventually eliminate the syllables to perform the messa di voce on a single vowel, as in Figure 1.21.
4. Conduct a steady beat, no other gesture. Singers perform the messa di voce on a single vowel, peaking in volume on beat five, striving over time for greater contrast within each singer's own dynamic range. (Once the voices are out of medium range, proper vowel modification becomes even more useful and necessary; see the Complete Vowel Modification Chart, p. 127.)

5. Shorten version 4 of this exercise to five beats, peaking on beat three.
6. Shorten further to three beats, peaking on beat two.
7. Conduct an unmetered messa di voce, varying the duration and intensity of contrast.

CHAPTER 2

Diction and Intelligibility

2.1   Acoustical Vowels versus Speech Vowels

Many of the troubles that plague choral directors in the area of diction and intelligibility are caused by the honest conviction that their choristers should sing as they talk. Aside from the fact that this is anatomically impossible, there remain each singer's problems with regional accents and bad language habits in spoken English, which would probably yield a diction that is, in any case, neither uniform nor clear.

THE COMPLAINT

What exactly is an acoustical vowel? Don't *pure* vowels ensure clarity?

Dx, THE DIAGNOSIS

Acoustical vowels are those that are harmonic with a specific pitch. Speech vowels only accidentally, if then, encourage the vibrations of the vocal folds to be harmonic with the pitch. The belief that singing is just speaking on pitch is erroneous. Regional accents abound in any chorus, and they often determine what each singer believes to be a correct vowel.

1. Singing a "pure" vowel is probably an impossibility; see the Discussion below.
2. Any tinkering with mouth openings or thinking one vowel while singing another are efforts at finding an acoustically compatible vowel; therefore they *are* vowel modifications, often just imprecise ones.

Using speech vowels or "pure" vowels exclusively can only result in vocal problems that undermine the singing of your choir. For both the choir and the director, the advantages of using acoustical vowels and vowel modifications far outweigh the task of learning to do them.

Rx, THE TREATMENT PLAN

Consider what you really mean by "pure" vowels. Acquaint yourself with the facts below about acoustical vowels and "pure" vowels, by which you may mean speech vowels. After reading the Discussion you will understand the difference between a perceived vowel and the acoustical vowel—the actual vowel—which is accurately discerned because of its frequency in the acoustical scheme of things. Directly following the Discussion you will find a table showing the relative merits of speech vowels and acoustical vowels.

DISCUSSION

The Cult of the "Pure" Vowel

The core of the vowel—which itself is achieved by the size of the jaw opening, the shape of the lips, and the position of the tongue—is the core of the pitch when that vowel is sung as opposed to spoken. Is there, then, such a thing as a pure vowel? The answer given by Richard Miller is, probably not: "vowel purity is the *optimum acoustical response* for a given vowel (emphasis added)."[1] Voice teacher and researcher Berton Coffin believed that the bel canto devotees, who insist that the basis of their art is pure vowels, really mean that they wish to have pure tone.

When considering the practice of singing only "pure" vowels, recognize that, acoustically speaking, speech vowels are not necessarily pure. In addition, because speech vowels vary considerably depending upon regional accents, results are less than uniform. Moreover, those who really understand the vowel issue—acousticians—consider a pure vowel to be the one that delivers beauty, stable vibrato, resonance, and ease on that particular pitch. Vocal pedagogue Virginia Morrow has this to say about speech vowels: "the requirements for singing far exceed the demands of speech. Singing is *not* simply sustained speech spun out over wide-ranging pitch fluctuations, except in the most simplistic and technically limited vocal styles."[2]

THE SCIENCE

Morrow elaborates on the specific nature of vowels. "[There is] the perceived vowel, taken from the IPA . . . used for precise identification of the various vowel sounds. . . . The acoustical vowel [is] measured in terms of partials or formants, and judged to be mixed or modified as it moves through a series of pitches. . . . Each vowel has a quality which is unique to that particular vowel, a quality which names the vowel or makes it what it is. The vowel core then, is the identifying quality of a given vowel. It is also an acoustical phenomenon; i.e., when the vowel is identified precisely . . . resonance chambers of the vocal instrument are immediately re-shaped (coupled) so that one hears optimum amplification of the basic sound; one has more volume, and potential for dynamic variation, and one has improved intonation and greater ease of production."[3]

Speaking and Singing

Remember that one cannot sing as one speaks. It is not enough to heed the frequent admonitions to "just spit those consonants out," or to "relax; it's just like speaking on pitch," or to "sing on the consonants" (Robert Shaw's immortal words).

Experiments have proven that each of the consonants b, d, f, h, s, t, v, m, and z averages only .058 seconds in speech, but .108 in song. The semi-vowels l, m, n, and r average .145 in speech, but .354 in song. Vowels average .280 seconds in speech, but .797 in song. When bidden to pronounce consonants just as if speaking, while singing notes in the high range or in very loud / very soft dynamics, singers will execute the notes neither comfortably nor well. In sum, the following paraphrase of Richard Miller's masterful discussion lists the reasons why speaking and singing cannot be done in the same way.[4]

1. Breath management responsibilities are far more stringent for singing than for speaking.
2. A vowel must be sustained for greater durations in singing than in speaking.
3. The range covered by the singing voice far exceeds that used for speaking.
4. The sounds of singing demand greater fluctuations of dynamics.
5. Singing requires a constant level of resonance not necessary for speaking.

Acoustical and Speech Vowels: A Comparison

Sometimes it happens that one or more sections will sing a different modification for a vowel that the composer wrote as one for all sections. At least one voice part is usually singing in its comfort zone. Furthermore, as Berton Coffin writes: Whereas spoken vowel values vary according to languages and dialects, in singing they cannot depart from the coincidence of a vowel pitch and an harmonic of the sung pitch. This is an absolute of singing. This is one of the reasons that a person can *sing* a foreign language without an accent but cannot *speak* it without an accent.[5]

Following is a comparison of the advantages of acoustical and speech vowels adapted from Coffin:

Acoustical Vowels

Acoustical vowels, wherein the harmonic of the sung pitch coincides with the pitch of the vowel, produce amplification of resonance and a physiological feeling of well-being.

The more ringing and vibrant we wish the voice to be, the more we should use the harmonic values of acoustical vowels.

Acoustical vowels give the voice more size and more carrying power (important to unamplified singing).

Singing with the best relationship of vibrator (cords) and resonator (mouth) is therapeutic to the throat, the ears of the audience, and the length of the air supply

Almost always, the use of acoustical vowels in singing produces tones that are in the center of the pitch.

Singers who use harmonic sounds (modified vowels) sing for a long time.

The use of acoustical vowels aids rather than detracts from understandable diction.

Speech Vowels

Singers who insist on singing absolute language values that conflict with the written pitches experience as a result, discomfort, an out-of-tune tone lacking in beauty, and a serious diminution of the air supply.

The more we approximate the sounds of speech vowels, the more nonharmonic our voices will be.

Speech vowels give the voice a reduction of carrying power, a fact no longer germane to music theater singers because of the prevalence of amplification

When the most resonant vowel on one particular and sung note is found, it is invariably different from the one used in speech patterns.

The use of speech vowels often gives rise to inexact pitches—flat or sharp—that may not be controllable, even by the singer's sensitive ear.

Singers who utilize many nonharmonic sounds, speech vowels, do not sing as long, because this practice is physically unhealthy over time.

Contrary to common belief, adherence to speech vowels does not promote clear diction, because the tonal interference produced by incompatible vowels masks the clarity of the diction.

2.2 Diction and Vowel Modification

There are many reasons cited for ignoring the use of vowel modification with choral singers, but the one by far most often employed is that it will exacerbate the diction problem. Yet the acousticians' evidence to the contrary is weighty: perceptibility studies have shown that above a certain note in each voice category the listener cannot tell the difference, for example, between one front vowel and another. This is partly because of the limited capacity of the human ear to decipher vowels on high-pitched sounds, and partly because the singing voice, functioning better with the modified vowel, will produce a sound without the acoustical interference that degrades listeners' perception.

THE COMPLAINT

Won't vowel modification further lower perception of the text?

Dx, THE DIAGNOSIS

Singers may complain about the difficulty of singing passages very loud, soft, high, or low. Part of the difficulty lies in executing clear diction. The cause is vowels that are incompatible with the pitches.

Particularly in climactic moments, when the pitches are often proportionately high for all sections, the words are often repetitions of previous phrases. These moments are not text events; they are musical and vocal events. In many cases strict adherence to the written vowels will hinder the vocalism, and thus the musical effect. Modifications will greatly aid the tone and actually provide for better comprehension of the words.

Clarity is also well served by identifying the diphthongs that the composer wrote and by modifying both vowels when the situation calls for it. The Saxon languages, English and German, are notorious not only for consonant clusters that initiate and close each word but also for comparatively impure or combined vowels, which produce less beautiful tone quality and less intelligibility when the execution is rhythmically imprecise.

Generally speaking, at any given moment when the score asks for all sections to sing the same word, one or more sections will be vocally uncomfortable with the vowel. The section that is not uncomfortable is doubtless singing a vowel naturally or accidentally compatible with the pitch. Sopranos suffer more than the other singers. (See the Science box, pp. 119–20.) Modifying their vowels as necessary will give them vocal relief and, at the same time, improve the diction. The audience cannot avoid gleaning the text primarily from the sopranos, who have the top line and often the melody. Sopranos will respond better with the diction when their vocal needs are met.

Rx: The Treatment Plan

1. Always begin by modifying all soprano vowels, starting with D or E♭5 in the upper passaggio and above. Once sopranos are comfortable, tend to the tenors and/or other sections as necessary for intelligibility. Vocal discomfort will always hinder the comprehension of the sung vowels. You will soon acquire an ear that indicates when modifications are in order. In those spots, tone quality as well as diction generally deteriorate.

2. One of the techniques called for in English-language diction is to execute diphthongs with a specific duration for the second vowel. Go through the score, deciding upon the proper rhythmic duration for the two vowels of all diphthongs that fall on notes long enough to warrant the treatment. Recall that most linguists prefer a division of 2/3–1/3, or failing that, 3/4–1/4, and in a fast tempo, 50/50. Inform each section of the selected rhythms and have them mark their scores accordingly.

3. In climactic vocal and musical moments, allow the singers to direct their focus to free vocal production and to emitting the best sound possible. Let diction be of secondary importance.

Discussion

Tone versus Diction

Responding to a questionnaire distributed by the authors before publication, choral directors cited the following five elements as the most problematic:

1. Inability to sing in tune in the area of register breaks
2. Adverse effects of consonant production on tuning and tone quality
3. Inability to sing at a *piano* level without losing the pitch fundamental
4. Breathiness in the middle register
5. Inability to "cover" the tone

If language comprehension were to be included in this list, one could say that these same factors have everything to do with vocal issues in both solo and choral singing. Vowel modification will contribute to the solution for each of these problems, including intelligibility.

It might be easier to accept that distinctness of consonant production would result in clear diction than to believe that vowel modification—changing to acoustically efficient ones—would aid intelligibility. Yet, the human ear recognizes words in many ways and under varying circumstances. Assuring the comprehension of a choir's enunciation is not a simple matter. It is actually highly complex, requiring knowledge of the workings of consonants and vowels as well as judgment regarding where to apply which techniques. This explains the fact that, many times, choirs are not understood by their audiences, despite all the enthusiastic "spitting out" of consonants.

When a choir's repertoire is sung in the language spoken by its listeners, it is much easier for the audience to guess at the words they are hearing, or to supply meaning to inaudible words. Note that theater goers do the same kind of intuiting. They manage to make sense out of inaudible words, of foreign accents, or of heavy accents from other parts of the country applied on top of the English language. This is how an audience for a choral program can successfully intuit words occasionally missed: by supplying them, either because the context is clear or because the language is colloquial and modern. On the other hand, when the audience is listening to a piece written in a foreign language or to a piece whose text is in English but written in complex language or with very difficult concepts, they will find guessing correctly virtually hopeless. As an example, poet T. S. Eliot's language yields less to hazarding a meaning than does Robert Frost's. At such moments listeners give up trying. On the other hand, there are times when the musical/vocal event is so powerful that the recognition of the word is the last thing the audience cares about. If the piece is written in a foreign language that the audience members do not speak, then they do not care what the specific words are. They will probably trust the music or a translation in the program to deliver the message.

So what is the answer to the choral director's dilemma?

1. Train your choir to execute the many necessary techniques of consonant delivery, but don't stop there.
2. Recognize when the musical event is more important than the word recognition, or when repetition of the text in climactic moments makes the diction less crucial. Particularly where tessitura is extreme, let your singers deliver the best tone they can in those places, approximating the consonants, singing a correctly modified vowel.
3. Have the choristers mark the necessary vowel changes in their own scores. Encourage them to execute the correctly modified vowels and diphthongs.

Why will the modified vowels in the register breaks and upper range transmit the word to the audience better than speech vowels? Because acoustical interference caused by a speech vowel in the wrong place will not allow the listener to intuit the vowel that could help them to understand the word. See Acoustical Vowels versus Speech Vowels, pp. 62–63. In addition, when the unmodified vowel is causing vocal difficulties, the amateur singer cannot rise above the distress to clarify the diction. Bear in mind that appreciation of vocal music depends far more on the lengthened vowel than on the short and fleeting consonant, despite the fact that a word is generally unintelligible without clear final consonant(s). At the least, 50 percent of intelligibility relies on recognition of vowels. Do not sell them short.

It is counterproductive to ask all members of a choir to sing the same vowel color in all cases. Vowels are ratios of vowel resonances that vary with voice classification. When a soprano sings [a], [ɑ], or [ɒ] like a bass, she feels choked and loses her top voice. When a bass attempts to sing the same vowels with the color of a soprano, he constricts his throat in such a manner that the tone becomes ugly and nonresonant. Pablo Casals once said that every note of the cello has its own timbre. Surely it is the same for the singing instrument. Great orchestras are built on the great techniques of the individual. Why not great choirs?

It has been proven many times, theoretically and empirically, that listeners better understand the words where modifications are in place—especially on high, loud, very high, or very low pitches—than the words where the vowels are unmodified, struggling against acoustical interference that masks identifiable sounds. Pitches in and above the passaggio will benefit immeasurably from modification of the vowels.

THE SCIENCE

When vowels obey acoustical laws, they are differentiated more efficiently. Consonants are also articulated more easily when they are accompanied by the sympathetic resonation of vowels to the harmonics of sung pitch. Speech vowels occupy two cavities located on either side of the hump of the tongue. Women sing approximately one octave higher than men. Therefore the frequencies of their mouth cavities are approximately 15 percent higher than the frequencies of men. Acousticians have designated the high resonance of vowels occupying the area in front of the tongue hump as R1. The R1 frequencies for various vowels are

roughly G5 for the vowels [æ], [a], [ɒ]
roughly D5 for the vowels [ɛ], [œ], [ɔ]
roughly A4 for the vowels [e], [ø], [o][6]

When a given vowel is sung on a pitch above its R1 frequency, there is a loss of intelligibility. Sung in that range, it will sound just like any other vowel in its series; that is, all front vowels will sound the same and all back vowels will sound the same. Vowels sung on pitches higher than the ones indicated will tend to be distuned, harsh, unstable in vibrato. There may be difficulty with timbre, pitch, and flexibility in dynamics. Since female voices sing nearer to the resonance frequency of vowels, they need more modification in their singing. Male voices, on the other hand, tend to need less modification, especially below D4. Basic modification for men should be toward open on low notes and toward rounded (corners) or closed on top.

Science in Application

Two stories illustrate the practical results of vowel modification and the tendency of some to believe that such a practice is misguided.

A soprano who had been away from her voice teacher for six months was suddenly required to sing a new aria within a few days. She elected to go to a coach rather than her voice teacher for help. The coach, familiar with and disdainful of the voice teacher's use of vowel modifications, erupted in fury after the first time through the aria. "You are singing those dreadful vowels of Mme. X! And that is why I didn't understand a single word. I want you to sing it again with the exact words on the page." The soprano, aware that she had not been singing Mme. X's vowels but rather the ones on the page, panicked a bit. Then she silently decided to do the proper modifications, although she did not tell the coach what she was going to do. When she had finished, the coach said with great satisfaction, "There. You see? Now I understood the words!"

A baritone came to his voice lesson with a friend from Paris. The baritone and the voice teacher spent an inordinate amount of time changing the vowels on the notoriously high pitches of the Poulenc piece he was singing. All the while the modifications were being discussed, the Frenchman's head was wagging negatively back and forth, his face expressing disgust. Both the baritone and the voice teacher assumed it was the usual case of French speakers not liking any changes to their beloved language, but it was a concern with intelligibility. When the baritone finally sang the piece through with the modifications, the Frenchman leapt to his feet, shouting, "Ah, but now I understand the words!"

2.3 The International Phonetic Alphabet (IPA) Vowel Chart

All common vowels, with some few exceptions, appear in every language, but are sometimes spelled differently. The IPA denotes specific sounds across linguistic barriers.

TABLE 2.1 The IPA Vowel Chart

IPA Symbol	English	German	French	Italian	Latin
ɑ (middle ah)	sh_ou_t	_a_ch		c_a_ra	qu_a_m
a (front ah)	Boston: p_a_rk the c_a_r		(ah claire) m_a_man		
ɒ (back ah)	f_a_ther	J_ah_r	_â_me		
ɔ	_aw_e	n_o_ch, G_o_ld	b_o_nne	n_o_tte, r_o_sa	D_o_mine
ʊ (ɔ, no corners)					
ɤ (o, no corners)					
o	b_o_at	T_o_d	_au_x	tes_o_ro	
u	s_ui_t, fl_u_te	R_u_he	c_ou_, j_ou_r	_u_no	_u_mbra
ʊ	f_oo_t	_u_nd, Sch_u_ld			
ɯ (ʊ, no corners)					
ʌ (no corners)	_u_p, _u_gly		c_o_mme		
(ʌ) (with corners)	_o_ther				
ə	_e_vent, _u_pon				
i	s_ee_	L_ie_d	tr_i_ste	f_i_dare	s_i_cut
ɪ	s_i_t	K_i_nd, n_i_cht			
e	r_ai_n, M_a_y	_e_wig	_é_té	v_e_la	
ɛ	_e_xtra _e_very	_E_rde D_ä_mmerung	po_è_me,	b_e_lla	ego Abrah_ae_
æ	f_a_t, _a_nd				
ø (e with corners)		sch_ö_n	c_oeu_r		
œ (ɛ with corners)		G_ö_tter	h_eu_reuse de, l_e_, j_e_		
ʏ (I with corners)		Gl_ü_ck			
y (i with corners)		s_ü_ss	d_u_, _u_ne		

Diphthongs

When singing a diphthong, the second vowel should be articulated as clearly as the first. When singing a sustained diphthong, much longer than a spoken diphthong, give the second vowel a rhythmic identity even though the diphthong is notated as one note. The second vowel should be placed at the very end of the note designated for the diphthong. Stress always falls on the first vowel, proportional durations being 2/3–1/3 preferred, 3/4–1/4 second best—these choices dependant upon a moderate tempo and the type of rhythmic divisions of the basic beat. For example, a compound meter such as a moderate 6/8 could conveniently support a 2/3–1/3 division, less easily a 3/4–1/4 division. When the tempo is too fast for the first two, an equal division of 50/50 is necessary. (The same proportions work for two Italian vowels written on one pitch [e.g., m*i*o, s*u*o] unless the first one is a glide, as in pi*e*tà, consigli*o*, and *u*omo, where the second vowel gets the full sound and the first is a glide.)

[a . . . i]	sigh, wine, by	sein, kein (German)
[a . . . u]	south, loud, glower	Raum, Auge (German)
[ɔ . . . i]	foist, boy, Goya	Freude, Traüme (German)
[o . . . u]	snow, phone, glow	only in English
[ɛ . . . i]	say, pain, raise	only in English

German Umlauts and French Versions of Umlauts

Written in German	German Word	IPA	Executed	French Equivalent
ü	süß	y	[i] with corners	u, as in *cru*
ü	Glück	Y	[I] with corners	(does not exist in French)
ö	schön	ø	[e] with corners	eur, oeur as in *coeur*
ö	Götter	œ	[ɛ] with corners	eu, eux, oeu, as in *yeux*

Note: The word "corners" signifies that the corners of the lips should be protruding forward.

2.4 Physical Properties of Vowels: How to Practice Standard Vowels

Back Vowels

[u] as in *clue, shoot, mood, threw, tomb*

> Tongue tip down, back tongue arched toward soft palate, soft palate in highest arch of all lip-rounded vowels.

[o] as in *coat, soak, hole, snow*

> For [o] Americans usually say [ou], a diphthong.
> To achieve a pure [o], drop the jaw farther than for the [u] and stop short of the American final [u].

[ɔ] as in *awl, tall, shawl, naught, laud*

> Protrude the lips easily. Allow the tongue blade to descend moderately.

[ɑ] as in *shout, calm, prod, God, sorrow*

> Drop the jaw and keep the tongue blade very low in the mouth with the front flattened.
> No protruding lips.
> There are many regional versions of ah in America, nineteen at last count. The first vowel sound of the word *shout* is a good model of the middle [ɑ], neither front as [a] nor back as [ɒ].

Neutral Vowels

[ə] as in *about, upon*

> The tongue is at rest in the central part of the mouth cavity, with the front of the tongue higher than [ʊ] and lower than [i].
> A part of the schwa species, usually occurring on an unstressed, short syllable in English. Some authorities state that the [ə] appears in the French words *le, je, de*. Other experts prefer [œ] (ε with corners) for the French vowel.

[ɜ] as in *earth, curl, shirt, girl, verse*

> To keep this vowel pure, do not let it run into an American [r].
> Sustain an [o]. Keeping the lips protruding and rounded, let the tongue move toward the position for [ε].
> The result will be a sound like the last syllable of *sugar*.
> Move rapidly back and forth between [o] and [ε], moving only the tongue. The resulting tongue position will be the [ɜ].

[ʊ] as in *foot, book, push, und* (Ger.), *thoughtful, pleasure, could, cushion*

Back of the tongue is raised, but lower than [u].
Sing [u] and drop the jaw, keeping the lips rounded.
When the tongue rises a bit, this will be the [ʊ].

[ʌ] as in *up, shut, numb, blood, trouble, among*

Tongue central in the mouth, neither high nor low, tip on the lower
teeth, no rise in the back nor arch in the front, no rounding
unless [(ʌ)], with corners, is requested.

Front Vowels

[i] as in *he, creep, sheen, leader, secret*

Front tongue arched forward, nearly to the hard palate, lips not
rounded but also not spread, sides of the tongue touching the
upper fourth tooth on either side, tongue tip on lower front teeth.
If the corners of the lips are moved forward, the vowel color will
darken, producing [y] as in German, *süss* or French, *tu*.

[I] as in *sit, miss, flimsy, pickle, inward, ill*

Singing the [i], let the tongue blade (center) descend slightly from
the high position to [I].
Lips unrounded.
Tongue sides remain on upper fourth tooth on either side when
blade descends.
This vowel is found in German and English, not in Italian or French.
When corners of the lips are moved forward, the vowel will be-
come [ʏ] as in German, *glück*.

[e] as in *late, paste, chaos, favor, bayberry, nature, slave, pavement*

Sustain an [i]. Let the tongue blade rise, lips unrounded, tip on
lower teeth.
Center of the tongue will rise while the sides stay up on the fourth
tooth.
Sing [je], [je], keeping sides up on the fourth tooth. Tongue is up
for [j], descending minimally for [e].
When corners of the lips are moved forward, the vowel becomes
[ø], as in German, *schön*, or in French, *coeur*.

[ɛ] as in *then, red, bed, said, bury, heaven*

Sustain an [e]. Let the center of the tongue descend a bit more than
[e] while the sides remain up on the fourth tooth. This will be
the [ɛ].

Sing [jɛ, jɛ, jɛ]. Tongue is up for [j], moving slightly back but not descending on [ɛ].

When corners of the lips are moved forward, the vowel becomes [œ] as in German, *Götter* or in French, *yeux*.

[æ] as in *fat, ham, man, smash, anguish, laugh*

Relax the jaw completely from [i] until the tongue arrives at the low position of [æ].

Sing [jae, jae, jae]. Tongue is up for [j] and descends for [æ].

[a] as in Bostonian dialect *park* the *car*

This is the front [a], one of the nineteen American *ahs*. In French, this vowel is called *ah clair*. The tongue blade pushes forward and slightly higher than for other [a]s.

2.5 Importance of the Tongue

We are treated to many artificial rules about the tongue, these among them: It should never move; it should be relaxed at all times; it should remain flat in the mouth; it should never be thought about. Speaking practically, it soon becomes clear that none of these strictures is valid. The correct positions of the tongue, which are vowels, are instrumental in producing precise intonation, blend, high and low range, intelligible diction, and beauty.

THE COMPLAINT

Is the tongue really so important in nonprofessional singing?

Dx, THE DIAGNOSIS

The question of whether choral directors must concern themselves with their singers' tongue positions and tongue tension is a valid one.

Fact: The tongue position is guiding the head/chest balance, and therefore the blend, intonation, range, and beauty. For singers, a short course in the proper tongue position for each vowel is probably a good idea, with reminders in the subsequent warm-up sessions. Adjusting the tongue by a mere eighth of an inch will make big changes in the tone. Precision is wanted. Precision will give much desired results.

Rx, THE TREATMENT PLAN

Acquaint your singers with all the IPA vowels and monitor their pronunciations. Disregard the ideas about tongue flatness, no movement, total relaxation. If a singer were to achieve total tongue relaxation, only a neutral vowel such as [ʌ] would be possible, that is, [ʌ] is the only vowel with a completely relaxed tongue. Be pragmatic: Find as much tongue relaxation as possible for each position.

DISCUSSION

Tongue Positions and Tongue Tensions

True, we do often hear that the tongue should not move in order to produce even tone quality, that it should remain flat in the mouth and be totally without tension to get a beautiful, warm tone, that it is counterproductive for singers to think of it. But "they" also say that head voice is important in the upper range, that on high notes intonation is crucial, that clarity of diction is much needed. Front vowels like [i] or [e] cannot be sung identifiably with a flat tongue, and the all-important head voice cannot be added in the upper range when saddled with a tongue that does not move from the position of the lower pitches.

Facts: A tongue position *is* a vowel; the tongue must move to create and/or accommodate all vowels; the tongue cannot be totally without tension and make a recognizable vowel. To sing an accurate vowel in a language not your own or a vowel without a marked regional accent, of necessity you will think about the tongue position. In addition, high notes depend in large part upon a higher, more forward tongue, and chest voice low notes depend upon a lower, farther back vowel. The tongue must move.

Pay special attention to the four vowels required to produce most of the modifications on the upper passaggio notes and higher pitches: [ʊ], [e], [(ʌ)], and [ɛ]. For specifics, see the IPA Vowel and Consonant Charts, pp. 69 and 92, as well as Physical Properties of Vowels, p. 71.

The Quest for Uniform Vowels

Choral directors complain that even when all their singers attempt to sing the same vowel, they still hear disparity. Regional accents will always change vowels somewhat. Your singers should understand what the correct standard vowel pronunciation is, and that lyric diction, of necessity, replaces speech-quality diction, no matter how erudite, for singing.

2.6 Demystifying Consonants

To be fully responsive to their conductor, choir singers must use their voices as musical instruments but also as a means of communication. The musical use of the voice necessitates a knowledge of how to maintain ideal conditions for a beautiful, musical, and expressive tone. In contrast, the communicative use of the voice requires a command of ever-fluctuating symbolic sounds—consonants—that are often noisy. Because singers must do both things at once, the art of singing is essentially contradictory. Herein hangs the tale.

THE COMPLAINT

Must there be a choice between tone and diction?

DX, THE DIAGNOSIS

Singers must not be led to believe that good singing diction comes without skill. Before they can produce a beautiful tone and excellent diction at the same time, they must be taught each skill separately.

Regular practice at diction principles is effective. Bottom line: It is very easy to have good diction while singing poorly; the real trick is to have clear enunciation while not letting it interfere with good singing.

RX, THE TREATMENT PLAN

1. Dedicate a small but regular part of the warm-up to learning the consonant skills until only reminders are necessary.
2. Consider providing a handout that outlines how best to execute the consonants. See the IPA Consonant Chart, p. 92.
3. Devote these minutes to teaching how best to execute the problematic consonants in the repertoire being learned, and, when these are mastered, move to the easier and more commonly occurring examples. Or, if persuasion is in order, start with the easiest and move to the hardest.

DISCUSSION

Tone and Diction: The History, the Present

The great William Vennard, singer, voice teacher, and scientist, bade us take a brief look at music history for a greater understanding of the issue of singing versus diction.[7] Voices and instruments were once treated equally. In the time of madrigal singing it mattered not whether someone sang or played his or her part. Words were engulfed by the contrapuntal themes. Soon, however, voices had to struggle to keep up with the increasing virtuosity of instruments. As voices became successful at this, the words became less important than the vocal display. In the bel canto era, which pursued technical virtuosity above dramatic expression, one syllable often went on for sixteen bars of virtuosic singing, rendering unintelligible and unnecessary the poetic content of the piece. Then Gluck put a stop to all this by means of his reforms. Before long, as composers began to separate what kind of writing was suitable for an instrument and what was best for a voice, long fioratura passages disappeared and the poem became an equal partner with the music. The lied and the opera—exponents of dramatic sincerity—flourished.

Those composers who were the great nineteenth-century writers of vocal literature believed that poetry and drama went hand in hand with music. Eventually, this view was no longer held by composers of vocal music, as they struggled to extend the peripheries of compositional techniques. Even the possibilities of an electronic sound that imitated a human voice were explored. Moreover, the dissonances then primarily used by composers created difficulty for singers, whose singing in tune depended solely upon their ears. Clearly, the singer has no geographical references for pitch: no frets, no valves, no keys. Only a few singers have perfect pitch, the possession of which is debatably not a practical asset for a singer. Despite this, many singers managed to accustom their ears to the new music and excel in its execution. Interestingly, the type of new music that used only phonemes for texts, such as some songs by Milton Babbitt, John Harbison, and others, returned singers to the bel canto days of negligible text importance. Today, in a development most welcome to singers, new music has begun to shift its viewpoint back toward dramatic sincerity, considering music and text to be equally responsible for meaningful vocal music.

Singing is a paradoxical enterprise. It is dependent for success upon comprehending the relative importance attached to the text by its composer. It can flourish only when beautiful sounds issue from the singer's throat, but most of the time those beautiful sounds must be accompanied by an illumination of the meaning behind the sounds.

When Diction Is Less Important

When debating the relative importance of a beautiful tone and intelligible diction, must there be a choice between the two? Speaking pragmatically, the answer will depend upon the era and style of the composition. In baroque music, or highly contrapuntal music and bel canto compositions, the diction is less important once the exposition section has been set forth. This style, where text is not so important, would also include contemporary compositions that adopt phoneme texts only, as well as those minimalist compositions that repeat short phrases endlessly. With this music, a decision must be made as to whether—following the expository material—there really is a necessity for good diction. Once the audience has heard the initial phrase, they tend to remember it, even when it is only roughly understandable in its repetitions, where the music and expressive tone are more important.

Identifiable Vowels or Clear Consonants?

Beauty of tone depends primarily on the vowel, whose role is to be comprehensible, perhaps by means of its modification. An efficient consonant contributes to vowel clarity by not interfering with the comprehension of the vowel. More important, consonants are the backbone of text clarity. Separating the study of vowel accuracy and modification from the work on consonant skills may be the most productive way to get results from both disciplines.

The singer's quest (at the behest of the choral director) for a higher level of expression defines the basic elements of singing. They are two:

1. The musical element of the voice: accurate, sustained, acoustically suitable vowels
2. The expressive communication of speech: accurately and cannily executed consonants with some help from the vowels

Singers and their directors seek diction that is as clear as speech. Truthfully, however, that diction will give only the illusion of being the same as speech; in actuality it must be quite different. William Vennard's felicitous phrase explains: "To sound 'natural' will require studied artifice."[8] See pp. 78–84 for suggestions of how to teach "studied artifice" to your singers.

The study of vowels will give your singers a better tone, a more varied choice of tone colors, and some intelligibility. The study of consonants will give expressivity and intelligibility. To choose between the two will deprive your choir of one or the other advantages.

How to Do It: General Principles

Even if singers have learned the IPA symbols for consonants in the singing languages, they have learned only the proper pronunciation. There is no chart indicating the proper modification for consonants. Solutions to these problems must be found on a case-by-case basis. Once the broad principles of consonant modification are thoroughly understood, it is simple to apply the proper solution to each question at issue.

The IPA is generally of more importance to the vowels than to the consonants. Most problems of intelligibility are solved by knowing in what way to execute the consonants. The correct IPA symbols for consonants are perhaps of less use in the rehearsal setting than is the instruction and training of their proper execution. Special training must be given for foreign-language consonants that differ from English ones.

It is clear that consonants come in two varieties: with and without pitch, that is, voiced and unvoiced. Those consonants that do not have pitch are, effectively, not sound, but rather noise. As such, they do not carry as well; for example, [f] will not carry as well as [l]; [f] cannot be sung on a pitch; [l] can be.

The enunciation and pronunciation of consonants is not covered by simply asking for good speech habits. Many amateur singers, even professionals, do not have good speech habits. Particularly in English and German (and to a lesser degree in the Romance languages), it is the final consonant that carries the meaning to the listeners, not the initial consonant. In Italian, French, and Latin, words most frequently end with vowel sounds, which tend to clarify the preceding consonant. When words in those Romance languages do not end in a vowel, the final consonant carries the meaning, as in English and German.

Indicate to your singers exactly where you want the final consonant to be sung and insist that they mark the music with the requested rhythm. Marking scores to indicate the exact rhythmic moment where the final consonants must occur, a favored technique of Robert Shaw, is a very simple method for getting more efficiency for your efforts (Figures 2.1, 2.2). When all singers utter the consonant at the same rhythmic instant, not only is noisy imprecision corrected, but the carrying power of that consonant is increased tenfold.

The often-heard instruction "Spit out those consonants!" implies tension in the tongue. The price of tightening the tongue in preparation for the consonant is not heightened clarity, but tension and fatigue. Similarly, the practice of combining an initial consonant with subglottal pressure or exploding it after a damming of the breath will not increase audibility. Damming of the breath simply creates more peripheral noise, which has the effect

lea - dǝ (pitch)	lea - dǝ
fee - lǝ (pitch)	fee - lǝ
mee - tǝ (air schwa)	mee - tǝ

FIGURES 2.1 and 2.2

of masking the real sound of the consonant. Tensing the tongue inordinately has the same effect: more noise, less articulation. (Note: This is not the same issue as doubling a consonant on a low pitch before an upward skip in order to defuse a consonant on the upper pitch. This particular execution, which is accompanied by pharyngeal compression, produces a consonant that makes very little noise but is recognizable to the listener.)

Regarding the forceful closing of the jaw for consonants (the "spitting out" of consonants), one should remember that there are more consonants needing tongue activity for clarity than there are those that close the mouth and use lips, teeth and bottom lip, and so on. Therefore, closing the mouth is often not efficient. It is also a perilous option when the pitches are high in the range.

Sopranos are most at risk. "The problem of singing diction is most acute among female singers, more prevalent in the classical styles, more noticeable in large concert halls with long reverberation times, [and] intolerable at high pitches," explains Ingo Titze. "A devastating reality for female singers is that on high pitches, above A5, the first resonance of the vocal tract is almost never energized. This makes phoneme perception problematic. It is amazing that the verbal mess is transmitted as well as it is."[9] Thus, training the sopranos in consonant techniques is most important for the director.

How to Do It: The Five Basic Rules and How to Practice Them

The conundrum posed by a desire to have good diction and sing well at the same time has, first, the three-word answer described in Rule #1:

Rule #1: Short but energized!

The greatest barrier to achieving a legato line is the presence of consonants. They are also responsible for three other technical deficiencies. Consonants tend to close your mouth, which ought to be open most of the time;

consonants tense the tongue, which ought to be reasonably relaxed most of the time; consonants (most of them) stop the air flow, which ought to be moving all of the time. Therefore, the standard consonantal movement must be short and rapid, not tentative or extended in length. In addition, the consonantal gesture must be energized, not lackadaisical—in sum, a fast, highly energized movement of the tongue or lips or any combination thereof. Richard Miller states categorically, "Clean diction is produced not by exaggerated consonants, but by *quickly occurring* consonants which do not impede the connected flow of well-defined vowels" (emphasis added).[10]

The only two exceptions to Rule #1 cover those occasions when the consonant is lengthened for expression, and those occasions when there is a large skip upward to a high note and you wish to defuse the consonant on that note; see p. 89.

How to Practice Rule #1

Under Rule #1, your singers learn how to wait to the last second of the vowel and then pronounce the next consonant as fast and energetically as possible. They learn not to let the tongue start inching toward the coming consonant in advance, but only at the very moment of the indicated beat. It is difficult to learn not to dwell on the consonant gesture or to extend its length (both of which are exceptions to Rule #1, the norm) unless bidden to do so by the conductor. To that end, the conductor could invent a practice, or delegate such a practice to one of his assistants, that features a tempo-keeping device (such as a metronome or the leader's hands clapping). Clearly, the skill is the rapidity of the movement from vowel to consonant and back again.

EXERCISE 2.1

Beating in a 60 to a quarter-note tempo and articulating the consonant on the beat without changing the vowel in the process, use the big, back vowels [a], [o], [ɔ] and one chosen consonant, first speaking and then singing.

AaaahDaaahDaaahDaaahDaaah
OooooLooooLooooLooooLooooh
AwwwTawwwTawwwTawwwTawww

By allowing one section to work while the others listen, the nonspeakers can hear the bad outcome each time one person starts the consonant imprecisely before or after the hands clap or the metronome clicks. Insisting that the sound be energized and rapid will accomplish the needed audibility without being behind the beat. Eventually commence singing, rather than speaking, the exercise.

Choral directors' usual instruction for consonants to come before the beat may be partially explained by the fact that singers consistently take too long moving from the vowel to the consonant, thus failing to maintain tempo. The common command for the vowel to release on the beat has the practical effect of speeding up the singers' execution, without the benefit of teaching them how to do it. This method may preserve tempo, but intelligibility and rhythmically accurate consonants may not necessarily be achieved. It may be a time-saving device under some circumstances. Training crisp, short, and energetic consonants is a better solution to the problem.

Start the training by using the five most often encountered consonants: [t], [d], [n], [l], [r]. They all (with the exception of the American [r]) touch the palate at the alveolar arch, preferably between the upper front teeth and the arch. To find this location, run your tongue from inside the bottom of your upper front teeth to the inside top of them. As the tongue leaves the top of the teeth, it touches the bony arch running behind the half circle of teeth. This is the alveolar arch. To clarify the issue: make a medium-sized mouth opening; leaving the jaw where it is, bring the tongue tip up to the space in front of the alveolar arch and articulate the consonant [l].

For the five consonants listed above, it is almost not necessary to close the jaw at all, except for [t] and rolled [r], which need a little jaw closing when the mouth opening that serves the vowel has been large. There are times in choral literature when the American [r] is mandated. However, care should be taken that the American [r] be softened, sometimes to the omission of [r] as in the British "dahling." The director's ear is the guide. One energetic short movement of the tongue up to the alveolar arch and down is not difficult.

Unless you are singing in a dialect, refrain from using the stopped [t]— which makes no sound at all. This consonant is one of the salient differences between British and American everyday diction. When British say, "I saw it," one hears the [t]. The stopped American [t] will not be heard in singing, for the surrounding vowels will obscure the [t].

As for the [d], the most important skill is learning not to dwell on it. Most Americans have a 2-beat [d], that is, they place the tongue up on the space between the alveolar arch and the teeth, leave it there for one silent beat, then in another movement, remove it, making the consonant sound as they leave it. They should be trained to do the [d] in one beat: up and off without the wait.

The American speech habit for [l] puts it farther back on the palate than are the French and Italian [l]s. [l], too, should be in that same spot just behind the upper teeth. In this way, it will be heard better and the line will not be disturbed.

When practicing the skill, make sure that the mouths are not closing when practicing [d], [n], [l], and minimally closed when practicing [t] and [r]. It is important that the singers learn to move the tongue without closing the mouth. Using the vowel [ɑ], an open-mouth vowel, enables the leader to observe who is not divorcing the tongue from the jaw opening.

Rule #2: Keep the tongue tip on the top of the bottom teeth, not on the bottom of those teeth.

Keeping the tongue tip on the top of the bottom teeth gives the singer a vocal position one-quarter inch higher and much further front. This seemingly small difference will make for clearer consonants and more carrying power with less force, therefore a more beautiful tone. Move the tongue (but not, unwittingly, the jaw) to execute the consonant when necessary, but return it to the top of the bottom teeth afterward. Use the exercise on p. 80, with all sections practicing the swift return of the various consonants on the beat.

Rule #3: Acquaint yourself with the knowledge of which consonants do and do not require the jaw to close.

Consult the following list that shows which consonants need the mouth to close loosely or minimally and which do not. (For quicker reference, phonetic terms such as fricative, palatal, and so on have been avoided, adopting in their place descriptive phrases such as "consonants that require only the action of the tongue," and so on). In the lists below, asterisks precede those that must close the jaw, however minimally.

> Consonants requiring jaw closure are *s, *z, *ks, *sks, *ʧ, *ʤ, *ʃ, *θ, ɚ. See The IPA Consonant Chart (p. 92) for translations from these IPA symbols.
> Consonants requiring tongue action only are t, d, n, l, r, ř, g, k, x, ʎ.
> Consonants using the lips only are p, b, m, ʍ, w. With experiments, you will see that these consonants can be executed by lips only, no closing of the teeth.
> Consonants using the teeth and lips are *v, *f, *pf. In order to use teeth and lips, the jaw must close.

Rule #4: Do not move the jaw unless absolutely necessary.

Learn how to snap the tongue rapidly and energetically to the proper area of the palate, whenever possible without moving the jaw—which action would of course change the vowel and thus the resonance and the beauty of the tone. When the vowel preceding or following a consonant that must close the jaw has required a large mouth opening, then the jaw must flop shut or open for the next vowel, carrying the tongue with it. The tongue tip remains on the cutting edge of the bottom teeth throughout the movement. Thus only the jaw moves, carrying the tongue with it and flopping loosely up and down swiftly. This loose flopping movement does away with the tensions acquired by the tongue trying to reach the palate when the jaw is very open.

Sizes of Jaw Openings

The size of the jaw opening required by the vowel has everything to do with what kind of closure one ought to make for the consonant preceding or following it. In general, the lower the pitch for a vowel that comes before or after a consonant, the easier that note is to execute. The opposite is also true; the higher the pitch for the vowel, the more difficult the consonant is to sing. For the most part, on extremely high notes one has an option: to be understood or to make a beautiful sound. In truth, in a moment defined by a very high note, the word scarcely matters to the listener. The sheer sound of the vocal tone itself carries that moment. Furthermore, it is the composer who must anticipate the problem that will be caused by a word that has been written on the high note. If the composer is well versed in writing for the voice, he or she will emulate Mozart and Verdi, repeating that word many times on lower pitches before setting the word on a high note, reserving the high note for tone, not import. This will free the singer to make a glorious tone instead of a clear word.

Numbering Jaw Openings

An easy way to have your singers remember jaw openings is to number them. The largest opening any singer can make (mouth sizes vary from one singer to another, so openings must be proportionate) should be labeled a 15 opening. The smallest should be the width of a fingernail between the teeth and is labeled a 1 opening. The thumb tip held up and down between the teeth should be a 5 for everyone, thumbs being reliably proportionate in size to other parts of each body. The other numbers can be figured out in comparison to the 1, 5, and 15 openings.

When the vowel preceding a consonant has a small jaw opening (1–7), almost any consonant can be executed without difficulty. When the vowel preceding the consonant has a large opening (8–15), care must be taken. A consonant preceding or following such a large vowel opening cannot be closed completely without giving difficulty in sustaining the tone. Therefore, the consonant must be fudged, and/or the jaw flopped swiftly (see p. 83). There are two occasions when the consonants should be fudged in aid of a better tone:

> when the import of the musical moment is more vocal than textual, usually at climaxes or in prolonged soft singing
>
> when a nonplosive consonant (one other than g, k, p, b, t, or d) preceding a high note is presenting the section with vocal difficulty

Rule #5: Consider the consonant's position in the word (that is, initial, middle of the word, or final) before deciding how to handle it.

This rule requires a more extended discussion, which we will turn to next.

How to Do It: Initial, Middle, and Final Consonants

Initial Consonants of the First Word of the Phrase

When starting a phrase with a word that begins with a consonant, do not prepare the consonant. Instead, prepare the vowel position with the mouth, then inhale, with the mouth position still faithful to the vowel. On the beat, snap your tongue, lips, or lips and teeth (with whatever movement the consonant demands) to the consonant, rapidly and energetically, but not in a sustained gesture, still without changing the vowel position. For example, with the words *Cantate Domino*, prepare the first [ɑ] position, inhale in that position, let only the center of the tongue make the [k] sound without changing the [ɑ] or the moving jaw, and attack the note. What does one achieve doing it this way? An easier attack, a better tone, less tension, clearer diction. Clearly, for choral singing the very fast snapping of the tongue is most important; otherwise the vowel will be late.

Exercise 2.2

The director chooses a vowel and a consonant. On one chord, all sections singing in a comfortable range, the director beats an empty 2/4 bar, cuing the choir to enter on beat 1 of bar 2. The choir silently prepares the vowel on beat 2 of bar 1 (the preparatory beat), executing the consonant and the vowel on the downbeat of bar 2. The dynamic levels and the consonants should be varied.

Consonants Beginning or Ending a Word in the Middle of a Phrase

The final consonant of any word aids intelligibility more than a beginning consonant. If you find this statement controversial, judge the consequent clarity of diction after such reasoning is applied to consonant tasks.

Those consonants that occur in the middle of the phrase are always delayed until the very last moment and then attached to the next word as swiftly and energetically as possible. When the next word begins with a vowel, the final consonant of the preceding word should be "plastered" right on to the next word's initial vowel. Occasionally, placing the final consonant of word 1 on the beginning vowel of word 2 will make a word that was not intended, thus garbling the sense. In practice, the incidence of such a result is rather low. If a new word is created, the initial vowel of word 2 must of course begin with a glottal, setting aside the suggested execution above. Example: one line from a duet by Henry Lawes with a text by Isaac Walton, the famous fisherman, is: "and angled and angled and angled again." If executed with the [d] of *and* placed on the word *angled*, the result will be an entirely different word, *dangled*, that totally changes the meaning. This example will require a glottal separation at the beginning of word 2.

When the next word begins with a consonant, the two consonants should be separated by a small schwah.

> *Example:*   Joan and Bill stood easily
> *Sung:*   ♪   ♪   ♪   ♪   ♪   ♪   ♪
>   Joa ... na ... nd[ə]Bi ... ll [ə]stoo ... dea ... si ... ly

Note the schwa [ə]—a very short "uh" sound without much character—inserted after each sounded consonant. Why do we do this? In English, German, and Russian, languages that are notorious for having more consonants per square inch than Italian, Spanish, or French, the real problem in deciphering sung words is that (given the obligatory legato) we sometimes cannot tell where one word ends and the next begins. A schwa sounded on pitch (when sung after consonants that have pitch, such as [d], [b], [m], [l]) or unsounded (when sung after consonants that have no pitch, such as [t], [p], [k], [f]), will separate the two words, such as a . . . nd[ə]Bill. Without the schwa, the [d] is inaudible, making it an'Bill; it might even sound vaguely like anvil or another word. So consonants or consonant clusters at the end of one word and at the beginning of the next word must not be bunched together without a schwa. The schwa will help the listener to separate one word from another and to comprehend the sentence. In the case of the unvoiced schwa after a consonant like [t] or [k], the energized puff of air executed between words will have the same effect.

Example: Both of them took their time
Sung: ♪   ♪   ♪   ♪   ♪   ♪
            Bo . . . tho . . . v[ə]the . . . m[ə]too . . . k[ə]thei . . . rt[a][i]me[ə]

Note the unvoiced schwa between the [k] of *took* and the [th] that begins the word *their*. There is no pitch, just barely audible air noise in the schwa, but the space does the job: It makes the *th* audible, separating the two words so that the listener can comprehend both. Note also the diphthong that finishes the word *time*.

Remember: However strange and unnatural this feels and sounds, you cannot judge its efficiency until listeners tell whether or not they have heard the word. That is the proof. Even the Italians, who do not admit the existence of the vowel schwa, adopt schwas when singing in their own supposedly schwa-free language. (For example, on the last page of Alfredo's *Traviata* aria, we have yet to hear an Italian tenor sing the words *in cielo* without executing them in this way: *in[ʌ]cielo*.) To do this well, the schwa must be executed as an extremely rapid [ʌ] or [ə] *on pitch*. On what pitch? The pitch on which the preceding vowel was sung (in this case, the [i] of *in*). The pitch will carry; a noise will not. Again, remember that the schwa is of extremely short duration. It is not perceived by the listener as a schwa. Rather, it allows the text to be understood. This recommended schwa bears no relationship to the overly emphasized and lengthy "uh" of the pop or rock singer.

So the rule holds: When the first word ends with a consonant or a consonant cluster and the next word begins with a consonant or a cluster (such as *and strong*), the task is to put a schwa between them on the pitch of the last vowel of the first word (the [æ] of *and*) and to move rapidly through the consonants at the beginning of the next word to the vowel of that word (the [ɔ] of strong, a . . . nd[ə]stro . . . ng[ə]). On the other hand, if the second word begins with a vowel (such as *and I*), then the final consonant of the first word *and* is attached to the vowel of the second word (a . . . ndI), unless it inadvertently creates another word. In this way two important results are accomplished. We understand the words better, and the vowel is elongated, not the consonant. Thus, the singing itself improves.

Two vowels can be used effectively, dictionwise, by changing them into consonants. [u] and [i] can double as the consonants w and y, as in *to us*, which can be sung as *to wuss*, and in *I am*, which can be sung as *Ah yam*. In this way the beginning of word 2 is clearly understood. To the singer executing this combination, it appears overemphasized, but to the listener it is totally clear and understood. (Note: Where consonant execution is lazy, this technique has a "Popeye" effect: "I yam what I yam." This is not acceptable. Where the consonantal gesture is swift and energized it clarifies the diction.)

Italian double consonants, a prime factor in authentic and authoritative Italian diction, must be taught as a rhythmic device. Double consonants are the single exception to the general rule of lengthening the vowel. The double consonant must be sung on the note before the notation of that syllable. The vowel following the double consonant is then sung on the beat of the second syllable. For example, if the three syllables of the word *spaghetti* were set with three quarter notes, the double [t] would be sung during the second quarter note and the [i] vowel sung on the third quarter note. In other words, rush the vowel preceding the double consonant so that the time is spent on the consonant. In the sample from Verdi's *Nabucco* (Figure 2.3) the chorus "Va, pensiero," the double [l] of *bella* must be executed on the second half of the third beat quarter note on C, leaving the [ɑ] of the next syllable to sound exactly on the fourth beat. That is, the time of executing double consonants must be subtracted from the first syllable, leaving only the following vowel to be pronounced on the next note. If done with the double [l] on the fourth beat, that syllable and note will be perceived as being late.

Consonants That End the Last Word in the Phrase

For the very last consonant in a phrase, the following principle must be invoked again. Especially in English and German, but also in Italian and French, we do not fully understand any phrase until the last word has been uttered or sung. This means that comprehensibility often hangs on the last word.

> In order for the audience to understand the phrase, the singer must sing a clear last word.
> In order for the audience to understand the last word, the singer must sing a very clear last consonant.

Singers often labor under the misapprehension that it is mainly the first consonant in a word that must be attended to. Some directors pursue this route, generally to little effect. A clear first consonant and first syllable

Oh mia pa - tria si bel - la e per- du - ta!

FIGURE 2.3

alone—even in a one-syllable word—does not tell us what the word is. Only the last consonant secures it. In addition, the schwa separating the first word from the beginning consonant of the second word will make the second word clear. Thus the same principles as articulated in the previous section, apply here. If the final consonant has pitch ([d], [b], [m], [n], [z], etc.), it should be followed by a tiny schwa on the pitch of the last note. If the final consonant does not have pitch ([p], [t], [f], [s], [k], etc.), it will be necessary to execute a triple-strength spurt of air to accompany the pitchless, unvoiced consonant. Anything less will not carry. The last consonant is where the command "spit them out" has some validity.

How to Do It: Defusing Consonants on High Notes

There are three methods for achieving ease (therefore better tone) on high notes together with a reasonably clear consonant; see pp. 83–84 for high note attacks. (An attack is an onset. However, the speed that delivers the sufficient air compression demanded by starting a tone on high pitches seems better described in this case by the word "attack" rather than the more serene word "onset.")

1. When everyone is singing *forte*, using the same phrase that has been repeated many times previously, as in a typical coda, let the sections who are on really high notes virtually abandon the consonants, leaving the enunciation tasks to the sections who are singing more reasonable pitches. Chances are that such a musical moment will be a vocal event rather than a text event. The sections singing in a lower tessitura will carry the text.

2. If a word such as *pacem* is repeated often, as in the "Agnus Dei" of the *Missa Solemnis*, then the need for intelligibility is lessened, and the director should realize this. Here, the best method for the high note that follow the [p] and [tʃ] consonants is to fudge the consonants on purpose (pronouncing them very clearly on the lower-pitched phrases). The best

"fudging" of consonants is done while imitating a ventriloquist, mouth open but only lazy tongue and lip movements.

> To "fudge": To avoid completing a consonant gesture. Examples: For the [p] of *pacem* in the word above (also [b] and [m]) do not let the two lips touch; just go part way to closure. For the [ʧ] of *pacem*'s second syllable, default to [ʃ], which may produce a less crisp [ʧ], but will be easier for the sopranos. Further examples: For [s] don't shut the jaw all the way; just go in the right direction part way, but swiftly. This will produce a slight lisp, a matter of no importance. For [t], [d], [n], [l], and [r] don't let the tongue actually touch the palate; just start the gesture without finishing it. For [f] or [v] don't allow the teeth to actually touch the bottom lip; just approach it, and leave. For [z], a voiced consonant, lessen the time spent on an actual pitch by defaulting to [s]. The same is true for voiced [ʤ] (*jest*) to unpitched [ʧ] (*chest*).

Not closing completely is a method that takes away the consonant's physical difficulty and releases the vowel into ease and beauty. It is, of course, a rhythmic problem. The fudged consonant must be done fast and precisely on the beat.

3. When the approach to the high note is by large skip and when the consonant on that note is a plosive, as in Figures 2.4 and 2.5, teach your singers to put the initial consonant on the previous lower note, singing only the following vowel on the second, higher note. For example a skip from Bb up to G, using the words *Oh, God*. Both the word *Oh* and the [G] of *God* are sung on the Bb. This leaves only the [o] vowel of the word *God* (or its modification) to be sung on the high note at exactly the right moment. The two words will then be: *ogg od*. This technique works best when the consonant is a plosive. Singing the consonant G on a lower note is easy, and the singer will be happily amazed at how much better the upper note is when the consonant has been left behind. Another example: On a skip of Bb to G a sixth above, using the words *to kiss*, put the [k] of kiss on the Bb during the note value for the Bb, arriving on the higher G with only the vowel [i] of "kiss," (or, if modifying correctly, [e] or [E], depending on the voice category), thus effectively transforming the words on the two notes into *tookk iss*.

When the high note is written as an entrance with initial consonant(s) beginning the word, such as "Glory to God" from *Messiah,* as in Figure 2.6, the same procedure can be followed. On the upbeat, close the [g], imagining it to be on an octave below, but making no sound. On the downbeat, release the [g] and put a swift [l] and the vowel on the intended pitch.

There is a further plus that accrues to the vocal tone when putting the consonant on the preceding pitch or an imaginary low note before an

FIGURES 2.4, 2.5, and 2.6

upward skip. A plosive that is simply lengthened (but not pushed or tensed with a strong tongue movement) will give higher pharyngeal pressure, thus giving the higher note more chest content and, therefore, a stronger, richer quality. The plosives—[g] and [k], [t] and [d], [p] and [b]—will give, when simply lengthened and placed on the first note of two, a stronger, more carrying tone. In contrast, the consonants [m] and [n], when lengthened, will produce a tone lighter and more heady on the following tone. Consider what result you would like to achieve and choose accordingly.

For the most part, singers are not equipped to do such precise movements without training. Nevertheless, the sooner they commit to learning the requisite movements in the proper fashion, the sooner they can hope to become skillful and productive choir singers. Tongues must be trained to do the singers' bidding. Teaching the technique as it is required in the music, then always calling for correct execution, makes the task less onerous and trains good habits. As architect Mies van der Rohe once said, "God is in the details."

How to Do It: Context as It Relates to Intelligibility

Accommodate this fact into your rehearsing: Without doubt, context helps listeners to understand the words. When one attends the theater, there is no way that every single word is understood. Rather, one guesses successfully at some of them because one comprehends the context. In the broad repertoire of choral texts, some poetry and prose is worded in an arcane fashion and requires study to comprehend the meaning. This kind of study time is not available to the audience, for the music is proceeding relentlessly. Some poetry is in accessible language and some is not. Adding inaccessible text to bad diction will produce disappointing results. Moreover, the audience will probably have problems understanding difficult poetry even when it is sung with excellent diction. This problem is well understood by composers of vocal music. It is one of the criteria influencing how they choose the poetry to set.

2.7 The IPA Consonant Chart

Groupings of Consonants Useful for Memory

[b], [p], [m]	lips meet with pitch for [b] and [m], without pitch for [p]
[t], [d], [n], [l], [r]	tongue strikes the frontest part of the palate between top of upper teeth and alveolar arch for all
[k], [g]	tongue strikes halfway back in the palate for both; [g] with pitch, [k] without
[w], [ʍ]	lips approximate, with pitch for [w](*with*), with blown air but no pitch for [ʍ](*which*)
[s], [z]	tongue touches upper side teeth and palate, air is blown across tongue tip with pitch for [z], without pitch for [s]
[ʃ], [ʒ]	tongue touches upper side teeth and palate, air blown across tongue with pitch for [ʒ], without pitch for [ʃ]
[f], [v]	upper teeth touch lower lip, air blown through with pitch for [v], without pitch for [f]
[n], [ŋ]	for [n] tongue at the top of upper teeth; for [ŋ] (*song*) tongue touches palate and upper side teeth; both have pitch
[dʒ], [tʃ]	tongue strikes behind upper front teeth; [dʒ] (*jam*) has pitch, [tʃ] (*cheer*) does not
[ð], [θ]	tongue touches bottom of upper front teeth; [ð] (*this*) has pitch, [θ] (*thin*) does not

TABLE 2.2 The IPA Consonant Chart

Symbol	Execution	English	German	Italian	French	Latin	Spanish
[b]	close lips, explode open; in Spanish, lips don't actually touch, close to a [v]	back burst	Bote beginnen	balsamo barbaro	bonbon débile	beata nobis	beso vaso cabo cavo
[ç]	form designated vowel; blow over it	human	ich Mädchen				gigante generale (before i or e)
[d] *	tongue tip wide just behind upper front teeth	dog dead	danke	donna	dinde tiède	dona laudamus	dice donde
[f]	lower lip under upper front teeth	fit suffer	für, viel Vater	fatto pifferi	femme lof	filius philosophus	fino cofia
[g] *	tongue center strikes center of palate	gave egg	geben Orgel	gola ragazza	galette mégot	ego gustus	gana cigala
[h]	short puff of air from diaphragm, cords open	hot	Hund hin	(silent)	hyacinth [h]s sometimes silent in French)	(silent)	(silent)
[j] *	consonant [y] is [i] say [i] and move to next vowel rapidly	yet yodel	Jedermann jung	ieri	feuille croyant	Jesu	vaya calle llamar

IPA	Description	English	German	Italian	French	Latin	Spanish
[ʒ] *	tongue center and sides up on palate	usual, pleasure	Genie, journalist		rouge, jour	gere	
[ʤ] *	tongue explodes from front palate	just, germ		giovane, raggio			
[k]	tongue center explodes from palate	keep, cat, knack	König, Glück	cosi, chi	cas, kiosque, cacao	sancta, mihi, qui, chorus, nunc	coca, que, kilo, quiso
[l] *	narrow tongue tip touches behind upper front teeth	lake, low, alone	löse, allein	lamento, salone	lupin, valise	lacrimosa	bala, largura
[ʎ] *	tongue moves from [l] through [j] to next vowel	million, value		agli, gl'occhi			
[m] *	lips together, humming sound	my, come	Mutter, Kamin	marmaro	marche, timide	Maria, Amen	mesa
[n] *	tongue tip touches behind upper front teeth	now, never, in	nieder, nein	notte, tanto	nomme, n'est-ce	nil, non	nube, andar
[ɲ] *	tongue moves from [n] through [j] to next vowel	onion, canyon		ogni	gagner	agnus, magnam	año
[ŋ] *	tongue center touches front palate and hums	singing	Ring, trinken				

(continued)

TABLE 2.2 (Continued)

Symbol	Execution	English	German	Italian	French	Latin	Spanish
[p]	lips together, explode air with no pitch	pet inspire	partei	opulente It. less forceful	polaire apéritif	Pater caput	poco Sp. less forceful
[pf]	lips closed for [p], move to [f]		Kopf Pfennig				
[r] *	American [r]	red, car					
[r] *	British/Italian [r], almost a [d], one flip	very merry	Ironie	mare originate	in singing French, use It. [r]	miserere	caro
[r]*	rolled [r]		Rast	guerra	arrière	Rex	rico
[s]	tongue sides touch upper teeth, blow	seat sense	es ist fliessen	subito essere	simple place	sanctus	casa servir
[v]	teeth on lower lip, with pitch	vixen sieve	wollen	vivere	veuve	vox	veloz (almost [b])
[tʃ]	[t] followed by [sh]	chicken witch	Witwe	accese caccia	sauvage	novum crucifixus	leche
[ʃ]	tongue sides touch upper teeth; more space than for [s]	show flesh	Fleisch Schopfer	sciagura	charme cheval	suscipe excelsis	
[t]	tongue tip touches top of upper teeth	top went	Tränen Mutter	tosse iterare	terrible thé	tanto Catholicam	tiempo retiro

Symbol	Description	English	German	Italian	French	Latin	Spanish
[ts]	[t] followed by [s]	lots	zahlen, zu	zucchero, nazione		gratia, tertia	
[θ]	tongue touches edge of upper teeth air blows without pitch	thick, thermal					cero, cinco (in Castilian Spanish)
[ɚ] *	tongue touches edge of upper teeth air blows with pitch	thou, within, therefore					
[w] *	lips protruding, blow with pitch	win, twine			oiseau		
[ʍ]	lips protruding, blow without pitch	which, why					
[x]	tongue hump high in the middle of mouth, air blows over hump		ach, noch, auch				
[z] *	tongue executes [s] with sustained pitch	zero, zinc, haze	sehen, Silber	casa	baiser, zèle	Jesu, prudens	
[dz] *	[d] followed by continuous [z]	bids, shades		azzurro, zero			

Note: An asterisk denotes a voiced consonant.

95

The German ch

There are two German consonants with which American choristers have some trouble. They are both spelled with a *ch* after a vowel. Many are the explanations of how singers should accomplish these consonants. Following is the simplest and most efficient, therefore best for the wide range of singing experience in choir singers. Place the tongue in the position for the *vowel* that will precede (or follow, as in *Mädchen*) the *ch* consonant, which is better written with the IPA symbols: [ç] (known as the *ich-laut*) and [x] (known as the *ach-laut*). Then blow air over the tongue without moving it from the vowel. [ç] is closer to the front, used for front vowels; [x] is farther back, used for the others. They will happen automatically when the correct vowel is adopted for the tongue position.

As Written in German	Tongue Position	As in the German Words
ich	[I] followed by [ç]	d<u>ich</u>, m<u>ich</u>
ech, che	[ɛ] followed or preceded by [ç]	bl<u>ech</u>, Mäd<u>ch</u>en
ach	[ɑ] followed by [x]	<u>ach</u>, n<u>ach</u>
och	[ɔ] followed by [x]	d<u>och</u>, st<u>och</u>ern
uch	[u] followed by [x]	a<u>uch</u>, r<u>uch</u>bar

2.8 Advantages of the IPA and How to Mark the Score

The Complaint

Is requiring my singers to learn the IPA, another whole written language, worthwhile for them and for me?

Dx, The Diagnosis

The advantage of using the IPA is that precise and accurate understanding of vowels makes possible better blend, better resonance, more intelligibility, a lessening of passaggio impediments, and better answers to range problems in all sections—all the advantages that accrue to vowel modification, ease of foreign language pronunciation, as well as uniformity despite regional accents. It is well worth the trouble. The two areas in which using the IPA will work most in your favor are

  when teaching your singers foreign-language diction;
  making vowel modifications easy for your singers to remember and
    to execute accurately.

Since remembering the consonants is not as demanding as remembering the vowels, it is possible that less time need be spent on them.

Rx, The Treatment Plan

Take a few minutes from each warm-up to discuss the IPA symbols for a few vowels and consonants. There are not so many that it cannot be done in a few months, especially those IPA vowels preferable for the passaggio notes. Start with the passaggio and high-note vowels. These number not more than six, an easy task. Begin with English words, then proceed to foreign-language words, tying the sounds and symbols to both. Add symbols and sounds to your singers' vocabularies as the situation warrants. Refer to the IPA whenever there are diction problems, especially in foreign languages. Use the symbols, not parallel transliterations into written English, during rehearsals. Accustom your singers to hearing, seeing, and using the IPA. Soon it will be automatic. Hand out copies of the vowel and consonant IPA charts.

Discussion

Advantages of Learning the IPA

A testament to the usefulness of the IPA is the fact that it would be difficult to find any major musical institution whose vocal department does not insist on the use of the IPA. Language awareness and accuracy of standard pronunciation are the usual reasons given for the adoption of the IPA symbols in the study of singing.

Thinking phonetically, however, has other advantages for singers. It centers their technical thoughts not on "producing" sound by various ideas about the larynx, (such as "opening" the throat, making "space" in the throat)—most of which are counterproductive because there is no possibility of exerting direct control over the larynx—but rather on the acoustical and resonation system, over which there can be substantial control.

This control makes possible the much-desired "blend," which is actually each section singing the acoustical formation that is best for its note. Consistently using this vowel posture basically creates control over the vocal instrument.

How to Do It: Marking the Score with IPA Symbols

The following sample illustrates a method for marking a foreign-language text with IPA symbols. The choral director will have taught or refreshed his singers' good vowel formation over a period of time by employing these vowels in the warm-up, and will have taught the singers to connect the vowel to its IPA symbol at the same time. Thus the singers will be prepared to mark their own individual scores as the director proceeds through the text with them.

We recommend teaching the consonants in context, explaining general rules and exceptions as each occurs. The singers, already familiar with the vowel sounds and symbols, will quickly become adept at marking only those that are particularly difficult to remember, or require special attention. The director's preparation has provided them with the skills necessary to mark the score as needed. We recommend this method for the ease of marking the score in rehearsal, the ease of reading a score so marked, and for the independent skills it requires of the singers. A text written fully in IPA, sound for sound, both consonants and vowels, is visually busy, and, for the average chorister, off-putting in its complex appearance. Therefore, encourage your singers to mark only the consonants and vowels for which they need reminders. In so marking, have them use a regular pencil for the foreign vowels or consonants expressed in IPA, but a red pencil for the marking of modified vowels. Another option is to mark the IPA for foreign vowels or consonants in the staff immediately above or on top of the text, but to mark the modified vowels above the staff.

The liturgical Latin pronunciation incorporated here represents current standard choral usage. It is an excellent place to begin teaching foreign languages to a choir that has not yet ventured beyond its own. A choir that has mastered the IPA symbols and the sounds for these vowels is well prepared to expand its diction skills into other languages (including Austro-German or French forms of Latin, which may be preferred for certain repertoire).

Sanctus

from the Ordinary of the Mass

aŋktu   aŋ u
Sanctus, sanctus, sanctus
ɔ i u   ɛ   ɔt
Dominus Deus Sabaoth
ɛ   tʃ ɛ   ɔ
Pleni sunt coeli et terra gloria tua.
oz   kʃ
Hosanna in excelsis

Consonants to Note in This Text

s   all [s]s in this movement are pronounced as in the English word *sing*, except the [z] sound in Hosanna

h   all initial [h]s are silent

k, t, p   pronounced in a drier manner, but less aspirated than in English

Although discussion abounds over which form of Latin constitutes authentic performance practice of Orff's *Carmina Burana*, school and community choruses often present the first movement, "Fortuna Imperatrix Mundi," alone. In those cases, it is frequently performed using Roman Latin, the form most familiar to many American choruses and directors. Without entering the discussion regarding that choice, it is offered here as another example of how to mark the score—with the reminder that as singers internalize the diction, they need mark only those vowels and consonants that continue to give them trouble. Thus the score of experienced, well-trained choral singers will have relatively fewer markings than what follows.

Carmina Burana, Carl Orff (1936)

Fortuna Imperatrix Mundi

ɔ   ɔ u ɑ   ɛ u   u ɑ   ɑ u   ɑ iɑ i i
O Fortuna, velut Luna statu variabilis,

ɛ   ɛ   ʃ   ɑu   ɛ ʃ   i i
semper crescis aut decrescis; vita detestabilis

u   ɔ   ʧiɛ
nunc obdurat et tunc curat ludo mentis aciem,

ɛʤɛ   ɔ   ʧ
egestatem, potestatem dissolvit ut glaciem.

ɔ z i   ɑ i
Sors immanis et inanis, rota tu volubilis,

i ɔ i i
status malus, vana salus semper dissolubilis,

ɔ   u   ɛ   iki kwɔkwɛ i ɛ i
ob umbrata et velata mihi quoque niteris;

u   ʃ ɛɛ
nunc per ludum dorsum nudum fero tui sceleris.

ɔ z u   k u ɔ
Sors salutis et virtutis mihi nunc contraria

u   ɛ ɛ u
est affectus et defectus semper in angaria.

	i		ɔ	i ɛ	ɔ	ɔ ɛ	u u	ʤ ɛ
	Hac	in	hora	sine	mora	corde	pulsum	tangite;

kwɔ				ɔ		ɛ u	ɔ	ʤi ɛ
quod	per	sortem	sternit	fortem,	mecum	omnes	plangite!

Consonants to Note in This Text

c   hard c as in *kite*

c   exception: pronounced ʧ as in *chicken* before e, i, y, ae, eu, and oe (*aciem*)

g   hard g as in *garden* (*angaria, glaciem*)

g   exception: pronounced ʤ as in *gel* (*egestatem, tangite, plangite*)

h   silent (*hora*)

h   exception: pronounced k as in *king* (*mihi*)

r   flipped when between two vowels (*mora*) or final (*semper*); rolled when initial (*rota*) or preceding a vowel (*umbrata*), or consonant (*corde*)

s   as in *sing* (*sortem*)

s   exception: pronounced z as in *zero* when between two vowels, or when final, preceded by a voiced consonant (*Sors*)

sc   pronounced [ʃ] as in *shell*, before ɛ, i, y, ae, eu, oe (*sceleris*)

t   dentalized as in Italian, not aspirated as in English (*tangite*)

v   voiced, as in *victor* (*vana*)

CHAPTER 3
Tone and Intonation

3.1 Beauty

Each musician has a personal definition for that elusive quality, beauty. There are certain elements of tonal beauty that inhabitants of the Western hemisphere honor, among them true intonation, free production, balanced vibrato, and a clear, focused tone. These are the qualities that singers seek to display, and they are closely connected to other technical skills. Therefore, in this chapter, beauty will be connected with breathing, with vowel modification, with diction, and so on, at the cost of some repetition.

The Complaint

Is a beautiful singing tone really important?

Dx, The Diagnosis

The vocabulary available to describe a singing tone, beautiful or not, is weak and nonspecific at best. Furthermore, the definition of a beautiful tone, which may include many factors, will differ from director to director. Yet a clear understanding of what he or she finds beautiful on a particular piece of music is helpful to a director and well worth the effort to clarify a personal aesthetic point of view.

Rx, The Treatment Plan

1. Decide how important beauty of tone is to you in your work. Perhaps this differs from composition to composition. Perhaps beauty's appropriateness to the meaning or to the achievement of a powerful effect seem more important qualities to you at times. Perhaps musical accuracy is the prime goal.
2. Come to a personal definition of vocal beauty.
3. Familiarize yourself with the various basic attributes of vocal beauty, carrying power, impressive size of tone, and so on. See the following Discussion.

Discussion

Defining a Beautiful Tone

Tonal beauty is indeed in the ear of the beholder. Every person will have an ideal tone, as does each culture. The Western hemisphere's epitome of tonal beauty is sharply at odds with the ideal of singing beauty generally held by the countries of the East. For those who do insist that a singing tone be beautiful in the Western manner, that beauty is characterized by several components, some of which are listed below:

1. true, just intonation
2. a "spin" in the tone (a balanced vibrato)
3. ease of emission
4. core, focus, clarity, carrying power
5. a warm, full tone quality

A lack of any of the above components would preclude beauty in the average vocal musician's mind. Couching the same list in the negative, we have:

1. no flat or sharp intonation
2. no wobble, no bleat, no straight tone, no vibrato that is too slow, too fast, or too wide
3. no forced or pushed tones, no excessive tension
4. no breathy, shallow tones, no unsupported delivery
5. no thin, shrill, harsh tones

Noting and defining the absence of beauty is only the beginning of a director's tasks when trying to elicit beautiful tone. After identifying what is missing from the choral tone—likely to be a combination of factors—a plan for correcting the vocal ills must be devised.

What to Do about the Absence of Beauty

When searching out underlying causes for tonal faults, each mutually dependent factor will hold part of the key to tonal and intonation improvement.

1. True, just intonation

    Choristers can frequently accomplish the task of raising or lowering the offending pitches by acute listening, but wavering pitches will be remedied far more efficiently by proper support, appropriate modifications, and precisely defined vowels.

    Accurately modified vowels make the high-range notes easier to sing by correcting the head/chest balance. Passaggio vowels, with their smaller jaw openings and their modifications, encourage entrance into head voice, usually defeating flat intonation. However, too much head content can produce pitches that stray toward sharp intonation and a concomitant shrillness. Advantageous and accurate vowels generally produce correct registration and accurate pitches.

    Flat intonation usually arrives as the result of too heavy an adjustment, a chest-predominant tone. Such a tone is accompanied by "pushed" or "forced" high-range pitches and a harsh quality. Singers tend to push just before, during, and just after the upper passaggio. Again, vowel modifications can ensure the use of head voice at a proper moment. Sufficient head voice content generally eliminates the flat intonation difficulties. The center of a vowel is the center of the pitch. When the vowel is not acoustically advantageous, intonation suffers.

2. A "spin" in the tone (a balanced vibrato), and
3. Ease of emission

    Ease of emission normally generates a spinning tone, or a tone that is not held tensely but vibrates almost imperceptibly. Clearly, a lack of ease or beauty will show more overtly on high-range notes. To achieve a vocal production that sounds easy, especially on top, a singer must not feel the need to fight a lack of support, an uneven vibrato, destructive vowels, or interfering consonants. This translates to the need for the appoggio, well-formed vowels in the easy range, the employment of acoustic vowels in the danger zones, and skill in using consonants.

4. Core, focus, clarity, carrying power

   Each of the four nouns listed here refers to the same element of vocal beauty. The right acoustical vowel helps, and the appoggio position magnifies the good effect of the modification. Habitually keeping the tongue in a forward position, its tip on top of the bottom teeth, moving it only for a swift consonant, and then returning the tongue tip to the teeth will enhance the work of the appoggio and the vowel modification.

5. A warm, full tone quality

   The adjectives *warm* and *full* are basically meaningless when it comes to learning how to produce those tonal attributes. In actuality, they describe only the resulting tone when it is not allowed to be harsh, shrill, or thin—nontechnical terms. Each of these pejorative terms describes a tone that uses a pushed or forced production, a tone that is fighting the proper registration, lacking the ideal balance of head and chest for that particular pitch. The appoggio position supports the tone without the need for resorting to force. Correct vowel modifications assure the balanced production that gives ease and beauty.

SCIENCE IN APPLICATION

Some years ago, the national convention of the National Association of Teachers of Singing featured an interesting experiment. Six hundred voice teachers from all over the country were asked to listen to a large number of small excerpts sung by various singers in differing stages of development. They were asked to mark their score sheets with one mark for "beautiful" and another mark for "not beautiful." There was no attempt to ferret out why the segments were beautiful or not or what qualities were perceived as beautiful—just an immediate visceral reaction from voice professionals, who are known to disagree with each other much of the time. The results were overwhelmingly in agreement for each selection, proving that vocal "beauty" has certain common characteristics recognizable to those whose profession—voice training—is ever conscious of beauty.

Do ordinary audience members respond in like manner? The choir director wants to give the audience a meaningful, if not thrilling, musical experience. Does that include a preponderance of singing that is beautiful? Directors must answer this question for themselves and train choirs accordingly.

THE COMPLAINT

Is it possible to get a beautiful tone from every singer in my choir? Can all high notes, especially from the sopranos, be beautiful?

DX, THE DIAGNOSIS

To be gifted with several singers in each section whose voices are inherently beautiful is a blessing for a director. It is more likely that truly beautiful voices will be in the minority. Two facts shed some light on beauty of choral tone and high notes:

1. In a choral section, one or two superb voices with carrying power and some beauty, surrounded by many less well-endowed voices, can make a great effect.
2. All high notes, even less-than-beautiful ones, generally carry very well; therefore the director must decide how important beauty is to the moment. This decision depends upon the spirit and design of the music.

Consider what you want to hear each time high notes are being sung. Beauty? Power and size? A softer, gentler tone? An electrifying *pianissimo*? Perhaps a more dramatic effect?

RX, THE TREATMENT PLAN

1. Do not fret about the vocal endowment of your singers, but do recognize which ones have been favored with beautiful voices. Place these special voices in advantageous positions so that they can easily bolster and carry along the less well-endowed voices. See pp. 154–56.
2. Institute the appoggio position in all the singers. Teach each section to use the suggested vowel modifications in and above the upper passaggio. This will enhance the beauty quotient for all your singers.

DISCUSSION

Beauty and High Notes

What qualities in addition to beauty might the director or the listeners want from high notes? *Brilliance* could serve as well as beauty in climactic or viscerally exciting musical moments. Directors and listeners are often less critical of the quality of high notes when they are secure and easily on pitch. We become uneasy when listening to tones with uneven vibratos, so the sound of *even vibratos* satisfies both our ears and our minds. When an orchestra accompanies the chorus, much of the decision making is determined by score study. Where the chorus is exposed, beauty may be of greater importance. At other times, when the orchestration is heavy in the exact pitch area where the part is written, *carrying power* (possibly less beautiful) is more important than beauty.

There are some musical moments when nothing but true beauty will accomplish the composer's ideal. The appoggio position and attention to the integrity of correct vowels will aid in this achievement. Because vowel modification answers some of the most pressing technical needs of the singers—gifted or not—when applied appropriately it will deliver what the choral director most wants: ease (therefore beauty), great blend (therefore beauty), resonance (therefore beauty), command of dynamic contrasts (therefore beauty) and, finally, intelligibility.

3.2 The Passaggio: Transitional Notes between Registers

What is a passaggio? This is a question frequently asked. Knowing that a passaggio is a region between registers only leads to more questions: How many registers are there? One? Three? Seven? None?

What does science say about registers? So great is the dissension on the subject of registers among voice teachers that choral directors cannot be faulted for their temptation to pay no attention to the issue. But the potential for these two complex factors—passaggios and registers—to be helpful to directors is very great.

THE COMPLAINT

What is a passaggio, and what should a choral director do about it?

Dx, The Diagnosis

The small group of notes called a passaggio—usually three half steps, during the singing of which the balance between head and chest content changes to accommodate the next register—has a great influence upon intonation, ease, and beauty. As the pitches rise, the balance should tip toward head voice; as the pitches descend, the balance should tip toward chest voice. When it does not, problems appear.

All the complex scientific jargon about registers can be reduced to a single highly pragmatic statement: A register is a group of notes that are sung with the same balance of head and chest content. Ongoing vocal research into the actual muscular activities that define the various registers will inform us properly before long. Meanwhile, be assured that a passaggio has been proved a real physical entity. Until research is completed, it suffices to know that the register changes most important to choral directors are those, in sopranos, tenors, and basses, that lead into head voice and, for altos, as they decide whether or not to go into chest voice. What is the precise usefulness of this knowledge? Failure to arrive at high notes with the proper balance of head and chest is a root cause of faulty intonation, shrillness, vibratoless shouting, and the notorious "lack of blend." Failure to descend to the low register in correct chest voice or in a head/chest mix will commonly make the altos and basses inaudible or out of tune.

It may be fruitful to think of transitional notes as they might be demonstrated by Alice's trips through the little door in Wonderland. When she was too tall, she had to drink from the little bottle that was labeled DRINK ME, becoming shorter in order to pass through the doorway (the passaggio). The sip of liquid (singing the proper vowels) enabled Alice (in our case, the tone) to pass into the next room (the next register). If she did not drink, she bumped her head against the doorframe (if singers sing inappropriate vowels, they flat or sharp, don't blend, shout, and so on).

The simplest method for Alice to make her way through the doorway was to drink from the little bottle. The simplest method for singers to make their way through a passaggio is to modify its vowels correctly.

Rx, The Treatment Plan

It is fairly easy to train the upper passaggio of sopranos, tenors, and basses for proper balance. A bit more arduous, but worth the effort, is the task of equiping altos with the ability to go into chest, or not, through their lower transitional notes; see Falsetto and Chest Voice, p. 110, for more details. To achieve this balance there is an absolute and precise solution that serves choral directors' need to be efficient in the use of their few precious warm-up minutes.

Trouble with singers' intonation and blend is often experienced in the simplified areas described below. The following diagrams for each part (Figures 3.1–3.5) encompass an area from one half step below the actual passaggio to one half step above the actual passaggio. The actual passaggios are the three bracketed half steps in the center of the area outlined. These areas lead into, through, and out of the important passaggios for the sections mentioned. Note that the passaggio vowels for all sections mandate as their common characteristics smaller mouth openings and vowels that sit well forward in the mouth. Thus the tonal balance between head and chest content changes for the better in a simple but reliable fashion. As the altos descend and need to be more audible, opening the mouth and letting the vowels sit slightly further back will accomplish this. The correct modification of these five notes will solve many vocal problems. For the entire span of the recommended modified pitches, see the Complete Vowel Modification Chart, p. 127. (This text uses the octave numbering system that starts at the far left of the piano keyboard with C1, C2, C3. C4 is middle C. C6 is the soprano high C.)

The lower passaggio is usually of lesser importance to choral sopranos. True mezzo sopranos singing alto have E5–F♯5 as their upper passaggio and D4–E♮4 as their lower passaggio. Second sopranos and heavier soprano voices have F5–G5 as their upper passaggio and E♭4–F4 as their lower passaggio.

Even though there are several types of tenors and baritones (lighter and heavier), the fact that all men sing in chest voice up to the first note of their respective passaggii makes choral male voices less problematic than the female voices.

DISCUSSION

Directors may find interesting a discussion of the various percentages of head and chest that are, practically speaking, most efficient. First, a caveat: The following figures are approximate and are intended to give a general and functional understanding of the register system. They are not meant to convey scientific certainty. In business, these numbers would be called "ballpark figures."

Since men sing in some type of heavier or lighter chest voice all the way up to the vicinity of C4, their upper passaggio must move the voice into a register that has a mix of 50 percent chest and 50 percent head content somewhere around C4. This is the mix with which they go through the passaggio and into high notes successfully. About four half steps above

Figures 3.1. 3.2, and 3.3

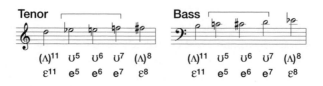

Figures 3.4 and 3.5

their passaggios, male voices move into a 40/60 mix, and the tenor high C (C5) is best accomplished in reinforced falsetto (not identical with true falsetto).

The various registers of the female voice reveal a more complex pattern of possibilities. The bottommost register is composed of 100 percent chest voice. Next comes a register with a mix of about 75 percent chest and 25 percent head content (commonly called chest mix), followed in the lower passaggio by the same 50/50 mix that men use in their upper passaggios. Preceding the upper passaggio is a register with approximately 40 percent chest content and 60 percent head content, an area where female voices frequently sing flat, caused by the difficulty in arriving at the 40/60 mix. The upper passaggio changes the balance to something like 25/75 chest/head mix. Above C6, high C, both the 25/75 register and the flageolet register (5/95) can be used. Above E♭6, super whistle, which has 100 percent head content, must usually be invoked in order to access those pitches.

3.3 Falsetto and Chest Voice

Confusion accompanies the naming of registers, especially with regard to the high range of male singers. There are three types of head registers: the thin-sounding natural falsetto of untrained voices, the delicate artis-

tic falsetto practiced by a countertenor, and the loud, full tone of a trained head voice with added resonance, commonly referred to as voix mixte. Falsetto is characterized by a breathy, flutelike tone lacking in overtones. Once the changes of the pubescent voice have been completed, the falsetto can be used to train high notes in young males.[1]

The safe use of chest voice in females is an issue of controversy. It is probably best to avoid the chest voice with young females. It can be difficult for the choral director to know whether the voice has actually matured sufficiently to ask for chest voice. Furthermore, many young female singers who have taken part in elementary or high school productions of Broadway shows have already acquired the habit of imitating the modern music theater "belt" voice, to the advantage or disadvantage of their vocal health. With clearly mature female voices, chest voice, either pure or in a mix, can be taught in a safer manner.

THE COMPLAINT

When should a male be asked to use falsetto? When can a young male be safely asked for a real (modal) tone?

DX, THE DIAGNOSIS

Tessituras in choral literature sometimes lie higher than amateur singers can comfortably maintain. Young male singers in the tenor section, and those in the bass section who are facing unattainable high notes, may resort to falsetto. Their modal voices are often not sufficiently strong or well trained to sing these pitches for extended periods of time. Further, a falsetto regime has been used for two centuries in training high notes of the male modal voice.

RX, THE TREATMENT PLAN

It is sometimes difficult to know just from listening whether a young male is singing in falsetto or not. It is best to take the individual's word for what he believes he is singing. In the case of a male singer who has difficulty accessing his falsetto, there are exercises for helping him isolate it. Although every male singer should be able to use falsetto, he should also be aware of when he is using it and when he is not. A smooth transition from modal voice to falsetto and back is more difficult for heavy, mature voices than for lyric, high voices. Falsetto, as we generally know it, is much more limited than the modal voice. Therefore, it is useful in a limited way for adult male singers. Caution: There exists a strong possibility that singing exclusively in falsetto is harmful to the vocal cords due to its basic inefficiency, which results in significant vibrato and intonation problems.

The decision of when to request falsetto from mature male singers is up to the musical discretion of the choral director. When falsetto is used extensively for pitches that could be sung in modal voice, the modal voice will be robbed of some of its power.

Discussion

The Use of Falsetto in Adult Male Singers

Falsetto singing is useful to adult male singers in the following ways:

> when singing folk music
> for countertenors and falsettists
> for so-called Irish tenors
> for comic effects when male singers are imitating women
> for yodelers
> to enable first tenors to stay in a very high tessitura for lengthy periods
> for pitches that are grossly above the normal male range for modal voice
> for pianissimo tones impossible in modal voice
> for training the high modal register

How to Do It: Helping Singers to Access Falsetto

Here are two helpful exercises for those few who have never found their falsetto.[2]

Exercise 3.1

Sing the melody in Figure 3.6, which is based upon the overtone series, starting in the key for each type of voice (given below), and going up by half steps, doing the entire tune on each of the vowels. The mouth should be quite closed, 1–6 opening. The top note should be in falsetto, and the bottom two notes should be sung in modal voice. The falsetto sensation is one of letting go of all controls except pitch. Indeed, the pitches will waver in the beginning, until some skill has been achieved. The difficulty of switching gears will eventually ease and the exercise can be sung rapidly, which is recommended.

> Tenor starts in the key of B (first note F#) and continues through the key of E.

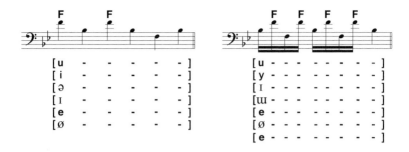

FIGURES 3.6 and 3.7

> Baritone starts in the key of A (first note E) and continues through the key of D.
>
> Bass starts in the key of G (first note D) and continues through the key of C.

EXERCISE 3.2

This exercise (shown in Figure 3.7) is sung exactly as in Exercise 3.1; only the melody is different. The high note will be in falsetto, and the lower two notes in modal voice. Use one vowel for each repetition, in the same keys as indicated above.

How to Do It: Training Male High Notes by Using Falsetto

In private sectional rehearsals or in individual instruction for those who need it, teach the techniques of going from falsetto to modal voice in the male high range, using the two exercises above. This need not be an isolated technique given only to the tenor section. The lower voices will appreciate accessing their high notes more easily.

The old masters used their falsetto regimes in this way: The kinesthetic feedback of singing in falsetto—easy, forward, and high—was used to give men a sensation of laryngeal ease. They then added only air flow and appoggio for their modal high notes. The teachers also used the ploy of extending the falsetto as low as possible to strengthen the laryngeal muscles by doing the opposite of modal high note execution. Singing falsetto down low is extremely physically challenging, but it contributes strongly to the ability to sing modal high notes.

When teaching male singers to find their modal high voice, there is no ignoring the effectiveness of a correctly executed trip through the passaggio. The passaggio notes must be sung with a smaller jaw opening, a higher fronter, vowel, and often with rounded lips. This affords the voice the opportunity to shift into a tone with more head content, or to "cover."[3] When the [e] passaggio vowel is executed properly—by resting the sides of the tongue on the fourth upper tooth on both sides of the mouth and keeping the tip against the top of the bottom teeth—the high modal voice generally opens up. The [e] vowel, tongue sides on the fourth tooth, is almost foolproof when this is accurately done. The high front [e], resembling the French aigu é, is without doubt the most valuable vowel for tenors in their upper range.

Another method is to start a tone in the falsetto voice, then develop it into a modal tone by opening the jaw, moving the tongue forward, and adding air. Both of these methods help the singer to feel the correct muscular setup. Nothing takes the place of experiencing the *feeling*. Some male voices cannot move from falsetto to modal voice without an obvious glitch. A glitch is not important and need not be corrected.

Then, when singing the actual music, the vowel modifications through the passaggio notes must be followed explicitly so that an incompatible vowel does not betray the forward, slender position. For example, large mouth openings and low, back tongues will play havoc with the passaggio necessities. Therefore, sing no back vowels—no [a], no [ɔ], but sometimes [o]—on the passaggio notes in order that the passaggio remain slim to protect entrance into the higher notes. Trust exclusively the [e] and [ʊ] for the passaggio until the feeling is captured. *See* the Complete Vowel Modification Chart, p. 127.

The Complaint

Is chest voice singing really dangerous for young female singers? What about chest mix?

Dx, The Diagnosis

Here opinions vary. By far the majority of practicing voice teachers in this country would not advocate letting young females sing in total chest. The ever-increasing cadre of classically trained teachers who instruct theater and pop singers exclusively would disagree. For those young girls who want to make a career in the theater, chest voice use usually translates to belting on the bottom, and often, on the few occasions when higher notes are requested, the temptation to sing in an unsupported head voice above. Many professional music-theater singers who have an extended range sing in an "imitation belt," a chest mix, which they find healthier.

Rx, The Treatment Plan

Reliance solely on true belting for young girls' lower notes is using chest voice to the exclusion of a healthier mixture of chest and head. This fact complicates the situation for some choral directors to the degree that they should send the singer to a voice teacher for sorting out. For suggestions on how to train the chest mix, see the following Discussion.

Discussion

The Necessity for Adult Females to Access Either Chest Voice or Chest Mix

Frequently, directors are at a loss when trying to coach their adult altos to go into chest voice on low notes without eliciting horrendous glitches in the process of changing registers. Teaching adult women the facility of either going into chest register or not, at will and without glitches, is likely to be a long-term project. Pure chest is much easier to access than is a chest/head mixture. Chest voice is uniformly regarded as dangerous by many, but the old master teachers were accustomed to teaching it. When more sound is needed from the alto section on low notes, there is no way to avoid dealing with chest voice. Although rather vulgar and ugly in sound, it will be loud and carry well. Thus the aesthetics of the situation have a place in the director's decision of whether to use chest or chest/head mix.

A possible solution is to find someone, either in the alto section or from the outside, who can demonstrate the chest sound and the mixed sound. Then have a sectional meeting in which you take the altos through the chest exercises.

How to Do It: Training Chest Voice and Chest/Head Mix in Female Voices

In private sectional rehearsals or in individual instruction, teach the techniques of discovering pure chest voice and the chest/head mix in the female alto (or soprano, if needed). Encourage them to recognize that chest feels low, back, and wide, and is accompanied, no doubt, by a slightly lowered larynx (probably best left unsolicited by the director). Chest/head mix feels as though one is singing in front of the face while adding chest content that comes in from that low, back, wide place—wide as the shoulders, tone felt at the nape of the neck, literally a dual position: singing in a front placement but willing chest voice to enter into the tone from the rear.

Lowering the larynx is helpful, but difficult to teach, and difficult to execute without holding or pushing the larynx down, which defeats the purpose. When making a deep inhalation, the larynx moves down to an optimal level. There it should be kept by mental imagery, not by physical holding of the musculature. The subtlety of this maneuver explains its difficulty.

Exercise 3.3

With regard to developing chest voice for the adult female singers, try the following exercises as a method. Start by singing up and down a major third (do–re–mi–re–do) from somewhere near low Bb3 in the low, back, wide vocal position, with a very open, deep [ɑ] vowel, allowing the tone to be spread and in vulgar chest voice. (Do not have your singers go higher than F4.)

Once the chest tone is achieved, repeat the do–re–mi–re–do tune, but let the third note (mi) break into head voice with an obvious glitch, as pop singers sometimes do. This will allow the altos to feel the laryngeal difference between chest and head tones, the difference being most observable on the fourth note (re) as they return to chest voice on the way down the do–re–mi–re–do pattern.

By doing the exercise above, they will identify the feeling of being in chest voice, and what they must do to get this result (a large mouth opening, a low, back tongue but tongue tip still on the lower teeth, no corners, and a feeling of singing in a deep and wide position in the back of the neck).

Then have them sing downward scales of an octave, beginning around C5 or C#5 in a quiet subdued head voice, eventually finishing as low as A3. As they sing down the octave scale, encourage them to inject gradually the just-learned feeling of chest voice into the tone, while still maintaining a front placement and without giving in totally to the low, back, wide position. This will be the chest/head mix. In essence, keeping the tone in an imaginary front-of-the-face position will ensure that there be head content in the mix. Let them sing the octave two different ways, one intending to end up in total chest, but migrating to chest voice gradually; one intending to end up in a chest mix, changing equally gradually. Soon they will be able to differentiate the two techniques.

Finally, once they have learned the technique, indicate to your altos the places where you want the low notes to be in chest voice, and where you want them to be in a mix. It should then be your aesthetic choice.

3.4 Vowel Modification

Artistic performance is dependent on the human spirit, the musical and poetic imagination, and health, but it also hinges on the physical events of vibration and resonation that are brought about by certain muscular activities related to the vocal instrument. The voice is a musical instrument, responsive to the laws of acoustics just as any instrument is.[4]

THE COMPLAINT

Why should choral singers modify vowels? Is the task too complex for a group?

DX, THE DIAGNOSIS

The same acousticians contracted to correct the deficiencies of a concert hall's acoustics tell us the salient facts about vowel modification. When the vowel being sung is compatible with the sung pitch, three advantageous things happen: the singer experiences more comfort, the tone is more beautiful, and the air supply lasts longer. When the vowel is incompatible with the sung pitch, the opposite happens: the singer experiences discomfort; the tone quality suffers; the air supply is diminished. Compatible vowels produce not only beautiful tone but also clearer diction. In addition, the tone actually carries farther without the use of brute strength and forced air, thus delivering a seemingly increased air supply to the singer.

An assumption that the composer invariably writes the best vowel for each note is rapidly dispelled by a clear-cut comparison between singing the printed vowel and the modified vowel. For example, in a strophic piece you may notice that certain notes in one verse are always more pleasing than in another verse. It is likely that in the text of that one verse more advantageous vowels accidentally fall to those more pleasing notes. The American national anthem, "The Star-Spangled Banner," offers an example. Many singers find "rockets red *glare*," usually on F4 for males or F5 for females, easier to sing than "land of the *free*." Yet both occur on the same pitch; only the vowel differs. In the same manner, you may have tinkered with a particular vowel, asking your singers to tilt it a bit more toward another vowel, such as, "Sing ee but think ih," or, "Put the ee into a tall place."

Dissatisfaction with a section's tone quality on a particular note and vowel begs the modification of the vowel. Additionally, complaints of fatigue or excessive vocal difficulties from your singers require an examination of the relationship between the pitch (or tessitura) of a passage and the vowel(s). Changing the mouth opening as well as the vowel is also a major way to change the resonance of the singing. The influence of these factors should not be underestimated. If you have ever experimented with any of these elements—changing the tongue position, the rounding or spreading of the lips, or the size of the jaw opening of your singers—you will have noticed significant changes to the tone, because you have used de facto modification.

Rx, The Treatment Plan

1. Acquaint yourself with the modification chart for each section. See the Complete Vowel Modification Chart, p. 127.

2. Make some experiments to convince your singers and yourself of the results of modifying. One good way to make a clear-cut comparison is this: use a strophic piece (different words in several verses set to the same music), to observe which tones are better in one verse than another. Teach the necessary modification, then let one-half of the singers listen while the other half sings that portion of music without modifying and once again while modifying. Then have the former listeners sing the same music with and without modifying. This example will acquaint the singers, perhaps you as well, with the rewards of modifying. They should find the modification easier to sing and the tone more resonant; you should find the blend better. A final experiment: With one-half of the singers again, demonstrate the resultant blend and the vocal ease when all the sections do not necessarily sing the same vowel at the same time, but instead each section sings the vowel mandated by the Complete Vowel Modification Chart; see the following Discussion.

3. Teach your singers the IPA symbols and monitor their skill at executing each of them, while you display patience. It will take time to refine awareness of the differences between vowels, and to link vowel and symbol.

4. During the warm-up, vocalize each section with the proper vowel modifications just below, through, and above the passaggio, the most responsive part of their ranges. Teach them to mark their music so that the modified vowels are part of their discipline when singing. At first, dictate the proper vowels; later remind them to do it themselves.

5. Instruct your singers to keep their tongue-tips on the top of the bottom teeth, that is, higher and more forward than usual, except during the milliseconds spent executing consonants for which the tongue is needed, after which it must return to the same position. Clarity will improve.

DISCUSSION

Why Modify Vowels?

Often choir directors believe it simpler to instruct their singers to use one mouth and tongue shape for all vowels. Regarding such a method, world-renowned vocal pedagogue Richard Miller states: "pernicious is the technique of distorting all the vowels throughout the range by assuming some one ideal mouth and pharynx posture through which all vowels must then be produced."[5] This is not a productive method.

Why then must vowels be modified, especially for louder, higher, softer, or lower notes? The late vocal pedagogue Oren Brown answers, "It is impossible to maintain one vowel position at all pitches. Vowel modification must be mastered to facilitate a smooth transition from low to high and soft to loud. . . . As a basic rule, the louder or higher, softer or lower a vowel is sung, the more it will migrate."[6]

It is entirely logical to believe that your choristers should sing the exact vowel written by the composer. However, to do so is not natural to the vocal instrument. When one hears a singer whose vocal resonance is even and consistently good from note to note—high or low, soft or loud—the vowels are changing semitone by semitone, and the vocal tract is changing form constantly, whether or not the listener can sense it, whether or not the singer takes note of it. This cannot be avoided. This is the way the voice works. As Brown reminds us, "Good singers, whether consciously or not, depend on finding an easy adjustment for the pitch. *This will be a modification*" (emphasis added).[7] Moreover, when choral directors ask their singers, for example, to sing [ee] but drop their jaws while doing it, they too are modifying the vowel.

There is no disputing the fact that the modification of vowels inspires much controversy. However, the conviction that modification is unnecessary is counterproductive to a director's aims. It is true that singers can sing any note on any vowel, only limited by the physical boundaries of their range, but some vowel forms will have constructive interaction with the vocal cords and other vowel forms will have a diminishing acoustical interaction.

THE SCIENCE

In the last forty years there have been many vocal researchers working on the issue of formant frequencies. Researcher Johan Sundberg is particularly adept at presenting this complicated subject in layman's terms, of which the following is our précis.

> The vocal tract resonator has different requirements for the sounds that try to pass through it, depending upon the

frequency of that sound. Certain frequencies pass through the resonator easily and, as a consequence, are given a high amplitude. They are called resonance frequencies. In the vocal tract these resonances are called formants. They and they alone determine vowel quality and donate personal timbre to the voice. Vowel color is determined by the two lowest formants; timbre is determined by the third, fourth, and fifth formants. *Tuning the formant frequencies is done by changing the shape of the vocal tract: the jaw, the tongue, the lip opening, the larynx, and the side walls of the pharynx* [emphasis added]. Formant frequencies are about 40% higher in children than in adult males. Adult females have shorter vocal tracts than adult males. Therefore their formant frequencies are 15% higher on average than those of the adult male.[8]

Adjusting the shape of the vocal tract is the most common method for tuning the formant frequencies.

The first formant is responsive to the jaw opening.

The second formant responds to the tongue shape.

The third formant is responsive to the position of the tip of the tongue, or to the size of the cavity between the lower teeth and the tongue.

The fourth and fifth formants are more difficult to control by these means.

Certain vocal researchers/teachers, among them Vennard, Appelman, Coffin, and Miller, have made strong efforts to transmute the results of their work into a functional language for singers. Coffin's writings do not constitute a "method," but show how to make the vowel modifications: Musical notation, jaw openings, and phonetics have been substituted for frequencies wherever possible. As such, they show a practical way to consistently productive singing that profits from the research. Coffin reminds us that an unknowledgeable diction teacher can undo a great deal by ignoring the laws of vibration and resonance. On the other hand, a knowledgeable diction teacher can accomplish a great deal by obeying the laws of harmonic pronunciation.

Another fact noted by Berton Coffin: When the vowels have achieved their best position, breath-coordination problems diminish. Freedom of function in one part of the vocal instrument induces freedom in others. Vowel modification brings the frequencies of the vocal cords and the vocal tract into concord on the various notes and vowels. "As a trumpet player must learn to vary the length of his tubing by use of fingering the valves on that instrument, or the trombone by the use of the slide, for best tonal results the singer must be able to vary the effective length of his instrument by the use of various vowel colors. These are formations of the vocal tract caused by movements of the lips, tongue, depressor and/or elevator muscles of the larynx, and action of the soft palate."[9] Or—the vowel shapes.

The crux of the matter is this: Modifications persuade the resonator (vowel) to work efficiently. When, vice versa, the resonator adjusts to amplify the sung pitch, the vowels are, in that instant, automatically modified. This explains why singers experience vocal unease and difficulty when asked to sing speech vowels in the more perilous parts of their ranges. If vowel positions are kept in a fixed state rather than modified, the voice will run into and out of resonance points, resulting in a sound that is at times out of tune, harsh, unfocused, and unsteady in vibrato. Furthermore, it is a truism that critics and audience members are more likely to point out bad sound than they are to mention slight modifications of language values.

Inflexible language treatment tends to impair the musicality, expressiveness, and survival of voices. You will find these conclusions in the Complete Vowel Modification Chart. With the aid of vowel modification your singers will have fewer vocal problems, including intonation.

A reminder: Because female voices, especially sopranos, sing in a range that is nearer to the resonance frequency of vowels, their singing will profit from a greater use of modification. In addition, for acoustical reasons this modifying will be visually evident: The word *benedicimus* sung on A4, for example, will look just as it does when spoken; sung on A5, however, the mouth opening will be quite large. Male voices, on the other hand, are actually playing the pitch of vowels by overtones most of the time. Therefore there tends to be less need for vowel modification, especially below middle C4. Basic modification for men should be large-mouth vowels on low notes, and rounded vowels (corners) toward closed vowels on the top, thus tending toward the much-desired "cover."

THE COMPLAINT

How do I teach my singers to do this complex task called vowel modification?

Dx, THE DIAGNOSIS

Instituting the practice of vowel modification study is made less complex by taking a logical approach. Experience shows that the difference modifying makes in their singing creates receptive learners. The resulting freedom of effort and better tonal quality increases the singers' confidence, motivates them to do the work, and gives them pride in the results.

Choir singers should have a knowledge of the IPA symbols. Without it, modifications will be imprecise. With it, breathing, blend, intonation, resonance, and intelligibility may be cogently addressed. The director should acquire a facility with the IPA and some personal experience with modifying, using his or her own voice. In addition, the director would do well to score his copies of the choir's music with the proper modifications in advance of rehearsals and request the singers to mark their scores accordingly.

Rx, The Treatment Plan

It is usually best to teach the choir the IPA symbols in a musical context, just a few at a time during the warm-up, through the following methods.

How to Do It: Teaching Vowel Modification to Your Choir

Method 1: Task-Specific, Low-Key

1. An effective way to introduce your choir to the principles of the IPA and how to modify vowels is to incorporate Exercise 3.4 in the latter part of your warm-up. It is a great "stealth" method. If you simply teach the singers to do it without any fanfare or lengthy explanations, they will soon ask you why and be curious about how it works. Having first experienced benefits in the warm-up, your singers' interest will be piqued and their receptivity increased as you advance into greater usage of the IPA and vowel modification.

2. Using a medium-range register, teach the entire group to sing the interval of a perfect fifth as a continuous ascending, then descending, slide on the vowel [ʌ] (*duh* or *up*) with a large mouth opening. Make sure that they make a true slide in each direction, pointing out that this is one time you do not want a nice, clean choral leap to the second note, but rather a real trombone "smear."

3. Next, teach the same slide on the vowel [ʊ] (*foot*) with a smallish mouth opening and rounded lips. Teach the word "corners" as a shorter direction for "rounded" or "protruding lips"—the sides or corners of the mouth literally come forward.

4. Once this is accomplished, explain that you are going to guide the various voice parts through the passaggio, using these two vowels in a pattern of 3-3: three big-mouth slides (on [ʌ]), three small-mouth slides (on [ʊ]).

5. Beginning the voice parts in the appropriate keys given on p. 199 results in each section navigating through its upper passaggio. You will have combined a healthy warm-up of the upper passaggio with a direct application of vowel modification.

6. At a later point, use the same exercise to teach the front vowels: big-mouth [ɛ] (*pet*), small-mouth [e] (_cha_-os). Your singers are then prepared to understand what to do and why when you teach them to make the same modification in their literature. From this starting point you may naturally increase their skill at vowel modification, adding vowels and their IPA symbols gradually, as relevant to the repertoire.

EXERCISE 3.4 THE PASSAGGIO WARM-UP

Continuous ascending and descending slide on the perfect fifth
Three big-mouth slides on [ʌ] or [ɛ] (*duh* or *pet*), ending before the high note hits the first note of the upper passaggio
Three small-mouth slides on [ʊ] or [e] (*hook* or _cha_-os) in patterns where each high note is part of the upper passaggio

For teaching the entire IPA and vowel modification, here is a method.

Method 2: Entire IPA, More Exigent

1. Copy the IPA master list and distribute it to your singers.
2. Call attention to each symbol and sound as you cite them in context of rehearsal. See Physical Properties of Vowels, p. 71.
3. For each rehearsal's warm-up period, the following exercise would be useful to ingrain the symbols and sounds into the singers: A simple five-tone scale, sung with arbitrarily chosen front vowel up and back vowel down on each tune, such as [i] and [ɑ], [e] and [ɔ], [I] and [o], [ɛ] and [u]; then neutral and umlaut vowels, such as [y] and [ʊ], [œ] and [ʌ], [ʏ] and [ə], pointing out to the singers when the vowels in question have corners and when they do not.
4. As skills improve, apply the alternating vowel concept to other exercises.

The following method applies the modifications in context.

Method 3

Once the IPA is learned, teach your singers how to apply the passaggio modifications in context. From the perfect fifth slide exercise of Method 1, they learned how to use only [ʊ] and [e] on the passaggio

notes. It will now be natural to continue using these vowels on those
pitches.

Next, proceed to teach the singers the vowels above the passaggio—
the high notes. These will be found in the Complete Vowel Modification Chart. It is now possible to make modifications in the score
where required.

Discussion

We readily acknowledge that there are many ways to accomplish habits
of modification. Generally speaking, singers can eventually be guided to
find the optimal resonance of each vowel for themselves. This quest is
regularly pursued by voice teachers using any number of indirect or nonspecific approaches. It is a much lengthier process. The modification charts
presented here offer a direct, specific, and fact-based approach. The correct vowel creates correct registration—a more efficient process. There is
another advantage to using vowel modification, aside from the already
stated results: blend, ease, intelligibility, resonance, and so on. As Richard Miller says, the "use of the IPA symbols requires the choral singer to
view so-called voice production more in acoustic than laryngeal terms.
Such concentration removes attention from the laryngeal vibrator, over
which no local control is possible, and directs attention to the resonation
system, over which there is considerable actual control."[10] In other words,
once your choir singers have experienced and become habituated to the
use of modifications and the IPA symbols with which to mark them in
their music, they will find it progressively simpler to intuit optimal resonance and ease.

The Complaint

Having opted for modified vowels in place of the written vowels, won't
this interfere with blend and diminish the intelligibility of the words?

Dx, The Diagnosis

Adopting a suitable vowel modification as required by the individual sections, whether or not it results in all voices singing the same modification,
is one path to good blend. The audience will hear the desired effect—one
single vowel sound—because each section is singing the most advantageous version of the vowel for vocal ease and clarity of diction. The need
for a modification is more acute on the high range notes, where a modification supplies the vowel sound better than the unmodified vowel it-

self. This unmodified vowel is often fraught with physical difficulties and resultant lack of clarity. With experimentation, both the director and the singers can be persuaded that this is true. The consonants, on the other hand, must be executed by all the singers at the same exact moment and in the same way. This method of enunciation, together with the correctly modified vowels, will produce a clarity of diction that is totally satisfactory. See Demystifying Consonants, p. 75.

Singers will always try to find the best modification for their difficult notes, whether or not they call it that. You do them a favor when you encourage them to search for that modification, or, better, teach them what the modifications should be. They will return the favor in the form of a better tone.

When blend is accomplished by reducing the choir's sound to the lowest common denominator in vocal resonance, this will actually cause vocal faults, especially among developing singers or amateurs, undercutting the desired results.

Rx, The Treatment Plan

1. Acquaint yourself with the basic vowel modifications for each section, using the Complete Vowel Modification Chart, p. 127.
2. At a particular juncture where the text and pitches indicate the need for one or more sections to modify, mark the necessary modifications for each section in your score. Spend some time during the warm-up period teaching the singers to mark their scores and to use these vowels. The use of a red pencil for these marks sitting above the notes to be modified will better catch your eye—your singers' eyes too, if practical.
3. If you remain unconvinced, let half the singers use their modifications while the others listen. Repeat without modifications. Note the opinions of the listeners and the singers. Follow with a turn-about.
4. Now put the chord together and decide whether it satisfies you as to blend. Do not insist on *piano* singing. Let the singers do several versions of *mezzo forte* and *forte*, then return to the written dynamic level.
5. Turn your attention to the consonants. Choose a slow tempo section for practice. Teach your singers to put the final consonants of each word, except the last one in each phrase, over to the right onto the next note, with or without schwas according to the demands of the text (unless, of course, this produces a different word from the one intended). See Demystifying Consonants, p. 75. Now

let the full chorus sing the passage, all sections executing consonants together and each section modifying vowels as necessary.

6. The outcome of this experiment should underscore the value of
harmonic pronunciation. Teach the modifications to your singers;
its benefits are especially advantageous to those singers who have
little natural resonance. Blend will come more easily by teaching
the nonresonant voices to have more, not by asking the resonant
voices to hold back. If choristers follow index cards indicating the
proper vowels for each section that have been prepared and distributed, lesser voices will achieve more resonance.

Discussion

Does Vowel Modification Destroy Blend and Clarity of Diction?

Those opposed or indifferent to modification include many choral directors and some voice teachers. Pressed for the reasons behind their objec-
tions, they generally cite lack of blend and unclear diction. In an effort to
promote the elusive "blend," directors sometimes subscribe to reducing
their singers' sound to the level of the least resonant voice in the group.

Seeking intelligibility of the words and recognizing that an audience
comprehends the words most often from the soprano section, choir directors frequently ask high voices for speech vowels. Not only is this difficult for sopranos but it also cannot give the correct and identifiable
linguistic sound. Difficulties in the upper range of the soprano and tenor
voices come about, especially in amateurs and young singers, because the
gradual thinning and elongation of the vocal folds increase with ascending pitches. To cope with this requires extra energy in the breath and great
skill, which amateurs and young singers do not possess until trained.
Speech recognition, which all directors desire, "is dependent upon the
changing shapes of the filtering resonator tracts above the larynx. . . .
Attempting to exercise *direct laryngeal controls* causes the articulatory
mechanism to malfunction" (emphasis added).[11] Consider seriously the
following basic truth: high notes and very dynamically intense notes are
musical events, not text events—musically effective, not textually effective. Asking for a text event on high or loud notes may produce an uncontrolled and unattractive result.

As for intelligibility of vowels in particular, research done on perceptibility tells us that, when each voice reaches the pitches near its high
passaggio, the human ear can no longer tell the difference between that
voice singing one front vowel or another, one back vowel or another. Why

sing a vowel that is incompatible with the sung pitch, thus more difficult to execute, if the listener cannot even tell that you are singing it?

SCIENCE IN APPLICATION

As undergraduates in the music department of a western university were preparing to perform in their yearly opera production, former fears about audibility and clear diction were stirred up. The complaints were the usual ones: It would be just the same as last year; the young voices were no match for the orchestra; the text was completely unintelligible. Using the new sound system to boost the singers' voices led only to amplified "booms."

Then one of the resident voice teachers recalled vocal researcher Johan Sundberg's words about audibility and how to enhance it. If all that is heard from the singer over the orchestra is the singers' formant range from 2000 to 4000 Hz, why not use the new sophisticated sound system to boost only that range of frequencies? Immediately, the voices could be heard, and beautifully. If boosting the singers' formant frequency made such a difference in the balance, why not add another boost to the Hz consonant/diction spectrum that lies between 7000 and 8000?

Again the result was miraculous. Especially advantageous was the fact that boosting only the relevant frequencies took away the listeners' annoyance at the obvious tonal interference produced by the usual amplification methods.

It is, in short, advantageous to sing with good interaction, where the vocal cords and the vocal tract augment—not fight—each other. Furthermore, this interaction releases the singer's spirit and energies for that suprahuman effort called artistic performance.

Recommended Reading

Apfelstadt et al., 2003, pp. 25–32
Simonson, 1992, pp. 103–122

3.5 The Complete Vowel Modification Chart

Lines 1 and 2 under each note give the best vowels—the most resonant, least disruptive—for that pitch in that voice category. Bearing in mind that jaw size will vary with individual singers, line 3 gives the suggested (individually proportional) mouth openings, based on the following scale:

1: the width of a pencil point *between the teeth*

15: the biggest mouth opening that each singer can muster

5: generally the distance of the thumbnail held sideways (up and down) between the teeth

What principles guide the choice of modification? Of the two possible vowels, choose the one that most closely resembles the written vowel. For example, if the syllable written for the soprano section on their G5 passaggio note were ri *from the Italian word* morire, *the choice would be* [e] *with a 6 opening. If the syllable written for the soprano section on their B♭5 were* Al *from the word* Alleluia, *the choice would be* [(ʌ)] *with a 9 opening.*

Parentheses indicate that lips should be protruded without changing the tongue position from the vowel indicated. This is the position that we refer to as "with corners."

These pages refer only to mezzo forte *and* forte *singing. For pianissimo singing by altos, tenors, and basses, refer to* Forte/Piano *and* Vowel Modification, *p. 130.*

The passaggios are in bold type, and they use only the small openings 5, 6, and 7.

Lyric Sopranos (Table 3.1)

Most choral sopranos, young or old, are lyric sopranos. The upper passaggio of spintos and dramatic sopranos, although virtually unimportant in choral singing, is one-half step lower, whereas that of coloratura sopranos is one-half step higher.

At D5 the human ear can no longer distinguish between two front vowels, or two back vowels. The reason for this phenomenon is the same as that for why sopranos' diction will never be as clear as that of the lower voices unless their vowels are modified at this point of their scale. The sopranos' high pitches have fewer overtones, hence less intelligibility without modification.

Altos (Tables 3.2, 3.3)

The passaggio that most defines alto duties is the low passaggio, somewhere between C♯4 and F4, depending on whether the singer is a mezzo, heavy soprano, or real alto. When the melody ascends through the lower passaggio, it is sensible to use the small openings indicated. They will add head voice to the tone and make the higher notes easier. When the melody

TABLE 3.1 Sopranos

D5	E♭	E♮	F	F#	G	A♭	A♮	B♭	B♮	High C6
(ʌ)	(ʌ)	(ʌ)	(ʌ)	ʊ	ʊ	ʊ	(ʌ)	(ʌ)	(ʌ)	ʌ
ε	ε	ε	ε	e	e	e	ε	ε	ε	ε
8	9	10	11	5	6	7	8	9	10	11

TABLE 3.2 Altos, Descending or When More Sound Is Needed

E♮	E♭	D		C#	C3	B♮	B♭
(ʌ)	(ʌ)	(ʌ)		(ʌ)	(ʌ)	(ʌ)	(ʌ)
ɤ	ɔ	ɔ		ε	ε	ε	ε
10	11	12		8	9	10	11

Note: The symbol [ɤ] under F4 signifies an [o] without pursing of the lips.

TABLE 3.3 Altos, Ascending

D4	E♭	E♮		F	F#	G	A♭
ʊ	ʊ	ʊ		(ʌ)	(ʌ)	(ʌ)	(ʌ)
e	e	e		ε	ε	ε	ε
5	6	7		8	9	10	11

goes down through the passaggio, or when more sound is required, the larger openings are preferable. The larger opening induces more chest content into the tone and gives more sound.

Since choral altos rarely sing much above E♭5, knowledge of their upper passaggio (E♭5 to F5) is usually unimportant to their choral duties. However, directors of high-school- and college-age women who do not study voice—and thus rely on the choral director for instruction—owe it to these singers to teach them access to their higher range. All singers deserve to know the full extent of their vocal abilities. More important, nearly every alto section contains singers who are not true altos. They may simply be good musicians whose reading skills augment the section. Or they may be true sopranos as yet unskilled in traversing the passaggio to the upper range. Including the alto section in the warm-up exercises that carry each section through their respective passaggios will benefit these women.

Tenors (Table 3.4)

Men sing in chest voice until they reach their passaggios, at which time the tone must shift into a mixture of chest and head voice in order to access the high notes that lie above the passaggio. Below the passaggio virtually any vowel can be sung. The tenor passaggio occurs on E♭4, E♮, and F. Note that parentheses around a vowel symbol mean to add protruding lips to those vowels that do not have them naturally, such as [o] and [ʊ]. When descending through the passaggio to lower notes, the substitute vowels are not so important as when ascending to higher notes. On those rare occasions, the best high C5 vowel for tenors is [ae]. Note that corners come off the [(ʌ)] at A♮.

Baritones (Table 3.5)

Below the passaggio, basses and baritones can sing virtually any vowel. Through and above the passaggio it is best to sing the vowels indicated. When descending through the passaggio, substitutions are not so important as when ascending.

Basses (Table 3.6)

The use of [ʌ] with protruding lip corners to substitute in the upper range for all back vowels (a, o, u, ɔ) and the use of [ɛ] to substitute in the upper range for all front vowels (i, I, e, æ) will provide vocal ease and better intelligibility. Neutral vowels are substituted for back vowels because the low tongue position of the back vowels (except for [u]) makes high notes more difficult to execute. Ascending through the passaggio, [e] substitutes for all front vowels and [ʊ] for all back vowels, making an ascent to higher notes easier. Remember: these modifications serve all singing languages; and the listener cannot distinguish between one vowel and another from each series (front, back, neutral) in the upper passaggio—and in the upper range, the listener cannot even distinguish between back vowels and neutral vowels.

3.6 *Forte/Piano* and Vowel Modification

Singers and conductors might prefer to think of forte *and* piano *in a very basic way: to sing* forte, *send more air and use more energy; to sing* piano, *send less air and use less energy. This simplistic view does not always bring*

TABLE 3.4 Tenors

E♭4	E♮	F	F♯	G	A♭	A♮	B♭
e	e	e	ɛ	ɛ	ɛ	ɛ	æ
ʊ	ʊ	ʊ	(ʌ)	(ʌ)	(ʌ)	ʌ	ʌ
5	6	7	8	9	10	11	12

TABLE 3.5 Baritones

C♯	D	E♭	E♮	F	F♯	G
e	e	e	ɛ	ɛ	ɛ	ɛ
ʊ	ʊ	ʊ	(ʌ)	(ʌ)	(ʌ)	ʌ
5	6	7	8	9	10	11

TABLE 3.6 Basses

B♮3	C4	C♯	D	E♭	E♮	F
e	e	e	ɛ	ɛ	ɛ	ɛ
ʊ	ʊ	ʊ	(ʌ)	(ʌ)	(ʌ)	ʌ
5	6	7	8	9	10	11

the desired results. Sending more air with more energy can make for pushed singing and strident tone. Sending less air with less energy can easily produce pressed, cracked, or off-pitch notes. The use of vowel modification and correct mouth openings is less dangerous and more productive.

THE COMPLAINT

What does it matter how my chorus sings *forte* or *piano*?

DX, THE DIAGNOSIS

A common viewpoint is that asking for *forte* from a choir may bring intonation or blend problems, but that it would be wonderful to get a true *forte* without those problems. Similarly, *piano* singing does not have to sound undernourished and incapable of intensity.

Paying attention to the size of the mouth opening, position of the tongue (the vowel), and presence or absence of rounded lips gives your singers better technical ability at dynamics. Vowel modification is a strong aid when executing these varied dynamic levels, especially when they must be executed in the high range.

Rx, The Treatment Plan

1. Acquaint yourself with the general vowel modification rules serving *forte* and *piano*.
2. Where high *forte* singing above the passaggio is required, encourage singers to use a large mouth and the vowels that produce a lowish, backish tongue position, the vowels indicated in the Complete Vowel Modification Chart, p. 127. The amount of sound that issues from such a mouth and tongue position will be a pleasant surprise and a great help. These results are absolutely predictable, which in itself gives singers all-important confidence in their abilities.
3. For a high *piano* section, the small mouth openings and high, front tongue positions allow the singers to use full breath but achieve a recognizable *piano*, which gives them confidence at this most difficult task.

Discussion

How to Do It: Teaching Reliable Methods for Producing Forte *and* Piano

Forte Singing

High notes and passaggio notes are most vulnerable to wrong vowels. When *forte* is requested on those notes, the singers should use exclusively those vowels presented in the Complete Vowel Modification Chart, paying special attention to the size of the mouth openings and the corners (rounded lips) or lack thereof, as listed. Singers' instinctual decisions as to the best openings are seldom totally right. Many will tend to widen the lips and draw them back, which is counterproductive. A singer who keeps a large mouth opening all the time will be wrong about 50 percent of the time. A singer who keeps a small mouth opening all the time will also be wrong about 50 percent of the time. The trick is to know when to open a little or a lot. These openings are clearly marked in the chart and are proportional to the individual singer's mouth size. A mouth opening marked 1 will be so small as to admit only a sheet of paper between the teeth; the 5 opening is measured by inserting the thumb, held with the nail vertical, between the teeth. A 15 mouth is the largest possible opening, and is used only above high C (C6) by sopranos and below G2 by basses.

Piano Singing

Regarding *piano* singing, one has a choice. Holding air back to elicit *piano*, the usual method, presents the possibility that one might remove too much air, which will stop the tone or make it unstable. To remove just the right amount, particularly on an occasion when illness, fatigue, or allergies have masked the condition of the cords or when performance stress is high, presents difficulties. *Piano* singing on high notes is a perilous maneuver at any time, and singers are only too aware of how "iffy" this is. The common individual method of dealing with such difficulty is surreptitiously to stop singing, with predictable results for the choral sound. Confidence is at a low ebb, which makes the maneuver even harder. Using vowel modification to achieve the *piano* has two advantages: first, one need not remove air at all; second, one knows exactly where to put the tongue, exactly how far to open the mouth, and exactly how the lips should be placed. There is no guesswork, no mental crossing of the fingers. If these details are learned precisely, the result will be exactly as expected.

The *piano* vowels are three: one, [I], for all front vowels; one, [Y], for the lip-rounded umlaut and French vowels; and one, [ɯ], for all back and neutral vowels.

> For front vowels and lip-rounded vowels such as umlauts, use [I] without corners as in *lift*, or with corners [Y] as in *Lüft* (German). The mouth opening should be from 1 to 4 only, recalling that a 5 mouth is as big as the thumbnail placed up and down between the teeth, and that therefore jaw openings 1 to 4 will be smaller than this.
> For back and neutral vowels, use [ɯ]. This is a complex vowel to explain. It is an [ʊ] *without* rounded lips or in a neutral relaxed position. It could also be described as the nonvowel that actress Lucille Ball used as a groan in *I Love Lucy* whenever she was caught doing something her husband had forbidden. Picture her face: The space between her teeth was very small (between 1 and 4); her tongue stuck out slightly between her teeth, lips not protruding, but relaxed.[12]

Using these three vowels for *piano* singing makes singers feel as though they were ventriloquists. Indeed, that is an easy way to accommodate *piano* singing: Keep the mouth opening very small like a ventriloquist's, but sing with normal air. The resulting sound will be soft, effected by an automatic register change.

It may take some time to persuade singers to shut their mouths for *piano*. It seems to them that opening the mouth would help more, but it does not, except for those who were initially gifted with this ability, or those whose voices are so small that it is not a problem—in short, those who are confident that they can do it and do it well. Those who are not always worry a great deal about singing softly. To find a method that works without fail does wonders for their confidence and eventually for their sound.

Summary

Not only does holding all voices back to the level of the least vibrant voice in the group diminish the sound it is also actively unfair to and dangerous for the larger, resonant voices. The noted voice pedagogue Dale Moore, whose studio has produced many fine singers and teachers, had this to say when he served as national president of the National Association of Teachers of Singing: "I would rather have a soprano of potentially operatic caliber serving as part of a cheerleading squad than have her singing in a group where the 'tonal ideal' for a soprano is the sound of a tired English choirboy."[13] Paul Kiesgen, eminent teacher of voice and vocal pedagogy, echoes Moore: "Loud singing with inadequate vocal technique can be harmful. . . . Poorly produced soft singing, however, can be equally harmful. . . . For most voice students, soft singing is the last skill mastered and one of the most difficult to acquire."[14] In addition, the result of improperly produced soft singing is often perilously close to pushing. Often, too, this adopted coordination for soft singing leads to the same faulty coordination being used in all circumstances, because singers have been convinced that their sound is loud and ugly. Add to this the fact that most amateur singers spend more time in choral rehearsals than they do singing as soloists, and you have a dangerous situation, one that also denies the choral director the results he or she expects to get. Yes, the more resonant voices will project over the nonresonant. This is why the better solution is to raise up the less resonant voices until all voices are projecting resonance. This will make the *forte* blend as available as a *pianissimo* one.

3.7 Carrying Power and Resonance, Loud or Soft

Regardless of the size of a singer's vocal endowment, to achieve tone with enviable carrying power is not out of the question. The first step toward understanding resonance is to define the terms carefully. Is a rich, deep, large, warm voice synonymous with a voice that carries well? Not neces-

sarily. The next step is to understand what will give carrying power to a relatively small voice—or to a large voice as well. Just as a flabby three-hundred-pound man is not stronger than a one-hundred-eighty-pound man who works out, a big voice can be large but flabby and a small voice can be slender but focused and carry well.

THE COMPLAINT

How can I get more sound from my singers?

DX, THE DIAGNOSIS

Carrying power can equalize the contributions of large and small voices in the choir, and is actually more important than natural voice size. All singers can learn to make the most of their natural gift and achieve greater carrying power. They can be trained to sing with an overtone somewhere between 2750 and 3000 Hz in their tone. Referred to as the "overtone of ring" and "the singer's formant," this frequency in a tone will allow it to carry through the piano, orchestra, or organ sound. It can be maintained regardless of the vowel being sung and its dynamic level. The human ear distinguishes 2750 from other overtones, hearing it as "louder." Resonance carries better than sheer volume.

Have you noticed that the pitch area in which the accompanying instruments play has a great deal to do with the audibility of your singers? When assessing what their tactics should be, solo singers never fail to note the level of competition from the orchestra. Choral directors should do the same. When the orchestra is playing quietly or when the choral writing is thin and transparent, all singers will be heard. When the orchestration is very thick, extra measures must be taken.

RX, THE TREATMENT PLAN

Some ways to find a measure of 2750 Hz in the tone are these. Encourage your singers to

> keep the tongue tip on the top of the bottom teeth
> try to urge the back vowels into a further front position
> use a larger mouth opening when *forte* is requested from non-passaggio notes
> eschew the vowel [ɑ] on the top notes, substituting [ʌ], preferably with "corners"
> modify the vowels according to the chart and mark them in the scores

Discussion

More Resonance from Your Singers

How many huge, resonant, dramatic voices can a choral director expect to be given each year? In the professional singer's world, such voices number perhaps one in thirty. It is probably more realistic for the director to prepare to give his or her normal voices greater power than to hope for more big voices, who might present the director with blend problems, in any case. The secret to getting what appears to be more sound out of average voices lies to a great extent in the tongue positions, mouth openings, and support.

On average, the choral conductor wants more sound on those occasions when the group is singing with an orchestra, not with piano or organ, or even a cappella. The writings of the many fine vocal research teams in the United States and abroad have made it evident that one particular overtone, when present in the singing tone, will permit that tone to be heard through the sound of the orchestra instruments—very few of which can play in the vicinity of 3000 Hz. The human ear distinguishes this overtone, the overtone of "ring," approximately 2750 Hz, from a group of other tones, making the listener hear the tone that contains it as "louder" than a tone without it. Carrying power thus relies on the ability to employ the vowels in a way that will produce 2750 Hz in the tone. Even those who sing a ringing tone often believe that they "just think it in the right placement," when they are actually—albeit unconsciously— changing the tongue positions.

Loud Tone versus a Tone That Cuts

Teaching this kind of singing to amateur choir members is possible, although results may appear only with time and continued attention. The following general rules can help your singers:

1. Other elements being equal, a forward vowel will carry better than a back vowel; front vowels include [i], [I], [e], [ɛ], and [ae].
2. Back vowels can be encouraged to move further front than their natural place, that is, closer to the front of the mouth; for example, the [a] spoken in Boston is much closer to the teeth than the [ɒ] one hears down South.
3. Maintaining the tongue tip on top of the bottom teeth for all vowels will keep the tongue in a more forward position at all times.

4. Modify the vowels in the passaggio and above to include 2750 Hz.
5. The high-pitched [ɑ] vowels should be modified because a real [ɑ] is progressively less useful as the pitches rise.
6. All passaggio pitches should be sung more narrowly: that is, front tongue position, smallish mouth, protruding lips—one or all of these.
7. Professional male singers can be observed modifying first toward [o] and then toward [u] as the pitches rise, as Caruso advised. Women will do almost the same: protruding their lips and diminishing the mouth size through the passaggio, then opening above it.
8. With one method or another, air support should be strong.

Professional singers who have a ringing tone will often refer to the result as "singing in the mask." By that term they mean the buzz that they feel on the bridge of the nose and across the cheeks—the mask. We remind you that this buzz is the result of keeping the 2750 frequency present as much of the time as possible. In order to be blessed with the "masky" feeling, adopt the above methods.

3.8 Vibrato, Tremolo, Bleat, and Wobble

Vibrato difficulties can be traced directly to air management and laryngeal tension, and indirectly to insufficient head voice content in the tone. Vocal skills being mutually dependent, incorrect vowel modification can also lead to tensions, and laryngeal tensions can contribute to unstable vibratos. Singing in pure head voice can be a healthy substitute for a straight tone where one is required, ameliorating the vocally unhealthy practice. Although relaxation techniques can alleviate laryngeal tensions and thus unstable vibratos, if support is lacking, another solution is required. The best answer is to attack all three elements.

THE COMPLAINT

What exactly are vibratos, tremolos, bleats, and wobbles?

Dx, THE DIAGNOSIS

A vibrato is the natural result of free singing. It is the laryngeal system's own process by which vocal strain is eliminated. A tremolo, bleat, or wobble, on the other hand, is the result of faulty vocal production and resultant tensions.

When a vibrato is neither too slow nor too fast, neither too wide nor too narrow, then the listener hears as the intended pitch one that is exactly halfway between the two outside pitches. Under these circumstances, and barring any other technical difficulties, it will be a just intonation. To blame the existence of a vibrato for its disturbing qualities is to assign blame to the wrong element. A faulty vibrato is the result of other failures—usually breath, tension, or vowel formation—not the cause.

Attempting to "control" the vibrato in singers addresses the issue from the least healthy standpoint. Few singers are capable of controlling vibrato without evoking more tension. This is demonstrated in the long, held tones of rock singers and some of today's Broadway singers, who make a point of removing vibrato. Ultimately, the larynx can no longer sustain the tension of a long-held straight tone, and we often hear the introduction of vibrato near the conclusion. The pattern of a straight tone evolving into a wide tremolo is a familiar one with these singers, to the extent that it is now considered by many a stylistic trait to be imitated.

Singing softly makes it seem that there is less vibrato, but in fact it is not so. The vibrato is actually the same; it just isn't as apparent when the tone is softer. This is not a real solution.

Younger voices naturally have less vibrato, and, of course, they have a genderless, immature sound that many prefer. Nevertheless, it is unnatural for adults to make a vibratoless sound. Asking adults to remove vibrato is as perilous as asking children to add it.

Rx, The Treatment Plan

For your singers' vocal health, do not insist that they control their vibrato. It is counterproductive to their technique to do so, and does not address—indeed may exacerbate—the underlying problem.

1. Watch for tension in jaws, mouths, tongues, and necks, and offer help in relaxation techniques. See relaxation exercises on pp. 271–73.
2. Do not encourage your singers to control the sound by constant *piano* singing or constant straight-tone singing. Instead, ask for a tone with high head content.
3. Take steps to instruct them about vowel modification, by which means they can bring more head content into the tone.
4. Insist by all the means at your disposal on improving their breath management.

5. Read the following Discussion for a full understanding of the practical answers to this problem.

DISCUSSION

Orchestral conductors tend not to address vibrato as a direct issue with the players as often as some choral directors do with their singers. Occasionally orchestra conductors might request narrow vibrato or no vibrato for a particular effect, indicating when to return to natural tone quality. They might ask string players for more vibrato in an expansive melodic line or perhaps as an expressive gesture, such as making an accent more with vibrato than with the bow. In other cases, the orchestral conductor might address instead the specific desired affect, such as more diminuendo or crystal clarity at a cadence. The well-trained professionals are trusted to, and prefer to, make the technical adjustments required by the conductor's aesthetic vision, and they are relied on to be sensible in the use of vibrato overall. Professional players possess finely developed ensemble skills; otherwise an obtrusive vibrato would eventually result in their losing employment.

Differences also exist between instrumentalists and singers regarding production of vibrato. String players effect vibrato by means of hand movement, often following an admonition to "make it sing." Wind players effect vibrato primarily by means of airflow. The flutist, for example, whose instrument possesses a fairly limited actual dynamic range, can create the impression of greater dynamic range through skillful use of vibrato. By speeding the rate of air flow—and accommodating the increased air flow with embouchure and jaw adjustments so as to maintain pitch accuracy— the resulting faster-spinning vibrato enhances the impression of a crescendo. Conversely, controlling the air to make a diminuendo—with the concomitant embouchure and jaw adjustments required to maintain pitch—and slowing, then stopping the vibrato as the tone fades, increases the effect of the decrescendo. *Piano* seems softer, *forte* seems louder, and the gradation of movement between the two levels seems more dramatic.

It is different for singers. The amount and rate of air passing through the larynx is but one component of tone production. There is the all-important matter of pitch. Instrumentalists change pitch by moving fingers or hands. To be sure, wind players also effect pitch-related changes in the pharynx, the embouchure, and breathing mechanism, but the vital element of producing a specific pitch lies in an external action.

Not so for singers. The essence of producing pitch occurs in the vocal folds. The frequency of the pitch determines how much inherent tension the vocal folds must sustain. Other factors—breath, support, the vowel (which is effectively the shape made by the tongue, teeth, jaw, and lips) enhance, or complicate the effort. For this reason vibrato is a natural component of well-produced vocal tone. Vibrato occurs spontaneously in free vocal production. Its organic purpose is to alleviate the concomitant strain placed upon the laryngeal musculature that occurs when pitch is healthily sustained—and more so when pitch is faultily sustained, hence the offending tremolo, bleat, or wobble. The ubiquitous pattern cited earlier—straight tone evolving into a wide tremolo—occurs most often among rock, pop, and some Broadway singers. As the late eminent collaborative pianist and author Stanley Sonntag observed, this phenomenon would have originated as a physical response to poor technique, but has become a stylistic trait to be imitated. As these singers advance in their careers, we hear the resulting deterioration, loss of range, lowered tessitura, inability to sustain long notes, increasingly wide tremolo, and raspy or nasal tone quality.

For some directors the vibratoless tone is an aesthetic choice. In those cases it can be achieved most safely when singers introduce as much head voice content into the tone as possible. This effort is made more or less difficult by requirements of pitch and/or dynamics. Immediate vocal fatigue and resulting damage, however, may in this way be avoided. Even so, a debilitation of vocal capability occurs over time when senza vibrato singing is the norm rather than the exception, particularly in larger voices.

A familiar presence in the voice studio is that of professional and nonprofessional choristers who seek a remedy for physical strain and loss of vocal capability brought on by extended senza vibrato singing. The professional singer can learn to accommodate the request by singing as much in head voice as is possible, and by taking frequent breaths to release the strain on the musculature. Nevertheless, he or she continues the practice of extended vibratoless singing over the long term at the peril of diminishing vocal capabilities.

The nonprofessional singer has less technical skill available and is far more dependent upon direction from the conductor for his or her vocal health—thus our firm belief that healthier singing results when choral directors limit how long and how often they require senza vibrato singing. If vibrato is problematic, directors should address the problem from the standpoint of the effect they desire, not by manipulating the vibrato itself.

Understandably, choral directors want blend and worry that vibrato will ruin it. Vibrato, however, is not the same as tremolo or wobble. When vibrato creates a problem of ensemble or blend, the remedies that may be applied to faulty vocal production or to placement of singers within the ensemble (see pp. 154–57) will be useful. Where individual ensemble skill is lacking, inculcating an awareness of the differences between performing as soloist and as ensemble member is in order.

When a director feels strongly that repertoire and aesthetic choices require senza vibrato singing, it is wise to recruit singers with smaller voices. The director is more likely to achieve the desired result with voices that are predisposed to deliver it. Otherwise, it is a bit like hiring a bass trombonist to cover a clarino trumpet part.

Defining the Terms Vibrato, Wobble, Bleat, *and* Tremolo

When the vibrato "pulsations are slower than five per second, the human ear picks them up as separate and unpleasant pitches," commonly referred to as a wobble. Such a wobble "can be caused by muscle fatigue, emotional tension, or excessive contractions of the intrinsic laryngeal muscles." When vibrato pulsations number "more than eight per second, being heard as a group of tones rather than one, another type of unpleasant sound like a bleat or tremolo is produced, caused by too much pressure on the vocal folds," the result of the larynx alternately resisting and releasing the excessive breath pressure. "Rigidly true intonation without any vibrato is uninteresting and intolerable to many."[15]

THE SCIENCE

Metfessel, a contributor to Carl E. Seashore's original study, had this to say: "Most singers cannot sing a tone that would have any semblance of desirability without using the vibrato. . . . They have not distinguished timbre from sonance, rather interpreting the vibrato effect as tone quality."[16]

Dr. Friedrich Brodnitz, a leading New York otolaryngologist of the fifties, agreed: "A well-trained voice exhibits always a certain amount of vibrato that gives changes, both in pitch and volume. By vibrato we understand small rhythmical changes in pitch and volume. These oscillations are more noticeable in *forte* than in *piano*. . . . If the wavering becomes excessive—up to twelve times per second—it is called tremolo."[17]

Nor do later scientific authorities disagree with Seashore's earlier findings: Appelman (1967), Large and Iwata (1971), Vennard and Hirano (1971), Hirano, Y. Yoshida, T. Yoshida, and Tateishi (1985), Horii (1989), and Kelly (1995) all consider a vibrato of from five to eight regular pulsations per second to be that of a good singer. They are in agreement that pulsations slower than that (called a wobble) are picked up by the human ear as separate pitches and unpleasant, and that a rate of more than eight pulsations per second is too fast, producing an equally unattractive sound (called a bleat or tremolo).

The Predilection for Vibratoless Tone

Some choir directors justify their dislike of a recognizable vibrato in a tone by citing a belief that singers of early music never used it. Before we accept the premise that these singers used no vibrato, we must ask several salient questions, as proposed by the American Academy of Teachers of Singing (see appendix 5):

1. Do contemporary writers from these two periods accurately describe in unmistakable terms the sounds they admired and those they disliked? There are no recordings from which we could draw our own conclusions.

2. Do they clearly indicate that there was or was not vibrato in the vocal tone? Or whether some singers used it and others did not? Do they indicate whether some singers may have used it part of the time for specific music and eschewed it in other music? Do we now understand exactly what was meant by the terms they used at that time? (Present-day voice teachers have considerable difficulty agreeing on exactly what constitutes a wobble, or tremolo, or even the desirable degree of vibrato.) Do we know exactly what Tosi meant by his treatise of 1723 ("Observations on the Florid Song, or Sentiments of the Ancient and Modern Singers," trans. into English by Galliard, 1742)? Both sides of the vibrato controversy have used this work as evidence: One group cites it as proof that early singers used vibrato; the other group, that they did not.

3. What does the music itself really tell us? We know that the use of the voice changed significantly in Rossini's day after the tenor Dupré demonstrated the possibility of the high C (C5) in full voice rather than falsetto. Could there have been a significant change at some earlier point between the early music we are discussing and that of, say, the Baroque?

4. Does the range used preclude the use of any particular type of tone? How about the tessitura of solo parts and the tessitura of ensemble parts? It is possible that some of the dissonances used were sung without vibrato for the sake of clarity and pitch accuracy. Was a distinction made between the tone adopted by soloists and by ensemble singers?

5. Do we have any reliable information on the vocal longevity of singers of that period? Did they go on singing well into their later years, as

some of our recent and present solo singers do? Were there in fact professional singers in the current sense at all?

All of the above questions seem relevant to the subject of singing early music and of possible vocal abuse in relation to that effort. Choir directors should know that, across the profession, voice teachers are very concerned about the vocal debilitation that occurs in their students who sing nothing but early music in groups that shun vibrato. For further information, see appendix 5, "Early Music and the Absence of Vibrato," a statement issued by the prestigious American Academy of Teachers of Singing in response to this issue. The assertion of questionable tonal preferences, or rehearsal procedures and performance practices that compromise a singer's vocal health and natural function are the concern of every teacher and director.

A final word about the belief that early music was sung without vibrato should come from two distinguished musicologists, the late Dennis Stevens and G. Moens-Haenen. Stevens, in answer to a question as to whether early singers in fact did strip all vibrato out of their sound, said, "No they didn't, and there are actual proofs. People thought that the vibrato was a very lovely addition to the voice. Those sixteenth-century pieces . . . say quite clearly that they should have a touch of vibrato."[18] In his article for *The New Grove Dictionary of Music Online*, Moens-Haenen has this to say: "During the sixteenth to eighteen centuries, vibrato was supposed to be small. According to some baroque treatises, a vocal sound without vibrato was an ornament, which suggests that a well trained baroque voice normally used minimal vibrato."[19]

THE SCIENCE

As long ago as the 1930s Carl E. Seashore initiated a study of the vibrato. Until only very recently, when the issue was raised again by researchers—without conclusions as yet—the results have stood as a hallmark. Seashore's definition of a vibrato is the traditionally accepted one: "A good vibrato is a pulsation of pitch, usually accompanied by synchronous pulsations of loudness and timbre, of such extent and rate as to give a pleasing flexibility, tenderness, and richness to the tone."[20] Several important points were revealed in the Seashore study, among which were these, roughly extracted from that study:[21]

1. The vibrato is a fundamental attribute of the artistically effective singing voice.

2. With the exception of trills, and an occasional note, every tone of every artist registers vibrato, whether long or short, gliding or steady, high or low, *pianissimo* or *fortissimo*. The upper and lower limits of each vibrato pulse are always present.

3. It is this fact—that the vibrato is not heard even by the best musician as it really is—that lies at the bottom of the confusion that has prevailed on this subject.

4. The impression that a vibrato disappears in *pianissimo* is false. When a vibrato is not detected in *pianissimo* tones, it is the fault of the ear. The vibrato is actually present in production.

5. Both the extents and rates of the vibratos of excellent singers are in a continual state of flux.

6. The whole problem of the prominence of the vibrato in a voice revolves around auditory fusion. Probably the fusion of the slower vibrato rates is not as perfect as the fusion of the faster. At the slower rate, the vibrato is less of a unity since it is completely broken. Too fast a rate, such as in a flutter, also attracts attention more than the artistic vibrato rates.

7. Although the vibrato consists of a frequency pulsation in the sound wave, it has only one salient pitch in perception. This perceived pitch is approximately midway between the extremes. There are individual differences. The vibrato that one person hears as in tune may appear to be out of tune to another person, pitch discrimination being equal.

8. Those who are most critical of the vibrato are generally those with very sharp ears for pitch discrimination. To those persons, a vibrato that is too slow or too wide is undesirable because the two notes cannot blend into one.

How to Do It: Recognizing Causes and Physical Manifestations of Unstable Vibratos

There is virtually no disagreement among vocal pedagogues and voice researchers regarding the cause of vibrato difficulties. The two main causes are

> unbalanced breath support. The solution to unbalanced breath support is the appoggio. Since proper vowel modification results in less laryngeal tension, it also plays a related part in vibrato stability.

excessive tension in the laryngeal mechanism. The answer to tension problems lies mostly in relaxation techniques, but vowel modification plays a part because of the adverse effect of an imbalance toward too much chest voice content.

Vibrato faults, which are not mutually exclusive, can be categorized as

defects of rate,
defects of extent, or
defects of breath energy.

Defects of Rate

Rates can be too fast or too slow. Rates faster than five to seven or eight times per second are generally judged to be unacceptable, as are rates slower than five times per second. When a vocal muscle tenses for too long and is not allowed to relax, it will begin to quiver and the singer will eventually develop an uncontrolled tremor in the tongue, jaw, larynx, abdominal muscles, and rib and chest muscles. If the quiver is fast, the vibrato will be fast, nervous, and insecure. Quivering in the larger muscles of the body takes longer to begin to develop. Therefore the vibrato will come in slow waves—a wobble—producing insecurity in the pitch and a tendency toward being too loud. Forcing the chin down against the larynx will change the vibrato rate for the worse, making it erratic and/or irregular.

Defects of Extent

The average acceptable vibrato displays an extent of one-quarter tone above and below the desired pitch. When the extent approaches a whole step, the perception is one of an unacceptable width of vibration. When the extent is less than a quarter tone, the perception is that of an almost straight tone.

Defects of Breath Energy

The aberrations rising from unbalanced breath energy are probably the most objectionable. Slow vibratos can be instigated by trying to produce a bigger sound than the voice is sized for, or by supplying too little support to a large voice, or by the larynx alternately resisting and releasing the excessive breath pressure. For example, forcing of the chin against the larynx will make the vibrato change extent unpredictably and inconsistently.

How to Do It: What the Director Can Do about Vibrato Aberrations

In your choristers who sing with objectionable vibrato you may observe signs of trembling or clenched jaws, a quivering larynx, veins standing out in the neck, chins pressing down onto the larynx, bad posture, or singing that is consistently too loud. All the above are tension-related vibrato problems, which arise because some particular muscle is being kept under too much tension for too long. A tremor is the result. Attempting to sing with a bigger sound than the voice can support, or supplying insufficient air to a genuinely big voice can produce either a straight tone or a bleat, both of which are caused by tension. Help your singers with relaxation of the laryngeal area, the tongue, and jaw. See the relaxation techniques and exercises on pp. 271–73. A training program in posture and breath support will help.

The director should be checking for both excessive tension and unbalanced support. The location of the various quivers is a clue. Audible but not visible vibrato faults indicate that the cause is in the larynx or the support mechanism. Most vocal authorities would vote for breath support as the likely culprit. Yet the bleat, for example, has more than one cause:

1. The tension in the abdominal muscles must be reduced. Teaching the choir singers to maintain an appoggio for inhaling and for singing is a must. Remember that the appoggio asks singers to concentrate on ribs and sternum, not abdominals.
2. The cords must be trained to stay in continuous phonation. This is another rationale for the importance of the legato. See p. 30.

The cause of a straight tone is tension in the larynx or the tonal model held by the chorister. Perhaps that singer was told at some time that his or her tone was too shaky, with the result that the singer is holding some musculature. Maintaining the appoggio and adhering to the ideal "empty throat" should help to alleviate the problem. The slow, wide vibrato—a wobble—is typically more troublesome for the choral director. The culprit, in addition to the absence of an appoggio, is lack of physical and vocal exercise. Bending and stretching exercises are recommended during the warm-up period and in private. This particularly helps the older singers.

Going through the passaggio well assures the proper amount of head content in the upper range and presents an alternate method for achieving a vibrato acceptable to those conductors who favor very little. In the lower range, smaller mouths and forward vowels will make head content available. If the dynamic level must be loud, however, the jaw opening will have to be larger, which makes head content more difficult to find. Objectionable vibratos are frequently evident in older singers. Nonprofessional choral singers, especially those who are older, should be singing ten or fifteen minutes a day—in the car, the shower, while cleaning the house or washing the car—any time that presents itself. Rehearsal once or twice a week is not enough to keep the vocal mechanism spry and responsive. The director should make a public statement about how he or she would like the singers to behave in this regard, and acquaint all the singers with these facts: They should sing ten or fifteen minutes each day, but singing too much and too loud in rehearsal or performance is debilitating.

In sum, balanced support and released tension are major factors in alleviating the vibrato problems of your singers.

The Complaint

How does the appoggio position steady the vibrato?

Dx, The Diagnosis

The high sternum, low shoulders, extended ribs (appoggio) position is probably the single most efficient technical skill that you can impart to your singers. It is the all-purpose vocal skill. It alone will make the most difference in their vibratos, intonation, endurance, agility, *piano* singing, and tonal beauty. A good singing posture is the prerequisite to producing that most important appoggio, whose many advantages include a steady vibrato.

Rx, The Treatment Plan

1. Acquaint yourself with the properties of the appoggio. If you do not now use the appoggio in your own breath support, learn how. Practice until you understand it thoroughly and can demonstrate it to your singers. Model it while conducting in rehearsal and performance.
2. Monitor their use of the appoggio until it is automatic. There is no greater reward for time spent.

Discussion

The Appoggio and a Stable Vibrato

Ralph Appelman, the late distinguished Indiana University pedagogue, vocal researcher, and a great singer himself, wrote in 1967: "Correctly produced, the vibrato is a vocal ornament that is directly related to the sensation of support. It is physiologically controlled by the muscles of respiration and is thereby basically a respiratory function assisted by co-ordinated laryngeal controls."[22]

The Science

Two eminent vocal pedagogues and researchers supply the reasons for relying upon the appoggio for help with objectionable vibratos, that is, reasons for holding the rib cage high and expanded so that continuing thrust from the abdominals will give a steady tone:

> Support of tone is dependent upon maintenance of subglottal pressure. This is done by maintaining balance and position of the rib cage, which in turn allows abdominals and diaphragm to function efficiently. An inexperienced singer . . . allows the rib cage to be drawn down by increasing expiratory effort.[23]
>
> A perfectly controlled vibrato rate is the result of a balanced musculature conceptually energized by the muscles of respiration (rib-raiser holding against the rib-depressors) assisted by specific laryngeal control, i.e., control of length, tension, and mass of the vocal folds.[24]

A statement from the authors: It must be recognized that the application of scientific advances in the knowledge of the vocal mechanism will perforce lag behind the publication of new discoveries. Those who toil on the performing front, nevertheless, will always need viable, effective, and practical methods for teaching the skill under discussion. The two quotes above belong to the former pedagogical school from the era when it was believed that vibrato issued from an involvement with the respiratory muscles. Although the present-day view of scientists is that vibrato is a laryngeal phenomenon, air flow continues to stabilize the vocal instrument and its vibrato. Wherever the research is leading, whatever the physiological origin of the vibrato turns out to be, the practical way of dealing with unstable vibratos remains a combination of air management and reduction of laryngeal tension.

The assurance with which Appelman makes his 1967 statement above should not cause us to ignore the complexity of the task facing the singer who is attempting to keep an optimal vibrato rate through the vicissitudes of

singing in many different musical styles: early music, mainstream, bel canto, jazz, Middle Eastern, etc.

changing dynamic levels, crescendos and decrescendos, sustained and nonsustained utterances: trills, staccato, marcato, martellato, etc.

fluctuating vowel and consonant demands of different languages.

activating glottal onsets, stresses, and unvoicings in languages not their own.

achieving the musical intentions of their conductor or of themselves.

executing extreme pitches, both high and low.

These are not simple tasks, and they are not made easier by doing them as a group. Each of the tasks influences the rate and extent of the vibrato. Each of the tasks is made easier by the maintenance of the appoggio, which generates vocal stability in many ways.

THE SCIENCE

The ordinary and extraordinary tasks for which a singer is often responsible present a variety of problems that impinge upon the desired stability of the vibrato.

1. The extent of the vibrato decreases when rapid pitch changes take place. If the vibrato frequency could be matched to the rate of pitch change in an agility passage, this difficulty could be avoided, but that would ask that the director choose his or her tempo with that principle in mind. This may well be why some directors intuitively ask for senza vibrato in melismas. However, requiring straight tone induces vocal tension. Better to allow the vibrato extent to decrease of its own accord.

2. Jazz singers commonly change from straight tones to vibrato by altering vibrato extent. See p. 145 for definitions of rate and extent.

3. Sustained, slow-moving music accepts more vibrato than fast-moving music.

4. Middle Eastern music asks that the vibrato extent be reduced even further in order to distinguish between melody and vibrato.

5. Whatever we perceive, neither the straight tone nor the vibrato tone is rock steady, although they are both steadier than a tremolo.

6. When pitches vary, intensity and timbre fluctuate greatly.
7. Classical Western singing styles have not always asked for the same type of vibrato; in fact, they have changed in the last century. In Seashore's day (early twentieth century) faster vibratos were common (6.0–7.0). Caruso's vibrato was near 7.0, whereas Luciano Pavarotti's average frequency is near 5.5 Hz.
8. Some shapes of the vocal tract—consonants—may affect phonation to such a degree that it is difficult to keep a stable phonation. Thus one could expect disruptions in vibrato during changing articulation.
9. Since vowels tend to have intrinsic pitch because of the tongue and hyoid bone height, rapid changes of vowels may cause some vibrato frequency instability, even when the singer's intent is to keep the frequency steady.
10. Vibrato extent increases with a crescendo; vibrato frequency increases with pitch and with level of excitement; a lack of excitement, poor muscle tone, or fatigue can elicit a wobble. This suggests again that physical fitness and good vocal conditioning are necessary, which points to singers' age or lack of fitness as a possible cause of vibrato instability.

What, then, is an acceptable frequency and extent for a vibrato? A simple answer, supplied by researcher Ingo Titze, is 4.5 to 6.5 Hz in frequency and + or −.05 semitone in extent.[25]

3.9 Blend

The issue of blend is a constant thorn in the sides of choral directors. How might the effect of one voice "sticking out" in a section be lessened? There are many answers: positioning of the singers; upgrading the resonance of weaker voices; teaching the singers to use forte *without lack of ease and focus; training all singers in vowel modification and the appoggio.*

The Complaint

Is it possible to get a consistently satisfactory blend from my choir?

Dx, The Diagnosis

Bringing weak voices up to match the strong voices certainly takes more work, more time, and more creativity than matching all singers to the weakest voices, but it is the best way to get dynamic variety and beautiful tone quality from your choir.

Often directors are more satisfied with blend when the dynamic level is *piano* than when it is *forte*. Relying upon *piano* singing much of the time from your voices can be injurious to their vocal health, and an injured human voice cannot always be restored to health. In addition, constant *piano* singing leads to the loss of vibrant tone. When singers are then asked for a real *forte*, it might be impossible for them to deliver it.

Unstable vibratos come in for their share of the blame for lack of blend. However, an unacceptable vibrato is very often caused by lack of an appoggio and/or singing an inappropriate vowel, or even a flawed onset—not by the dynamic level at which the pitch is being sung.

Singers' poor hearing is sometimes singled out as contributing to blend problems. Although it is seldom the actual cause, it remains a possibility. Clearly, how well the other singers are heard can influence what each individual does with regard to blend. The various ways of grouping your singers will influence their capacity for listening.

Rx: The Treatment Plan

Observe your singers' response to their own vocal ease and improved aggregate tone when you train:

the use of the appoggio position for breathing (see pp. 20–23)
habitually keeping the tongue on top of the bottom teeth
improving the onset and thus the tonal core (see pp. 27–29)
using vowel modifications for ease and better resonance (see pp. 122–24)

Discussion

A Satisfactory Blend

When referring to lack of blend, the primary complaint is that some particular singer can be heard as an individual voice. Two basic methods could help to achieve a better blend from your singers:

1. Teach the nonresonant voices to have more resonance.
2. Insist that the resonant voices hold back in order to match the nonresonant voices.

The first is clearly the preferable method, but demanding of the director. The resonant voices will always project over the nonresonant. Asking them to undersing in order to blend is a more onerous task for the singers, tiring and potentially vocally dangerous if made habitual. The necessity for resonance does not mean that the dynamic level must be *forte* at all times. To the contrary, young voices in particular should not be asked to sing too loud or too long. The voice works optimally when resonance is present at a *mezzo-forte* level, and when an appoggio position (expanded ribs and high sternum) is supporting the tone.

The eminent choral director Robert Page, who sees to it that his choristers use vowel modification by means of acoustic vowels, has said, "I don't believe in blend. Good singing is good singing. Period." In other words, blend is a problem only where good vocalism does not reside. Christopher Raynes, choral conductor, voice teacher, and opera director at Boise State University, whose splendid and amusing essay, "Blend," has inspired an eminently practical viewpoint on that subject, believes that the word "blend" is simply a catchall for a wide variety of problems that are likely to arise in a choral situation. Ideally, he would like each singer in a given choir to sing with his or her best production.

Raynes identifies four categories of problems that can be associated with, or contribute to poor blend:

> *Physiological* problems that can contribute to blend dysfunction include singers with actual aural or vocal disabilities, i.e., a physical inability to sing in tune or even to match pitch. These are relatively rare. Specific strategies are needed.
>
> *Musical* problems, the accurate singing of the notes in the precisely correct rhythm can be dealt with by teaching the music carefully. Although these problems certainly continue to creep in now and then and are often misidentified as blend issues, their significance is fairly minimal, given the conductor's proper attention to detail.
>
> *Spatial* aspects of the singers' physical placement relative to their singing colleagues should be considered. It can eliminate some potential difficulties immediately. For instance, try having the singers stand approximately thirty inches apart, both side-to-side and front-to-back, in a two-row semi-circle with the back row raised, the voices in a mixed formation. This arrangement allows the sound waves from each singer to travel without being absorbed by the next singer . . . [and] not needing to worry about whether or not they sound like the next singer in the section. One major advantage of the full semi-circle mixed formation is that hearing other parts becomes less of a problem: the old adage—if you can't hear the other parts, you're singing too loudly— becomes less of a ball and chain, less of a hindrance to good singing.
>
> *Vocal* problems . . . comprise the primary category of consideration for blendedly-challenged choirs, and are probably the most misunderstood. Vocal skills that are blend-offenders are four:
>
> > vowel (resonating space),
> > dynamic imbalance,
> > pitch,
> > tone quality.

These are the main reasons choirs are taken to task for "blenditis." And the greatest of these is vowel.[26]

What happens to the singer whom the choral director singles out to chastise for the sin of having a distinctive and resonant tone that obliterates the tone produced by others? Raynes contributes this scenario as an answer: "Igor, I can hear you above everyone else, and I don't want to!" Igor, humiliated, promptly begins to sing with an unsupported whisper that blends perfectly with the less than impressive output in his section. The result: No one is singing with optimal vocal production, and no one is contributing to the choir's best tone.

What exactly do choral directors fear about letting everyone sing with his or her best tone, the process recommended by every vocal professional? They fear that anarchy will take over. It may initially. But with some work and technical improvement, the result would serve the vocal needs of the singers, construct a choral tone of beauty capable of dynamic variety, and satisfy the goals and desires of the choral director.

It is absolutely possible to achieve the ideals inherent in the word *blend*, but this does require that directors find adequate time to give some technical vocal training to singers, that directors equip themselves with technical knowledge, and that consideration be given to the physical arrangement of the singers in both performance and rehearsal, about which more follows. In sum, after tonal necessities have been resolved, reassess the positioning, keeping in mind voice sizes and quality of musicianship.

THE COMPLAINT

I am satisfied with the voices in my choir, but less than satisfied with the resulting tone.

DX, THE DIAGNOSIS

Even in a choir composed of first-rate singers, choral tone can be problematic. The best solution is to find the best placement of the singers. Positioning makes it possible to achieve choral blend and also to enjoy the richness of tone that results from individual timbres united in choral singing.

RX, THE TREATMENT PLAN

Prepare a seating plan that takes best advantage of individual vocal attributes by following the guidelines provided in the Discussion. These precepts of positioning will also contribute to healthy vocal technique.

Discussion

Positioning and Choral Tone

Directors might vary the positioning of the sections of a choir based on the style, texture, or other requirements of the repertoire. The power and clarity of massed sections in contrapuntal passages is exciting, just as the closely meshed harmony of a chorus of quartets singing homophony is rich. Each is perfectly right in its own context. Each offers its own aesthetic, a different sound experience, resulting from the considered placement of the sections. This sort of positioning is familiar.

Varying the positioning of individual singers within their own sections, however, may be a less familiar strategy. Just as moving the sections creates new textures, so does the deliberate positioning of singers within the sections create new tonal sonorities. Further, considered positioning of singers not only improves choral tone but also helps the singers themselves, we believe, by providing an immediate aural environment that enables them to sing well, and which allows them to exert optimal influence upon the rest of the section.

Satisfaction with the choir's blend usually ensues when the aggregate sound is homogeneous and possesses the director's preferred tone. The most obvious source of dissatisfaction is the individual whose voice stands out, whether for its large size or poor intonation or ill-preferred timbre. A less obvious source of dissatisfaction is the smaller-voiced person, who may be unaware that he or she has abandoned proper technique, or whose contribution may be purposely diminished. Judicious positioning of voices prevents any number of maladies that are frequently incurred when singers attempt to match the director's concept of blend by changing their vocalism. Attention to positioning promotes healthy vocalism for all the voices, regardless of type, and satisfies directors by enhancing choral tone.

In terms of the broad concept, place stronger voices behind smaller voices. Positioning the largest and best voices at the rear of the section ensures that

> their tone filters through the rest of the choir;
> the common tone of the section is improved;
> each singer hears him- or herself more accurately and other voices
>   better;
> rehearsals and performance are easier for the big voices because
>   they no longer must constantly hold back; and
> very small voices are not tempted to push.

When the strongest voices are dispersed throughout the section, their effect on the aggregate tone is diluted, and those who stand in front are heard by the audience as a solo effort. In a sense, the effect of their singing gift is wasted. As for the best musicians, when they are dispersed throughout the section, they influence the largest number of singers for the good by shoring up their accuracy and raising their confidence—particularly important during the rehearsal period.

How to Do It: Deciding on Placement and Positioning

In one section of the choir at a time, have each member sing alone a short phrase—just enough to hear the individual timbre. Pull any two members with similar tone quality, that is, with larger or smaller voices, softer-focused or bright, forward-focused voices, and so on. Have them sing the phrase together; then trade places. One position will immediately sound more unified and more resonant than the other. Add a third person and try each combination. Again, one placement will immediately sound the most homogeneous and resonant. This technique has been pioneered and championed by pedagogue Rodney Eichenberger. It is adopted by everyone who observes its effect firsthand.

According to the size of the section and its placement on risers in performance, continue until you have a full row you are satisfied with, or continue to form small cells of, say, three to five singers, each of which pleases you. If intonation is a problem, place two who sing well in tune together with weaker singers on either side. Avoid putting those with poor intonation or weak vocal technique together, according to author/director Jean Bartle. Place them on either side of better singers. If height and visual presentation require consideration, apply the concepts to singers of similar height. Then group the cells variously, keeping larger-voice groups at the back—or, if height is too disparate, behind smaller-voiced groups of similar height. The tone quality of the section will change as you shift cells. Choose what pleases you, whether in general or with a specific work or effect in mind.

One choir director works this process as the penultimate session of an early season team-building weekend. Two sections work on positioning while the other two are on recreational break. Because the effect of positioning is dramatic, interest among the singers is keen. The task is engaging, and enthusiastic participation ensues. Those being positioned will often comment, "It feels better this way," or "I hear better the other way." The comments usually confirm the preferences of the listeners.

A chorus of eighty can be positioned for the most homogeneous, most resonant choral tone in about thirty minutes per section. The process can be accomplished over several rehearsals by working one section per rehearsal. Plan to keep one section fifteen minutes longer than usual while dismissing the others fifteen minutes earlier. The time is well invested; problems of balance and blend will require less time from future rehearsals.

How to Do It: Ad Hoc Positioning

Not every singer is present for every performance. Church choirs are especially prone to changes in personnel. One director is frequently called upon to provide subsets of the full chorus for last-minute high-profile events. Under changing circumstances, repositioning the singers who are present for the task at hand is particularly advantageous. Take the mindset of an organist, who must rework registration of his or her repertoire according to each organ, each hall. Achieving the desired artistic result is dependent upon judicious registration choices using the pipes and ranks at hand. For a chorus, make the most of the available singing personnel by positioning them for maximum effect.

Have the section leaders maintain seating charts, update any changes, and provide you with copies. Ad hoc changes are sometimes necessary. A master chart makes it easy to restore standard positioning when circumstances allow.

SCIENCE IN APPLICATION

For many years the original Robert Shaw Chorale performed on an annual Christmas Eve midnight broadcast with the CBS Symphony. One year Shaw had an unbreakable engagement out of New York and left the CBS program in the hands of his assistant, William Jonson. Jonson placed in the front row one of the sopranos, whose powerful voice usually caused Shaw to relegate her to the back row. Thirty minutes after arriving at her apartment following the radio show, she received a phone call. Shaw's voice said, "The front row, eh?" He had an infallible ear for balance and knew every voice under his command.

Vowel Modification, Appoggio, and Blend

A salient issue too often overlooked when discussing blend is vowel modification. A fact that may be difficult for choral directors to accept is this: For acoustical reasons, a better blend will be gained when all sections are not bidden to sing the same vowel in all cases. A lack of blend often occurs precisely because, for example, the basses should not be singing [i] when the tenors should.

Breath management is another very important element that surfaces in a discussion of solving "blend." Conquering the physical attributes of the appoggio and singing constantly in the appoggio position (expanded ribs and high sternum) bestows on all singers, regardless of their technical prowess, the capacity to control each dynamic level, even though a *mezzo-forte* level is the one at which good vocal production is most easily maintained.

Similarly, improving each singer's tonal core—that is, training a focused tone—allows for blend despite differences in timbre. Substituting unformed, undersupported singing for the sake of "blend" results instead in "bland," an unexpressive choral tone. Bringing all of the singers to their best, focused, and supported singing makes vibrant, expressive tone possible.

CHAPTER 4
The Individual Singer

4.1 Older and Younger Voices

Inevitably, choral directors face the dilemma posed by loyal but aging choir members, especially when they begin to lose their vocal skills. When directors acquire some knowledge about the physical effects of aging on singing, they can help their choristers sing well and longer.

The topic of older singers, though not lengthy, presents yet another opportunity for directors to exert a positive influence on their singers. It is, of course, even more important that directors of young singers be knowledgeable about the physical elements influencing young voices, concerning which there is much more to say. The great responsibility of training young voices carries with it the possibility of imposing danger to their vocal mechanisms. Concrete information on the subject decreases the risk of damage and ensures healthy development.

THE COMPLAINT

What is the director's responsibility toward his or her older singers?

Dx, THE DIAGNOSIS

For much of the twentieth century it was believed that nothing could halt the vocal deterioration caused by growing older. The latest research on the aging voice now mirrors the research on health and aging. It states that proper vocal health habits can stave off the effects of aging. Older singers who wish to retain their skills as long as possible should also assiduously follow informed principles of nutrition and exercise.

The research also notes that many older singers habitually sing only at rehearsals and performances. To restore and retain their vocal fitness, it is essential that they vocalize or sing a bit every day. Just fifteen minutes every day is the prescription. The old adage applies to singers, too: use it or lose it. As otolaryngologist Daniel Boone states: "the older professional voice user keeps a surprisingly stable vocal pattern when compared to the voice of an untrained age peer."[1]

Rx, THE TREATMENT PLAN

Clearly, part of the choral director's dilemma regarding older singers stems from concern about embarrassing them in front of their peers— not to mention concern about their vocal contribution to the choir. Since the vocal instrument is the whole body, choral directors' best contribution to keeping older singers agile is to teach them how to do it. An excellent plan is to distribute among all choristers a hand-out delineating how to keep the voice in optimal condition, not necessarily aimed overtly at older singers.

First, consult appendix 1, section 1.1, Vocal Health Guidelines for Singers, p. 291, and the following Discussion to learn the physical facts. Perhaps have an assistant put together a handout for distribution to all members, containing both the methods of keeping the voice healthy and a strongly worded plea from you, exhorting them to attend to the methods of preserving the singing voice into older age.

These appropriate words have been seen prominently displayed in a Boston otolaryngologist's office:

Vocal Longevity

Attend to the process of *healthy* voicing.
Follow a vocal hygiene protocol.
Warm-up adequately/exercise the voice.
Strive for optimum health.[2]

The following information could be put before older choristers with tact:

1. Appropriate exercise helps maintain muscle function and coordination and helps the vascular, nervous, and respiratory systems.
2. Weight control and proper nutrition contribute to the conditioning of the body and the voice.
3. Conditioning of the voice and body can eliminate flat pitch and tendencies toward wobble. These are not caused by irreversible aging changes, but by poor respiratory and abdominal muscle condition that undermine the power source of the voice.
4. Contributing stress to the life problems of the mature singer are grueling work schedules, caring for children and aging parents, professional competition, and self-imposed demands to do it all.
5. Fortunately, hearing loss alone is usually not severe enough to influence singing skills.
6. Hormone replacement therapy, when and if counseled by a physician, is an excellent antidote for the lowering of fundamental frequency that results from increased androgen in perimenopausal and menopausal women, provided no androgen is part of the medication. Because of controversy surrounding HRT, a thorough medical consultation is in order.
7. Gastroesophageal reflux is more prevalent in older than in younger singers. Almost everyone—singers or not—experiences reflux problems with aging. See appendix 1, p. 299, for an easy-to-follow regime that offers relief.
8. As people age, they take more medications, virtually all of which have some laryngeal effect such as the most common, excessive vocal tract dryness. Diuretics and beta blockers also produce a side effect of serious mucosal drying. If the vocal folds are adequately hydrated, vibration occurs more easily. Dehydration causes stress on vocal fold tissues because greater subglottal pressure is required to initiate phonation.
9. A proper vocal hygiene protocol includes these steps:
   Increase vocal fold lubrication.
   Identify and reduce vocal misuse.
   Avoid laryngeal irritants.
   Use vocal pacing.

Discussion

The Problems of Older Singers' Voices

Why do athletes reach their peak performance level in their teens or early twenties, when singers reach their greatest ability in their thirties and maintain this level for years? The answer is that singing depends on efficiency, coordination, and precision, whereas athletic endeavors are often related to strength. The aging process, beginning in the thirties, might actually work to the singer's advantage by giving more stability to the framework of the vocal cords, resulting in vibratory patterns that are more periodic and smooth.[3]

Of the many symptoms of aging beyond sixty years that everyone experiences, singers are especially vulnerable to these:

> A lowered vital capacity that issues from poor posture caused by slouching, which is common when optimum health is not present. Breathing exercises help.[4]
>
> The lowering of the habitual pitch range occurring in older women ensures that an insult to the larynx happens innumerable times throughout the day.[5]
>
> Both men and women experience respiratory limitations and hormonal influences, progressive calcification in the cartilaginous structures, muscle fiber reduction, even frequent bowing of the vocal cords.

Yet studies have demonstrated that intensity, fundamental frequency ranges, and vocal quality can be sustained into the sixties, provided that good health is actively pursued and that singing is done daily.

The very best news for older singers is that almost all these vocal changes are reversible. The sharing of this information and the directors' encouragement toward embracing the remedies will obviously benefit the entire choir. Directors find themselves in a difficult position when a loyal chorister ages and vocal skills begin to deteriorate. Not wishing to ask the singer to leave, but facing a lack of skill that is affecting the whole section or the choir, what is the answer? Perhaps a proactive stance—keeping the precepts of vocal health's vitality ever before the singers—will prove preventative.

The Science

The eminent otolaryngologist Dr. Robert Sataloff and a group of his colleagues have published a valuable compendium of facts concerning the aging voice:

Aging is associated with deteriorating bodily functions. Among them are accuracy, stability, speed, endurance, strength, co-ordination, breathing capacity, nerve conduction velocity, heart output, and kidney function. . . . Ligaments atrophy, and cartilages turn to bone (including those in the larynx). . . . The vocal folds themselves thin and deteriorate, losing their elastic and collagenous fibers. This makes them stiffer and thinner. . . . [and] the vocal fold edge also becomes less smooth. . . .

Throughout adult life, mean fundamental frequency of the [female] speaking voice drops . . . from ~225 Hz in the aged 20–29 group to ~195 Hz in the aged 80–90 year group. In males, fundamental frequency . . . drops until roughly the fifth decade, after which it rises gradually.

In older singers one should not be "surprised to hear breathiness, loss of range, a change in the characteristics of the vibrato, the development of a tremolo, a loss of breath control, vocal fatigue, [and] pitch inaccuracies." In trained vocal professionals, however, the changes appear to be less severe.

One of the surest principles of intervention into the aging voice is that of hormone replacement in females. Estrogen replacement therapy can avoid for years the changes in the mucous membranes of the vocal tract as well as the muscles. In light of changing medical opinion on the use of hormone replacement therapy, however, evaluating the most current research and consulting a physician is important.

Older singers should seek to be in peak physical condition. When breath support is weakened, one sees neck and tongue muscles used excessively. Appropriate exercise not only helps "maintain muscle function and coordination but it should also help the vascular system, nervous system and especially the respiratory system."[6]

Writing of conclusions gained from their research study based on the Stemple vocal function exercises, another group of authors stated, "The isometric-isotonic principle can be of benefit to the singing population to modify and improve the overall functioning of the vocal mechanism. . . . [These exercises] will help the singer to maintain optimal vocal efficiency."[7] (The Stemple exercises are found in appendix 2.)

THE COMPLAINT

How can a director be sure that young voices are being treated properly?

Dx, THE DIAGNOSIS

When choral directors are concerned about having a firm grasp of the physical guidelines for young choristers, several questions should be addressed:

> What technical and musical factors are appropriate to ask of young singers?
> Is use of the breath a primary technical skill?
> How can directors recognize what a child may be doing technically wrong?
> What dynamic levels are appropriate for prepubescent singers?
> May young singers sing in the same ranges with the same intensity for the same length of time as adults?

Rx, THE TREATMENT PLAN

It is in the children's choir that many receive an excellent vocal and musical foundation as well as an enrichment of their lives. Yet the possibility that singing in a choir might erode the voice of a young person is very real. For this reason, children's choir directors should have specific knowledge of a child's vocal physiology and musical psychology. The director should take responsibility for acquiring the necessary knowledge of proper training methods and the pitfalls. Here are some suggestions:

1. Do not ask a treble voice for singing that is too loud.
2. Select well-written repertoire of developmentally appropriate tessitura (generally about C4 to F5).
3. If possible, allow each child to keep his or her own characteristic timbre of voice by

   teaching good breathing skills;
   encouraging freedom in the treble range;
   teaching vowel skills that bring resonance; and
   using music with more than one dynamic.

4. At any age good posture and good breathing are the top priorities for vocal health. Train all your singers to have these skills.
5. Clear diction, musical phrasing, and experience with text interpretation are important at any age. Take advantage of the fact that young singers will probably enjoy working with imagery.
6. Train your own voice to provide a vocal model: resonant, supported, without tension, and with an even scale throughout the range. Learn how to correct basic vocal problems.

7. Do not ask children to sing very softly much of the time, for any reason.
8. Do not expect young singers to sing for long periods of time. Give them frequent breaks.

DISCUSSION

How to Do It: Some Advice from Experts on Younger Voices

A great voice teacher with much experience teaching younger people, Pearl Shinn Wormhoudt, has this to say about the ways in which the young voice is special:

> In the "best of all possible worlds," children's voices would be carefully trained; then both boys and girls would receive knowledgeable and special vocal treatment through the changes of puberty, and all high school students would be given further opportunity to develop more basic singing technique in suitable repertoire. The joy of singing would be everywhere. Clear, free voices would arrive at college studios for the crucial stabilization and building years. The usual tiny, most musical percentage would go on to become professional singers. For the rest, every community would have many more amateurs in all voices who love to sing and do it well.
>
> The potential is there in human voices. Where our ideal world falls down is through the "system." If a child begins to show interest in music, he/she may or may not get support at home. He/she may or may not have an elementary music teacher who understands how to train the child voice, and who with elan and imagination engages his/her excited interest. He/she may or may not attend a junior high school where the administration provides enough time and staff for a good experience during this time of great physical and psychological change, and where the staff understands and guides wisely through these changes. The potential singer may or may not have a high school choral director who is a trained singer and understands the instrument, who is patient to continue the basic developmental process, and who carefully chooses repertoire and choral placement to build and not tear down the individual voice.[8]

Indeed, choral directors' responsibilities are grave:

Their ears should be good enough to detect what the child singer is doing wrong.
They should understand the vocal instrument.
They should understand the physical and mental issues of the age level.
They should set vocal and musical standards for the children.

One of the most common mistakes made by choral directors is to ask too much of their young singers. Singing too loud puts stress on a treble voice because the cartilage of a child's larynx is still soft. Experts say that the average comfortable singing range for ages six to twelve, for example, is the octave from A3 or B3 to A4 or B4. Let the children's voices dictate the choice of songs; do not let the songbook impose repertoire on the children. On the other hand, singing softly does not serve the young voice. *Pianissimo* is more difficult and tiring because the voice works most efficiently when the singer's formant (2750 Hz or thereabouts) is present at a *mezzo-forte* level, even in young voices.

Later, says Wormhoudt, the onset of puberty brings changes of physique, feelings, and vocal functions. Many boys drop out of the choir, presenting the director with real problems. If the few boys that remain are not trained to stay in head voice, the director may have to ask the baritones to push up, thereby imposing a harmful stress. When the voice change occurs, many boys drop to bass and lose their high notes for a while. They should not be pushed to do more. Girls of about fourteen may have a light, breathy sound, but they should not be asked for a bigger, stronger sound. They, too, experience physical changes in the laryngeal structure, although the effects are less marked than in males.

The problem of having too many sopranos and not enough altos is universal. Often the director selects some sopranos whose low notes are not too light and who are musical enough to handle the harmony to sing alto. This is not bad for a time, but if these sopranos stay in the alto section their voices may begin to be too heavy on the bottom, resulting in the loss of high notes. These sopranos may eventually believe that they are indeed altos and never develop high notes. Wormhoudt has an intriguing solution: Give more harmony/reading practice to all the voices; shift the girls from one section to another on each piece—soprano on one, alto on another. Each girl utilizes her full range. The result: no danger to the young voices and better training as singers and musicians.

THE SCIENCE

The larynx of both the male and female singer continues to mutate after puberty. The female larynx does so less radically. By fourteen years of age, females have a greater vocal stability as well as more general maturity than males. Vocal pedagogue and researcher Richard Miller offers three basic principles for singing through adolescent changes, which he considers to be all right as long as the singer does not feel actual discomfort vocally. They are that the singer should remain chiefly in middle range, avoiding low and high tessitura extremes, with only occasional modest exploration of upper and lower ranges,

not attempt high-decibel intensity levels, and

not sing too long at a time.[9]

Miller, among many other experts, cautions against "unmonitored vocal activities that are patently injurious to young . . . voices." As examples, he names "popular ensembles and 'show' choirs . . . self-generated teen-age troops modeled on . . . vocally destructive pop-music styles. . . . contemporary gospel or emotive religious choruses . . . [relying] on heavy vocalis-muscle participation."[10] Miller knows that the director who overtly disapproves of the popular repertoire will be ignored by the young singers, but believes that the director can find ways to minimize the injurious practices by helping the singers improve breath management, laryngeal response, and resonance balance between chest and head.

A research project by Spiegel et al. gives us these corroborating facts:

"Puberty usually begins between the ages of 8 and 15 in American females and between 9½ and 14 in American males. It is usually complete by 12 to 16½ years in . . . females and 13½ to 18 in . . . males. Voice maturation is most active between the ages of 12½ and 14 [in both males and females], and is usually complete by age 15. . . . Male vocal folds grow 4 to 11 mm. or as much as 60% in length, whereas female vocal folds grow 1.5 to 4 mm. (as much as 34%). . . . The angle of the male thyroid cartilage decreases to 90 degrees, whereas the female thyroid cartilage remains at 120 degrees. In both sexes the epiglottis flattens, grows, elevates; laryngeal mucosa become stronger and thicker. During puberty the female voice drops about 2.5 semitones and averages ~220 to 225 Hz when voice change is complete. The male voice drops approximately one octave, averaging about 130 Hz at age 18. . . . [T]he vocal tract continues to grow in length and circumference through puberty and into adulthood. Full growth is not complete until age twenty or twenty-one."[11]

Choosing Repertoire for Young Voices

Musical parameters are not the only criteria for choosing repertoire for younger voices—a heavy responsibility. Vocal health must be part of the choral director's decision making. Less is probably always better than more for young choirs, except for the debilitating process of adopting a uniform *pianissimo* for all their singing. Smaller range and less time singing *forte* are good guidelines.

In choosing repertoire,

> make it your task to know the vocal status of all the singers;
>
> consider which pieces will build, not tear down young voices;
>
> choose music that suits the voices at hand, rather than make the voices fit the music;
>
> consider how much loud singing is required;
>
> research the ideal singing range of the age level of the singers;
>
> when attempting to answer their desire to perform music theater and pop music, consider the tessitura, range, dynamic levels, and length of time they will be in use.

A current trend is for school authorities and parents to be eager for their children to take part in music theater productions that were successful on Broadway. This is a risky undertaking for the director. Music theater producers are notoriously more interested in big effects than good vocal writing. Most important, they write for adults. They have enormous numbers of adult singers to choose from, all of whom will do almost anything—even something injurious to their voices—to get and keep their jobs. In addition, today's chorus singers in professional music theater productions are very often better vocalists than the lead performers. The result is that solo music is often written in quite low keys and chorus music is often vocally demanding, neither course suitable for young voices.

With regard to adult theater music being performed by children, the choral director's position is difficult at best. It is the choral director, no one else, who is responsible for the young voices in his or her care. To balance the prevailing parental desire for music theater productions against their very real dangers to young voices requires great skill. The director's greatest aid is a solid knowledge of what is contraindicated for the young voices in his or her care.

4.2 Working One on One

Directors who habitually address vocal problems during the warm-up and training sessions should anticipate individual requests for help that are best handled outside of rehearsal. Sometimes a singer's lack of skill poses a problem not tactfully remedied in rehearsal. A private meeting or two is better. Working with individuals is a gateway to an improved choir that should be welcomed. The more vocal knowledge possessed by the director, the easier and more rewarding he or she will find individual sessions.

THE COMPLAINT

Why and how should I initiate private sessions with an individual singer?

Dx, THE DIAGNOSIS

To address an issue involving one singer, consider the following questions:

Is the problem continual or situational?
Under what circumstances does it occur?
When did you last hear the singer individually?
Do your current observations represent a change in the voice or the exacerbation of an earlier fault?

Any individual vocal problem that affects the total choral sound should be addressed. If general instruction given in the choral rehearsal does not produce improvement, the director should work with the singer individually.

Rx, THE TREATMENT PLAN

Consider the nature of the problem and possible causes. Determine what remedies you can offer. Schedule a pre- or post-rehearsal minilesson. During the session remain observant for details you may have overlooked in rehearsal. Continue to analyze as you employ the remedies. Determine whether a further session, a referral to a qualified voice teacher, or medical advice is warranted.

DISCUSSION

Singling Out Individuals for Special Instruction

Once you are a choral director who addresses vocal issues in the rehearsal, you can expect that some singers will bring to you questions about their own voices. Consider these an opportune path to an improved choir. Model good tone or demonstrate with your own voice faulty tone exaggeratedly, remembering that young singers' notion of good vocal tone has been formed by a steady barrage of pop and rock music. Increase their perception of their own technique. Regardless of your own training, whether singer or instrumentalist, your willingness and ability to use your own voice confidently and competently encourages self-confidence in the singers. It is possible to create a productive, cooperative atmosphere in which attention to individual voices is normal and in which singers feel free to address vocal problems. Higher levels of individual self-awareness coupled with confidence in your instruction only serve to improve the choir.

Occasions may arise when the director should initiate an individual session. Do so without trepidation. Even the least talented choir member desires to sing well and with self-confidence. Among the great pleasures of choral singing is the sense that one is contributing to the general high level of performance. Having created an atmosphere where singers feel comfortable with your casual but effective individual sessions, you'll discover that amateur singers enjoy improving their skills and appreciate discovering more about their voices.

How to Do It: The Giving of Minilessons

If you've never worked with individual choir members before, except to help them learn parts, how do you begin? Here's an example. While working with the tenor section on a difficult spot, you observe one singer whose tone is harsh and out of tune on several notes. Perhaps you hear nothing offensive but see a reddened face and straining neck muscles. Find a moment after rehearsal to comment: "I notice that the high G and A at the beginning of "Glory to God" [*Messiah*] are uncomfortable for you. If you have a few minutes before next rehearsal, I can help you with that."

In the minilesson, teach (or reteach) the necessary vowel modification for the two high notes. Be sure also to align the posture, review breathing, check for tension anywhere in the body but particularly in the face, mouth, tongue, jaw, and neck, and adjust registration, which should coincide with the correctly modified vowel. (See the Complete Vowel Modification Chart, p. 127.) Attend to each as needed, remembering that although the act of singing may be neatly divided into categories for discussion, the components are complexly interrelated in practice.

Take additional advantage of the one-on-one session to reevaluate the singer's voice classification. Misclassification, though not uncommon in choirs, results in hamstringing the singer and thus the choir. Directors, owing to time constraints, often classify singers on the basis of a hasty range check, without taking time to discern tessitura, or to consider timbre and register shifts (passaggios). Regularly singing outside one's tessitura is both debilitating to vocal quality and capable of causing varying degrees of real damage to the mechanism itself.

You may find it advantageous to repeat the brief session once or twice. Or, you may discover larger vocal issues that need to be addressed. In the latter case, suggest that if the singer is interested, he or she could certainly benefit from further work with you, or with another qualified voice teacher. Directors are sometimes unnecessarily hesitant to suggest voice work to amateur singers, fearing the singers will feel themselves criticized. Experience demonstrates the opposite, that amateur singers often respond with enthusiasm to the idea that their voices can improve and their director is willing to help them.

How to Do It: Hypo- and Hyperfunction

Individual vocal problems may relate directly to any of the components of the singing process: posture, breath management, phonation, vocal registers, intonation, resonance, or diction. The problems may have to do with the functional coordination of the various elements. Or they may have to do with a dysfunction of one or more elements. Where dysfunction is present, it will be the result of either hypofunction, (underuse) or hyperfunction (overuse).

When it comes to corrective work in the area of hypo- or hyperfunction, directors should proceed with some caution. General traits and the general corrective steps that can be undertaken follow.

Hypofunctional Breathing

Hypofunctional breathing is found in singers who demand too little of their breath mechanism and probably fail to take air in deeply enough. There are several causes:

an anemic concept of tone
lack of awareness of the actual physical demands
a slumping posture
no appoggio
a timid approach to singing

Educate these singers in the physicality of singing and employ exercises that energize the body. Movement facilitates engagement that carries over into breathing. Invoke often the ritual of arms-over-the-head to refresh the appoggio position (see pp. 19–22). Induce physical involvement that is fluid, resilient, and balanced. Take care to monitor the singers' responses—hyperfunction occurs all too easily.

Hyperfunctional Breathing

Hyperfunction in breathing describes the singers who overexert the physical action of breathing. The appoggio inhalation technique solves this by setting the chest and rib cage in place for appropriate air intake without undue effort. Usually the first reaction of singers using the "sideways" direction is to feel that they did not get enough air, although that idea proves to be wrong in practice. Why do these types of singers try to take in too much air?

> They may be trying to make their voices bigger.
> They may be pulling in their upper abdominals.
> They may have excess posture tension.
> They may have too muscular an approach to breathing.
> They may favor a trying-too-hard manner of singing.

They should be guided to stop exerting too much effort in the upper abdominals. When they remove the familiar sensation of tension, however, it makes them feel that they are doing too little. Often it helps to encourage them to sing as though they were singing to a baby.

Ironically, some singers are virtually crippled by the belief that support is everything. James McKinney reminds us that "efficient tone is basic for efficient breath control."[12] Actually, laryngeal efficiency can supersede support issues, but if a singer believes that support is the universal answer, he or she tends to ignore other singing systems. What *should* happen is the following:

> The ribs should never collapse.
> The shoulders should never move up and down, inhaling or exhaling.
> The singer should never try to control the diaphragm; that is impossible.

Hypophonation

Hypophonation fails to demand the appropriate activity of the laryngeal mechanism, which translates physically to an inadequate closure of the glottis. Breathy tone and lack of breath control signal inadequate glottal closure. Such a singer must train the cords to close properly. Clearly, directing the laryngeal muscles to act a certain way is not possible. This closure must be done by indirect means:

by changing thought patterns
by acquiring conditioned reflex actions

In one helpful method, the choral director can instruct his or her singers to prepare to hum. The mere thought of humming will bring the cords together, and this can be trained into a reflex action. The onset exercises on pp. 28–29 will train the adequate and efficient closure of the glottis for those who have lost the natural gesture.

Hyperphonation

Hyperphonation demands too much activity from the laryngeal mechanism and results in a pressed, tense, edgy, or strained sound—a result of tension in the cords and the surrounding musculature. The signs of hyperphonation are

tight, edgy, strained tone;
hoarseness;
loss of range after singing for a while, which is most evident in range extensions; and
an involuntary straight tone, which is always an indicator of vocal problems and tension.

Parenthetically, this last fact is a good indication of why asking for extended vibratoless singing in early music or any other kind will produce vocal problems. Common causes of hyperphonation given by McKinney are the following:

singing in a wrong voice classification, especially in too high a tessitura
speaking far above or below optimal pitch
singing or speaking often in a noisy environment
habitually singing or speaking too loudly, screaming, shouting, or yelling
wrong concept of breath support
postural tension and rigidity
incorrect breathing technique
wrong vocal models
tension resulting from personality problems[13]

Correcting this kind of phonation must include relaxation techniques and a supportive environment. Also helpful are onset exercises. Two useful exercises that induce the opposite action are: (1) directing singers to imagine that the tone starts in their heads rather than in their throats; (2) instructing singers to start the air, not tone. Good posture is a must.

Awareness of these issues and their correction equips directors to address them as part of the warm-up regimen or as needed in the rehearsal. These tenets will also come in handy when giving individual instruction to choir members, or when directors must solve obtrusive singing by a choir member.

How to Do It: When to Help, When to Refer

To determine whether to offer individual help, consider these guiding questions:

> Do I recognize the root cause of the specific problem?
> Do I have the expertise to deal with it?

Directors should equip themselves to work with individual singers in the following areas:

> posture
> breath management
> warming up the voice properly to ensure healthy singing
> diction
> vowel modification
> recognizing common problems of hypo- and hyperfunction

Singers with more deeply ingrained vocal problems in all likelihood exhibit technical dysfunction and should, unless in the hands of a vocally trained choral director, be referred to a qualified voice teacher. Such cases would include

> chronic tension audible in the vocal tone;
> chronic tension visible in the body (overall, or in the shoulders, neck, face, jaw or mouth);
> chronic pitch problems; and
> chronically restricted range.

These may signal varying degrees of real damage to the mechanism itself.

Some directors feel that by referring to a voice teacher they undermine their own authority. A healthier outlook is to compare the choral director to the general physician. The family doctor treats common ailments and keeps the patient in the best possible general health. At some point, however, he may say, "This indigestion has gone on long enough. We've exhausted our remedies. It's time to see the gastroenterologist." Thus the patient's trust in the physician is well founded. The same is true for the aspiring, but frustrated singer. Choral directors who recognize when to refer singers to more specialized help garner the trust and respect of their singers and colleagues.

Some symptoms, if chronic, are danger signs that warrant sending the singer to a physician:

pain during or after singing
hoarseness during or after singing
soreness or burning in the throat during or after singing
inability to sing notes known to be part of the range

Hoarseness is a common symptom of various maladies: allergies, the result of temperature changes, sinusitis, air pollutants, gastroesophageal relux, or vocal abuse. Only a professional medical person can determine the cause. Directors who put their present levels of knowledge to use, whatever level that might be, begin to develop their "detective" skills (what is the cause?) and their "doctor" skills (how can it be remedied?). They improve by keeping eyes, ears, and minds observant of what goes on with their singers during the varying requirements of rehearsal and performance, and by availing themselves of learning resources such as professional journals, books, workshops, and association with other respected directors and voice teachers. Professional organizations—the American Choral Directors Association (ACDA), Music Teachers National Association (MTNA), Choristers Guild, the National Association of Teachers of Singing (NATS), Chorus America, and the American Guild of Organists (AGO), for example—deliver professional periodicals to members' mailboxes and provide up-to-date information regarding research, workshops, and opportunities for continued learning. Expanding knowledge and experience should be a continuing process.

Making use of readily available resources, directors can learn to recognize confidently the causes of common vocal problems. Their expertise at dealing with the problem should center on discerning what they themselves can appropriately remedy, and what should be referred to a qualified voice teacher, speech therapist, or otolaryngologist.

4.3 Auditioning and Classifying

The Complaint

Auditions are rushed and nervous-making. I'm not certain I learn what I need to know about a singer.

Dx, The Diagnosis

The audition process yields maximum benefits when vocal and musical skills are accurately assessed. Judicious planning of the audition is key. Skillful assessment of singers' abilities makes available an in-depth knowledge that informs repertoire choices and rehearsal techniques. The director is thus prepared, first, to select singers confidently, then to take advantage of the choir's strengths and to work toward improving weaknesses.

Rx, The Treatment Plan

1. Determine what personal/vocal/musical information is needed.
2. Develop an audition procedure that tests the required skills.
3. Prepare an audition sheet that gathers requisite data and serves as a vocal assessment reference.
4. Incorporate into the plan the facts and suggestions presented in the Discussion and the How to Do It sections.

Discussion

Auditioning voices for the new season brings a whirl of activity: enlisting help with recruiting, scheduling, and preparing orientation materials (rehearsal/performance schedules and your expectations of the singers), holding auditions, making the decisions, and, finally, notifying auditioners of the outcome. It's a time of expectation, marked by anticipation of the concert season ahead, and the new voices and personalities that will join returning members to make the year's experience different from any other.

What, Why, and How to Assess

The director's primary concern for the audition itself is how best to ascertain the singer's vocal and musical abilities within a very limited time, and how to use that information to the choir's best advantage. The more knowledge the director has of each choir member—the voice, its strengths and weaknesses, musical and extramusical skills, personal interests, and so on—the better equipped he or she is to work toward an ideal sound and an ideal organization.

The sample audition form provided here (see p. 182) is used regularly to audition a nonmusic-major college choir and will be useful for other auditioned nonprofessional ensembles such as school, community, and church choirs. The top portion is completed by the singer before entering the audition room. With a quick glance, the director will find some detail upon which to comment that will put the singer more at ease—a hometown, an all-state experience, or perhaps a musical in which the singer played a lead. Knowledge of the singer's musical background identifies where strengths lie and what other abilities he or she brings to the group.

The bottom portion of the form is annotated by the director during the audition. If the form appears too complicated for hurried auditions, please read further to learn that the procedure actually progresses rather quickly, and that its usefulness to the director does not rely on copious annotations. A few salient observations made while attention is focused on just one singer will be useful later when recollection has faded. Perusing the audition sheets after rehearsals have been underway refreshes the director's memory of individual vocal characteristics and musical skills until all have become familiar.

The audition process outlined here pertains to nonprofessional singers or nonvoice-major students. In the case of professional singers, technical mastery is quickly evidenced and the director may use a personal tonal ideal to guide selection. Voice majors at college, university, or conservatory will be under the careful tutelage of voice teachers who will attend to classification. Those college directors will develop an audition process that suits the circumstances. The director of a required choir, for example, will probably choose to conduct auditions in order to hear the individual voices and perhaps to assess reading skills. He or she will not, however, be concerned with classification.

Classifying the Voices

Classification of the voice is of paramount importance because it results in the development or the deterioration of the voice. The importance of proper classification is stressed by McKinney:

> The first rule of classification is: "Don't be in a hurry." This is a very important rule, but what if you are giving choral auditions in which you must evaluate fifty singers in three or four hours? In order to protect the

voices of your choir members and to obtain the best choral tone possible, it is essential that you be able to make an on-the-spot evaluation of
considerable accuracy. As many as possible of the traditional criteria—
range, tessitura, timbre, and transition points—will need assessment.[14]

Note that as many criteria as possible are taken into account in classifying the voice. A light or dark timbre does not necessarily indicate a
high or low voice part. An extended range does not indicate that a male
may be classified as either baritone or tenor. Tessitura must be considered. In what part of the range can the singer dwell comfortably? Where
is the voice at ease for long periods, not accounting for the occasional
extreme high or low note? A good rule of thumb is to designate a "warm-
up" range of a minor third higher than the usable range.

Evaluating timbre and tessitura of the voice occurs throughout the
audition. Taking those traits into account, along with range and location
of the upper passaggio (register shift, transition point, break), will determine the classification. By design, the audition form does not ask the singer
to indicate a voice part, allowing the director to listen without precon-
ception. The law of averages dictates that there will be more baritones
than true basses or tenors. There will be fewer actual altos than one might
expect. Some will be sopranos who never learned to negotiate the
passaggio to access their high notes. Still others will be sopranos who are
deemed altos because their reading skills or strong voices are needed in
that section. Some will be mezzo-sopranos. Mezzos, wherever possible in
the choral setting, should be allowed to switch between alto and soprano
parts, according to the tessitura of the piece.

The Science

Difficulties in classifying are sometimes complicated by untrained voices
with minimal range, an excellent reason for not using range alone as an
indicator. Research is underway into classifying by timbre. Since the
color of the voice depends upon the unique vibratory pattern of the vocal
cords of each singer as well as the distinct resonatory properties of that
individual's vocal tract, it may one day be possible to determine voice
classification by means of the formant frequencies in a voice.

How to Do It: Step-by-Step Audition

Start with a simple mid-range warm-up, such as a descending five-note scale,
or a descending 5–3–1 arpeggio on a syllable such as n[u] or b[o] or m[ɔ].
Work upward then downward, a short distance in each direction. Assess

tone quality and intonation. Look and listen for faults of breath management, tension, nasality or breathiness in the tone, and so on.

Next, ascertain range and upper passaggio by having the auditioner sing "Happy Birthday" as you move him or her through various keys. Because the upper passaggio has a greater effect on choral singing and its location is a critical factor in classifying the voice, this is an important step. Start in a key that allows most voices to reach the octave span comfortably.

Male Voices

Start in the key of E♭ (range: B♭2—B♭3). If the high and low notes are easy, the singer is probably a baritone or bass. Move down by whole or half steps until the lowest note disappears, and mark the low range on the audition form. Then go to F major (range: C3–C4) and move up by whole or half steps. A male voice untrained in negotiating the passaggio will typically flip into falsetto at the register shift. Having sung up the range at full voice to impress the director, the larynx has no choice but to shift into the falsetto gear to continue its ascent. For basses and baritones, this will occur in the vicinity of C4 and D4. Notate on the audition sheet the first pitch at which that event occurs. Continue moving up by whole or half steps to discover the usable upper limit of the range and mark the sheet accordingly.

If, in the starting key of E♭, the low note is weak or nonexistent, the singer is probably a tenor. Go to the key of A♭ (range E♭3–E♭4), and move by half or whole steps to locate the passaggio, which generally occurs on or near E♭4 in the tenor voice. Mark the audition sheet and note also the lower and upper limits.

Female Voices

Start women in the key of A♭ (range: E♭4–E♭5). If the upper note is weak, move down by whole or half steps to determine the limits of the lower range. Then go to A major (range: E4–E5), where the alto upper passaggio will probably reveal itself. In most sopranos the upper passaggio will occur at F♯5.

Because the untrained female voice displays less contrast at the upper passaggio than does the untrained male voice between its modal and falsetto registers, it may be more challenging to pinpoint the female passaggio. The male falsetto register is devoid of chest register content, marking a dramatic difference in tone quality. The female head voice, however, retains a variable percentage of chest register content, sometimes making the identification of the transition point trickier to accomplish. (It is important to do so, however, not only for purposes of classification but also because training the singers to sing correctly in the passaggio improves the tone quality of those notes and makes the high notes accessible.)

If the passaggio is not clearly revealed via the birthday song process, have the singer perform a slide with the suspected passaggio pitch as the upper note of a perfect fifth interval. Hear the slide first on [Ã], then on [U]. When the [U] vowel is properly executed on the passaggio note, the pitch will feel easier to the singer and will sound easier and better focused than the [Ã]—the smaller, fronter vowel [U] inviting more head content into the tone, thus enabling a smooth shift through the passaggio. Experiment with both vowels on pitches just above and below until you hear that you've found the transition point. Continue up by whole or half steps to identify the usable upper limit of the range.

With experience, you will develop an ear that moves the process quickly.

Third, test tonal memory with several examples of pitch sequences of increasing difficulty. Play the sequences in the singer's easy range. The difficulty of the examples should be relative to the general skill level of the choir. An excellent discriminator is the succession of four whole steps—the first five notes of the whole tone scale—for example, unexpectedly raising the fourth and fifth degrees of the diatonic scale to a pentatonic scale.

Mark the example numbers on the audition form with a check or a slash, indicating correct or incorrect recall. Check and slash marks require similar hand motion. Avoid the X, easily inferable by the singer from the hand motion or sound of the pen against paper, thus avoiding a disheartening observation by the auditioner. With more experienced singers, go directly to the most difficult examples, or move to one or more short phrases containing melodic leaps and strong rhythms, so as to keep it interesting and challenging. If less experienced singers are adequately challenged by the pitch sequences, omit the phrases and move directly to sight-reading. Leave unmarked the sequences or phrases you did not test.

Fourth, select several examples of sight-reading material at different levels of difficulty, four to eight measures in length. Present the singer with an excerpt appropriate to the skill level you have assessed thus far. Play the starting pitch and allow a few moments for the singer to look it over. Use the time to record your observations about tessitura, tone quality, intonation, and other notable attributes. Indicate any deficiencies and whether they may be improved through your work in rehearsal. An excellent reader with great pitch but breathy tone, for example, may be preferable to a person possessing a beautiful voice but exhibiting poor reading skills or phrase recall.

When you have completed your notes, proceed with sight-reading. It is often useful to have less secure auditioners sight-read from a choral score while the director plays all parts, thus supporting the singer but also eliciting whether he or she can hold the part. The numbers listed next to Sight-Reading on the audition form refer to measure numbers. Mark a slash through any incorrect bars. In a choir where entry is competitive, a comparison of phrase recall and sight-reading scores provides an objective measure to add to other more subjective conclusions.

Before or at this point, you will have determined the classification of the voice, putting together the clues from your evaluation of range, tessitura, timbre, and passaggio. Note that the audition sheet allows for eight voice parts. Making the classification with that specificity—even if your choir sings only non-divisi SATB—will show you which sopranos have the top notes, what soprano may sometimes be added to an alto line; which baritones can occasionally traverse to second tenor, which basses are true basses, and so on. In such cases circle the two categories and underline the voice part where the tessitura really lies, then assign the singer to the underlined voice part.

This marks the end of the audition.

Demeanor of the Director

It must also be said that the director's demeanor is of singular importance in conducting successful auditions of nonprofessional singers. Because the person/singer *is* the instrument, stress and apprehension impose a negative effect on the instrument—the voice—and on the ability to focus on performing well the tasks of the audition. The director's tact and personal warmth contribute to the possibility that auditioners will represent themselves and their abilities well under circumstances that even professional singers find unnerving. Putting each singer at relative ease produces a better audition and a clearer picture of the singer's capabilities. The director's demeanor also sets the tone for the year. A genuine and positive aspect will invite the enthusiasm and loyalty of choir members.

Please fill out top portion only.

NAME _____ CLASS _____

(Please list name as it should appear in concert programs.
Indicate the name you prefer to be called, if different.)

HOMETOWN and STATE _____

PREVIOUS CHORAL EXPERIENCE
(Please list all choral activities, including high school/church choirs or ensembles and how many years, all-county/state/regional participation, solos or
roles performed in musicals, honors, etc.)

OTHER MUSICAL EXPERIENCE
(Instruments played, length of study, any student conducting or accompanying experience, etc.)

TONE QUALITY _____

INTONATION _____

PITCH SEQUENCES   1   2   3   4

PHRASES   1   2

SIGHT-READING   1   2   3   4   5   6   7   8

S1   S2   A1   A2   T1   T2   Baritone   Bass

FIGURE 4.1   Sample Audition Form College Choir, Nonmusic Majors

CHAPTER 5
The Warm-Up and Training Period

5.1   The Warm-Up and Training Period

The chapters of part I have provided thus far ample exercises for establishing correct technique in all components of the singing process. Frequently we have advocated taking a few minutes of the warm-up time to teach, train, or refresh a skill. Here we address the warm-up, how and why to structure it, and we include a number of additional exercises. The comprehensive issues are the integration of the requisite skills for singing, and the preparation of singers to best advantage for the situation at hand.

Why Warming Up Is Essential

There are some who posit that choral singers actually have little need to warm up, that the music itself will train requisite skills, and that only the greater vocal demands placed upon soloists require a warm-up. Still others feel a responsibility to address the warm-up issue, but are nonetheless uncertain of the effectiveness of their efforts. Many directors search for the "perfect" warm-up exercises to settle the question. No single such warm-up regimen exists, underscoring the need for directors to develop their ability to diagnose and prescribe, that is, to assess a situation and be equipped to address it.

Singers should no more attempt to plunge into rehearsal without a warm-up than a quarterback would start to run with the ball or a hurdler to begin his race without a warm-up. Simply because the singer's muscles are, for the most part, invisible to the eye does not mean that they require less attention than the muscles of any other athlete, for singing is an athletic event. Prominent vocal researcher Ingo Titze has said that a singer's vocalizations are exactly like the stretching warm-ups never, ever skipped by other small-muscle athletes such as tennis players and golfers. The professional lives of these athletes depend on their muscles being at tip-top readiness for action. To them, readiness means winning or losing. To singers and their conductor it means the difference between a good or bad performance.

Choir singers are probably using their voices for 95 percent of a rehearsal or performance, whereas solo singers are not usually asked to use their voices more than 50 percent of the performance time in most orchestral concerts, oratorios, or operas. A hallowed rule of health for singers is not to use the voice for more than two hours a day. (Actual singing time for a major role in an opera other than one of Wagner's is usually just that.) Many choir rehearsals last longer than that. Many choral concerts last longer than that. Many rehearsals that shortly precede a three-hour choral performance last longer than that. Thus choir singers' voices are stressed by the very length of their rehearsals and performances.

In addition, choristers sing constantly in a group, which affords them very little opportunity to check their own personal vocalism. Often they cannot hear themselves. Since the vocal instrument has little or no visible record of the physiological processes involved in singing, singers can judge their output only by kinesthetic or auditory feedback; that is, they must feel it or hear it. The small amount of acoustical feedback given them by their voices when singing in a group increases the likelihood of singing poorly for some meaningful portion of the time. Moreover, the outcome (slow but sure vocal debilitation) is unchanged by the fact that some untrained choir singers—just like rock singers—take hoarseness after rehearsal in their stride. They expect to be hoarse—but they are mistaken. Hoarseness is not normal after singing.[1] Ultimately, the voices suffer, as do the performances.

Of course, the best way to ensure a short warm-up that saves rehearsal time is to ask choir members to warm up before they come. However, many choir singers are amateurs, not professionals, and the probability is low that they will find time to so. The choral warm-up should provide not only for the stretching of the vocal muscles but also for the vocal mechanism's changeover from speaking to singing. The warm-up also benefits the rehearsal or performance in a very practical way. Choral singers often arrive directly from the office, or even the kitchen. The problems of ordinary living may be uppermost in their minds. The warm-up serves to transfer attention from life problems to the kind of concentration and other mental skills needed for rehearsal. For a productive rehearsal to take place, the singers must put aside distractions and join in a community effort aimed at doing justice to the music.

In a 1948 letter to the original Collegiate Chorale, explaining the beautiful tone achieved by another chorus he was conducting, Robert Shaw said, "it has built its tone with two rehearsals per week by *consistently elaborate warm-up sessions* and the most intense attention to tuning" (emphasis added).[2] It is evident that Shaw depended upon a warm-up period for many types of good results.

The larger questions here are

1. Must I teach vocal skills to my choir?
2. If so, when should I do it?

The short answers are

1. Yes, to preserve their vocal health and to raise your chances of getting a better rehearsal or performance.
2. Primarily during the warm-up.

SCIENCE IN APPLICATION

A college choir composed of nonmusic-major students performed jointly with a prestigious amateur choir in a major New York City concert venue. A "ringer" from the amateur choir, a professional singer performing in concert with the group, approached the college director post-performance. "I am astonished at these college singers," he said. "Their breathing, their singing, their diction is so professional. As I stood among them, I kept wondering, 'Who trains these singers?'"

Perhaps the telling aspect of this real-life anecdote is not that the college students performed so well but that the professional singer wondered how and by whom they could possibly have been trained. The answer did not occur to him: the choral director.

Taking the Time to Train

As a director, you must take a position on teaching vocal skills and let that decision color the content of your warm-up period.

The changeover from talking to singing requires a physical tuning up of the thirty-nine pairs of muscles inside the larynx, the fifteen pair outside the larynx, and the thirty-six or more muscles of the breathing mechanism. All must be functional for the singer to respond effectively to the director's requests.

A celebrated voice teacher and highly experienced choral conductor, Robert C. White, Jr., expresses his opinion on improving choristers' vocal abilities:

> Choruses, no matter how large, can be treated as mass voice classes for at least part of each rehearsal period, but this requires proper warm-ups, a conductor sensitive to physical signs of stress in individual singers (all it takes is a trained eye), and an approach to rehearsing that considers interpretive and diction problems concurrently with the correct physiological approach to vocal tone. Vocal damage has seldom been a result of how much a choral director demands, but of the *way* in which these demands are made.[3]

The major concern of singers at the outset of a rehearsal is to find their head voice and high range, which has not been used while talking all day. Most people speak at least an octave below where they sing, except for baritones, most of whose ranges are within the talking spectrum. The warm-up must provide some kind of fail-safe exercise that enables the singers to ride through the upper passaggio and into the high range without strain. Smaller mouth openings, a front position for vowels, and protruding lips around the vowel will usually aid in this effort. This confidence in the upper range is the state of readiness that singers refer to as being "warmed up," whether they recognize it or not.

Achieving Better Results from the Warm-Up

Because so much can be achieved during a warm-up it is necessary to plan effectively for the issues you wish to include. The bare necessities are

    singers' bodies need to be awakened and mobilized;
    posture and breathing should be implemented anew;
    singers need to reestablish a sense of community with their respective
        sections;

a singing tone, as opposed to a speaking tone, must be activated; and proper diction must be redeployed.

New information can be imparted and old information should be reinforced. The warm-up period is a pedagogical moment, a group voice lesson, but it is also the time to forge a strong link between choir and conductor. Therefore, warm-up exercises must be presented as an activity that conductor and choir participate in equally. A collegial attitude should permeate the atmosphere.

The warm-up period can be used to identify

common goals of the organization: long-term, intermediate, and
   short-term;
the choir's present status;
recent progress;
readiness for scheduled performances;
vocal or musical techniques that need attention.

Community spirit expands exponentially with the number of times the conductor shares with his or her singers the overall concerns.

Efficiency is served by parts of the warm-up being geared to the piece(s) coming up in rehearsal. Particular skills may be readied by means of a tailored exercise. However, once the skill is directly applied to the piece, move directly into rehearsing the piece itself. Performance psychologist Alma Thomas tells us, "Taking a section out of context to rehearse a particular skill is very effective, but the section must be returned to context immediately after the skill is executed correctly, or it will not be retained."[4]

SCIENCE IN APPLICATION

In a letter to the Collegiate Chorale, Robert Shaw wrote:

> I'd like to say after the fact my thanks for the intensity of last night's rehearsal. We accomplished a great deal in a very short time. . . . The music, of course, was not difficult, but it required extreme agility and flexibility. Thanks.
>
> At the same time I feel rather ashamed about the tenseness of the rehearsal—my fault, not yours. I'm terribly anxious for us to become a really professional instrument, and that calls for a lot of high-grade habits: the habit of absolute intonation, of putting each tone in its one and only relation to key and chord—which calls for a terrific conscious effort—the habit of reading ahead of the music dynamic indications, tempo marks,

phrasings, the habit of rhythmic releases, of phrasing (breathing) before attacks so that rhythm rolls on, the habit of overprecise phonetic enunciation. All of these things I want us to handle as habitual tools, part of us, so that we can move immediately into that area where song becomes spirit.[5]

How to Do It: The Regular Warm-Up

Each of the following topics should be addressed in any warm-up. Select one or more exercises from each category to provide an adequate warm-up that enables singers to establish and train high-grade vocal function habits. Healthy and beautiful singing throughout the rehearsal depends upon smart warm-up techniques. In the course of long rehearsals, periodically insert one or more of the stretching or breathing exercises to rejuvenate bodies and minds—including your own.

The stretching moments are a good time to cement your relationship with the chorus members. Stretching and breathing exercises shed tension and induce energized relaxation. Coupled with the anticipation of the music-making ahead, these moments are perfect for sharing light-hearted banter and general comments that shift the singers' mental focus away from everyday life and toward the shared work ahead. As the mood settles, provide a brief assessment of the choir's latest achievement or its current status, and a broad overview of the work to be accomplished that day. Remind your singers how many days or rehearsals are left until the next performance or stated goal deadline. As the rehearsal progresses, provide the short-term goals for each piece of repertoire rehearsed. See p. 273 for a discussion of goal setting.

Throughout the warm-up, watch and listen for any tensions or faults that require correction. Short reminder phrases work best, such as, "Up!" for the appoggio and "Sideways!" for the inhalation. When you stress a particular facet of the warm-up, briefly explain why, for example, "Keeping the rib cage expanded and up provides enough air for the entire phrase." Tie the purpose of an exercise to some part of the music to be rehearsed, such as, "This steady stream of air is how to keep the air spinning through the dotted quarters of 'The Battle Hymn.'" When singers hear the improved results and understand what they are doing and why, then you are working together as a team.

> *Keys to warm-up success:*   Keep it friendly.
> Keep it organized.
> Keep it productive.

How to Do It: Exercises for the Regular Warm-Up

STRETCHING AND BREATHING EXERCISES

1. *Initial gentle stretches (to ready the body for singing, release tension, and increase the blood's circulation)*

   Place feet a comfortable shoulder-width apart.

   Hands at the waist, turn the upper body side to side.

   Bend over at the waist, allowing head and arms to hang like pieces of fruit from a tree. Then gently roll upright as though one vertebra at a time.

   Lean the right ear toward the right shoulder, the left ear toward the left shoulder and gently stretch.

   Shrug and release the shoulders.

   Roll the shoulders forward, then backward.

   Roll the head gently in an arc in each direction.

   Move the jaw down and up slowly, gently massaging the mandibular joint.

   Stretch the facial muscles outward as though delightfully surprised, then release.

   Stretch the arms over the head, reaching high.

   "Scrunch" the facial muscles inward toward the nose, then release.

2. *Establishing the appoggio posture (keeping the chest in the appoggio position requires the abdominals to work properly and well without further attention)*

   Explain the principles of the appoggio: it depends upon isolating muscle groups. (Once the principles are explained, combine appoggio with other exercises.)

   Standing with arms over the head, lower arms to their resting position without moving chest from its elevated position.

   Relax shoulder muscles without moving chest. (Back may be sore for several weeks. Then, habituated and trained, the muscles will cease hurting.)

   Standing, inhale sideways without lowering or raising the chest (sternum).

   Exhale (or sing) without lowering chest (sternum).

   Standing, continue to inhale, exhale several times.

3. *Checking other postural elements*

   Shoulders back and down, not rising with the chest.

   Body balanced on both feet, weight on the arch.

Knees not locked.

Head comfortably over the body; neck neither extended nor retracted.

Chin neither tucked nor lifted.

Body vertically aligned.

4. *Releasing remaining body tension; preparing the breathing mechanism for singing*

Hands around waist, index finger under bottom rib in front, thumbs on the back, pinkie on hipbone, note the expansion/contraction that occurs under the hands and in the ribs when the forceful sucking in of the air has put the appoggio in place. No raising chest or shoulders in an attempt to force more air into lungs. No "topping off the tank."

Appoggio chest position maintains. Breath intake does not disturb the sternum. Initially, sideways inhalation will make singers believe that they do not have enough air, which impression is erroneous, as they will soon discover.

Blow out a steady stream of air through the mouth.

Exhale on continuous sssssssss.

Exhale on shhhhhhhhh.

Exhale on whhhhhhhhh.

Exhale on unvoiced sigh (a sigh that employs only air, no sound).

Exhale on voiced sigh (a sigh that employs the voice).

5. *Energizing, when indicators point to the need*

Walk in place, keeping balls of the feet in one place, pumping the arms.

Hang arms loosely at the side; shake the hands.

Bounce lightly up and down on balls of the feet.

Rock the knees gently.

Onset and Legato

1. *Connecting voice to breathing mechanism*

Sustain [i] vowel as long as possible on F3 (males) and F4 (females).

Glide from lowest possible note to highest possible note on the word *knoll*, singing *pianissimo*; repeat, ignoring any breaks.

Glide from highest note to lowest note on *knoll*, singing *pianissimo*; repeat, ignoring any breaks.[6]

2. *Roller coaster slide*

   On a tiny [o] glide up, then down, up higher, then down, up highest, then down.

3. *Lip trill slides (see p. 321, note 11, for definition; to ensure a gentle stretch of the laryngeal muscles under balanced air pressure)*

   Slide on a lip trill, ascending and descending in octaves or perfect fifths, elongating the glide between the lower and upper pitches.

4. *Humming*

   Hum 4-note scales at *mezzo piano* dynamic level (1–2–3–4–3–2–1).[7]

5. *The sustained "S" exercise*

   Use an elongated [s] followed by a vowel on one pitch, followed by the [s] and then the vowel again (SSSSSSSaaaaaaaaSSSSSSSS aaaaaaaaa).

6. *5–3–1 on vowels*

   Sing the 5–3–1 pattern on [ɔ] preceded by a set of consonants [fm] in descending and ascending keys [fmɔ, fmɔ, fmɔ].

7. *Open mouth hum (to alleviate pushing/pressing and to train forward focus; see note 7, p. 323)*

   Employ the [ng] on various patterns (Figures 5.1 and 5.2).

8. *Balanced onset exercises*

   Employ one or more of the balanced onset exercises on pp. 28–29.

MESSA DI VOCE
(to balance breath and tone, to increase expressivity in response to director's needs)

This messa di voce exercise is based primarily upon vowel modification. For a messa di voce exercise that uses breath only, see p. 56.

All parts sing a single comfortable note, perhaps one pitch for sopranos and tenors and another for altos and basses.

During the messa di voce, the mouth goes gradually from very small to wide open and back again, as the dynamics change gradually from *pianissimo* to *forte* and back again, while the vowels (for words written with a back vowel) change from [ɯ], gradually shifting to [ʊ], and then to a rounded [ʌ] and back again.

[ŋ] (ng - open mouth hum)   [ŋ]

FIGURES 5.1 and 5.2

The small mouth [ɯ] will successfully deliver a *piano* sound and the rounded [ʌ] will deliver a *forte* sound, but the air will remain constant, the appoggio very strong throughout, allowing the mouth openings and the vowels to do the work. (For a detailed discussion of executing the vowel [ɯ], *see* p. 133.) For words written with front vowels, shift from [I] to [e] to [ɛ] and back again.

Exercising on the messa di voce trains the singers in the skills needed to replace the habit of removing or overblowing air. They should be trained to

keep the appoggio constant;
focus keenly on pitch;
vary the jaw openings; and
vary the vowels as determined by the director.

EXTENDING RANGE

1. *Passaggio notes into head voice*

   a. Lip trill slides ascending on a perfect fifth or octave, as in Figure 5.3.

   b. Slides on a perfect fifth using [ʊ] or [e] in the passaggio, [ʌ] with corners and [ɛ] above and below the passaggio. (See p. 110 for passaggio pitches in all voices.) This exercise is noted on pp. 123–24.

   c. Staccato arpeggio pattern of the Queen of the Night from Mozart's *Magic Flute* on the front [a], as in Figure 5.4. (This is the "Boston ah," as in that city's rendition of *park the car*. See p. 48 for explanation of "silver ah.") Do not ascend by half steps; rather, alternate high and low keys.

2. *Extending range downward*

   a. Lip trill slides descending on a perfect fifth or octave.

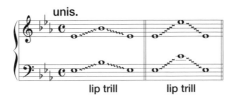

FIGURE 5.3

FIGURE 5.4

    b. The "donkey" glide, so named because its two vowels [i] [ɔ] re-
mind one of a donkey noise. Glide down a descending perfect
fifth on [i], modifying this vowel as shown in the modification
charts on pp. 129 and 131, ending on [ɔ].

    c. Staccato arpeggio patterns as in Figure 5.5.

AGILITY
(to prepare the voice for energized melismatic singing)

1. *The chuckle method for agility (see pp. 44–45 for details)*

    a. Close the mouth and chuckle on a moving stream of air.

    b. Close the mouth and chuckle on pitch on a nonstop stream
of air.

    c. Select a sixteenth-note pattern of suitable length and tempo to
match your choir's current ability. Gradually lengthen the
pattern, increase the tempo, or both, as illustrated in Figures 5.6
and 5.7.

DICTION
(to train vowels and consonants systematically over time)

Make a purposeful choice of vowels in the initial warm-up exercises above. Illustrate by example and by a brief explanation
of tongue positions.

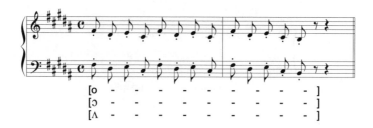

FIGURE 5.5

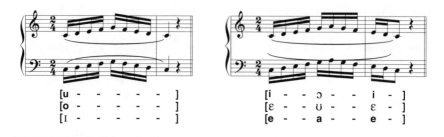

FIGURES 5.6 and 5.7

1. *Redeploy crisp diction*

   a. Review the consonantal gesture:
      swift, energetic motion of the tongue
      no tense preparation of the consonant
      avoid closing the jaw unless absolutely necessary (see also
         p. 83)

   b. Chant a 1-syllable word ending in an unvoiced consonant (e.g.,
      at, *up*, *oak*), blowing a puff of air (the unvoiced or "air" schwa)
      past the consonant.

   c. Chant a 1-syllable word ending in a voiced consonant (e.g.,
      awed, *in*, *save*, *sell*, *babe*) followed by a tiny voiced schwa.

   d. To train energetic articulation within a legato line, sing repeat-
      edly a word(s) with both initial and final consonants, separated
      by half rests, until both articulations are mastered. Then repeat
      the words without rests.

Note that in Figure 5.8 the final consonants on the words *red*,
cup, *big*, and *book* are rhymically notated together with the added
(voiced or unvoiced) schwahs, as are the interior consonants between
words.

re - də   re - dəcu - p
bi - gə   bi - gəboo - k

FIGURE 5.8

Watchword: Keep the tongue in a correct but nonrigid position. Move it quickly!

INTONATION AND ENSEMBLE

Connecting singers' awareness of pitch to vocal technique should begin immediately in the warm-up, signaling that you will accept nothing less than excellent intonation. Other issues that also contribute to poor intonation but are separate from aural skills include posture, breathing, consonants, and vowel modification.

Limit piano accompaniment to starting pitches and/or chordal harmonic underpinning throughout the entire warm-up (see Pianist and Partner, p. 206). Always allow adequate time for singers to internalize the pitch.

Focus the choir's attention more keenly on intonation and ensemble singing

1. Use a familiar four-part warm-up exercise (e.g., Exercise 1.2, p. 29); shift to random, unrelated keys. Provide the chord only briefly for starting pitch.
2. Use a familiar chord progression, chorale, hymn tune or homophonic passage from performance repertoire. Then provide tonic pitch only.
3. Sing the passage staccato but in real time, so that singers must concentrate.
4. Do a quick "body scramble" so that each singer stands between singers from other voice parts than his or her own.
5. Call for unusual pairings of voice parts to increase awareness of voice-leading and harmonic motion.
6. Pause on beat preceding an intonation challenge; adjust the tuning carefully on both chords.

7. Sing the passage on an open mouth hum (ng; IPA: [ŋ]).
8. Sing the passage omitting consonants, using only text vowels.

Summary

Thoughtfully take the singers through your choice of exercises in each category of vocal warm-up outlined above to prepare for the standard rigors of the rehearsal. Improved tone, intonation, and mental focus will result. Singers should end rehearsal feeling as though they could have sung on and on. Fatigue and hoarseness are not to be expected. Those are by-products of poor vocal or rehearsal techniques.

How to Do It: Shortcut Exercises to Technical Training

The warm-up becomes a training period whenever it is designed with purpose. The ideas below are supplemental to the many techniques presented in earlier chapters. They represent quicker methods for the initial training or reinforcing of a skill.

Posture

Reciprocal observation by choir members

Choir members choose partners.
Singer #1 observes; #2 performs.
#2 attempts to assume position of plumb line running from crown of head to heel.
#1 pulls up lock of #2's hair on crown of head and checks that line runs directly to the heel.
(Wrong positions: chin jutting high and out of line; shoulders high and tense; derrière pronouncedly back; chin forcibly back into neck.)
Option: combine exercise with singing repertoire or other exercises.

Additional Breath Management Skills

1. Reinforcing the appoggio position

For inhalation, attention to unmoving chest; sideways breathing with a strong sucking inhalation is sole requirement.
For exhalation (singing), attention to stable chest is sole requirement.
Sit and stand without dropping chest.

Sitting, inhale/exhale without moving chest or shoulders.

Sing any favored warm-up tune, all singers together, concentrating on appoggio position and vigorous sideways inhalation between key changes. Conductor's command: *Up!* before inhalation; *Sideways!* on inhalation; *Stay up!* during inhalation.

2. *Shortcuts to appoggio position*

Inside the shoulder blades imagine magnets straining toward each other.

Roll shoulders up, back, and down.

Hold hands behind the back while standing.

3. *Preparatory and catch breaths*

Train singers to take adequate preparatory breath.

Teach singers to inhale through nose slowly but vigorously when time permits. Train the habit of nose inhalation during breathing exercises at start of warm-up.

Teach singers to inhale for catch breaths with mouth in position of initial vowel shape. Train this habit while doing onset exercises. See pp. 28, 29.

Teach rhythmic preparatory and catch breaths so that entrances do not impede rhythmic integrity of the piece. Train habit of taking breath at both small and large pulses by tying it to conductor's preparatory beat in the warm-up exercises.

NEGOTIATING THE PASSAGGIO

Among choral singers, negotiating the upper passaggio well is most important to sopranos, next most important to tenors, as their parts are more likely to demand singing in and above that passageway. However, every voice part may be taught the skill, thus equipping altos and basses to take high notes in their stride. The preliminary skill needed is mastery of the two alternate vowels [e] and [ʊ]. Utilize the two vowels in various warm-up exercises over a period of time until the singers have command of them. Refer to the passaggio charts, p. 110, and the Complete Vowel Modification Chart, p. 127.

1. *Training the passaggio on a series of slides on the perfect fifth. (A description of this exercise is on pp. 122–23.)*

Teach the choir that each section will sing three slides on [Ã], three on [U] (the passaggio). Later, change the vowels to train the second acceptable passaggio vowel modification [e] in the passaggio,

[e] above. Both [U] and [e] will transfer the register into head voice, needed for high notes (Figure 5.9).

Starting pitches for other voice types is shown in Figure 5.10.

2. *Preparing the choir to spot-rehearse any modifications required by the repertoire with passages in or above the passaggio.*

Accomplish this by these means:

Conductor marks score with modifications he or she has selected.
Conductor gives out the proper vowel changes and rehearses them.
   (The chart showing modifications for all sections before, during, and after the passaggio notes will be found on pp. 129, 131.)

Intonation

(See also Pianist and Partner, p. 206)

1. *Connect aural skills to vocal technique—the ears to the voice—by employing these exercises extracted from Johnson and Klonoski's Subvocalization (silent singing) Applications.*

   a. "While singing a familiar tonal pattern, add random subvocalization. On a specific cue, the singers stop making sound but continue subvocalizing the pattern. At the next cue the singers resume singing the pattern as if they had never stopped making the sound."

   b. "Subvocalize an entire vocal exercise, but randomly stop and have the choir sing the next pitch in the pattern."

   c. "When singing familiar patterns, modulate to unpredictable keys, such as C major to F♯ major to A minor. This activity keeps singers mentally engaged in generating new tonal centers that are far removed from the previous keys."

   d. "Sing a major scale by sections (sopranos sing do; altos, re; tenors, mi, etc.). This is an advanced activity that requires singers to subvocalize all of the pitches so that entrances are accurate."

   e. "Repeat the preceding exercise, but instruct the students to sustain their pitch until their next note to be sung in the scale."

   f. "Sing and subvocalize patterns against sustained notes, such as bass and alto sustaining *sol* while soprano and tenor sing *sol-fa-mi-re-do*. This reinforces the importance of hearing the tonal center. Intervals are not disjunct events, but are heard and understood as part of an underlying harmonic context."[8]

Soprano

FIGURE 5.9

Alto   Tenor I   Tenor II   High Baritone   Bass Baritone   Bass

FIGURE 5.10

2. *Build an ensemble awareness of pitch by allowing time for singers to internalize starting pitches, then accepting nothing less than dead-on-pitch entrances. Illustrate and invoke often the habit of awareness not simply of where the pitch is but also of where it is going.*

    a. Subvocalize a familiar chorale or homophonic passage but randomly stop and cue the choir to sing the next chord.

    b. Sing a challenging passage staccato at a slow tempo. On a specific cue, the singers sustain; at the next cue they resume singing staccato.

    c. Pause often during a 2- or more-part exercise to focus attention on tonal relationships.

    d. Bend a particular pitch upward, to center, downward, back to center to demonstrate the range within a perceived pitch.

    e. Partner the exercise, one singer sustaining the pitch, the other bending it above and below the sustained pitch. Trade parts and repeat.

    f. Break large chords into duets, then trios of voice parts, in a variety of patterns so that the various relationships may be comprehended.

    g. In problematic passages, have accompanist create tone clusters comprising the pitches of the phrase or subphrase. Singers listen, then subvocalize, then sing.

    h. In problematic passages, one section "drones" the root or tonal center while others sing the melodic line and/or harmony.

    i.   "Scramble" into quartets after accomplishing the previous two exercises.

Diction

When time is available, train more specific diction skills, such as any or all of the following. See also Demystifying Consonants, p. 75.

1. *Improving singers' threshold of vowel awareness*
   a. Select a vowel from the repertoire that requires improvement.
   b. Illustrate the sound by presenting the extremes, both more open and more closed, then the desired quality.
   c. Teach the tongue position for the correct sound.
   d. Sing the vowel on random pitches and patterns, then sing in context.

2. *Training crisp, short, and energetic consonants (see also pp. 79–81).*
   a. Train initial consonants by pairing each with a vowel, then sing the syllable on a warm-up scale or arpeggio pattern.
   b. Train final consonants by teaching voiced and unvoiced schwas on single syllables set to a half-note, half-rest pattern.
   c. Eliminate the half rest to put consonants in the middle position.
   d. Systematically train the choir over time to execute all the consonants.
   e. Reinforce proper execution of consonants in middle positions alongside the word, tapping a sixteenth pulse to accommodate schwas. When clarity is achieved, resume normal speed.

3. *Practicing the above with larger mouth openings*
   a. Minimize and relax jaw movement.
   b. Maximize swift tongue movement.

4. *Practicing the execution of consonantal gestures on high pitches with large mouth openings, flopping the jaw, for which the previous exercise prepared.*

5. *Working any offending phrase from the repertoire as a warm-up exercise (to improve specific diction problems in the repertoire)*
   a. First, put the problem text to one of your regular warm-up patterns to lend variety to the warm-up and to indicate that you mean business about inarticulate diction.
   b. Then put the text back into the phrase from which you extracted it.

6. *Unifying group diction*
   a. Train rhythmic placement with precise instruction such as, "Place the [t] on the upbeat of count three." Demonstrate. Have

singers tap feet, tap sternums, or pat knees to the eighth-note pulse in order to routine correct execution. Put the word back into the context of the phrase.

b. Use rhythmic placement training to improve not only final consonants but also middle and initial ones.

c. Use rhythmic placement to train diphthongs, indicating on which specific pulse to place the second vowel of the diphthong (the "vanishing" or "glide" vowel).

LEGATO

To rely on rhythmic accuracy, especially as regards placement of consonants, is to accomplish a tone-improving legato. The main principle is move the air at all times, including during long notes, fermatas, slow-moving tempos, and other challenging maneuvers, such as large melodic skips. See also Legato and Breathing, p. 30.

1. *A physical reminder: extend the forefinger of the right hand and push it forward through the air as the phrase is sung, through pitch changes, consonants, tempo changes, and so on, starting a new gesture each time a breath is taken.*

2. *Separating diction tasks from legato tasks. (This is Part Practice. See p. 256.) First, rehearse the rhythmic placement of the problematic diphthongs or consonants. Then reunite diction with the moving air, as below:*

   a. Adopt a slow tempo, at first singing only the vowels.

   b. Then add the consonants, executed at the precise rhythmic moment. Move the air through the vowel and through the consonant, even if just in imagination, as on p. 34.

   c. Now sing the words with swift, energetic consonants on the pulse.

   d. Next, move the tempo more quickly.

   e. Director exhorts: "Straight ahead! Move the air!"

How to Do It: Combining Technical Skills

It can be extremely effective and time saving to adapt any of the exercise concepts from the regular warm-up to a specific technique the choir needs to improve. Simply select the vowel or consonant, melodic or rhythmic pattern, phrase that needs more legato, and so on, which needs to be worked on, and adjust the exercise accordingly. Once correctly executed, put the skill immediately back into context. For example:

Train the [e] (closed e) used in German, French, Italian, and some
forms of Latin diction, but less often in English diction, except as
a modification in the passaggio.

Used the second balanced onset exercise, p. 29.

Sing the exercise on this series of vowels: [i], [e], [ɛ], [e], [i].

Give brief reminders about tongue position and aural cues for the vowel
sounds, such as *meet* for [i], *chaos* for [e], *pet* for [ɛ]. Move quickly
to singing a portion of repertoire requiring the closed [e] vowel.

Recognizing the technical overlap between a standard warm-up component and the specific spot in the repertoire you wish to improve is not
only a time-saver; it raises singers' awareness that warming up is not to
be taken for granted or treated as rote repetition.

Following is an example of combining the skills of breath management, consonant precision, onset, and ensemble within the course of a
few seconds of warm-up time.

A rather slow piece with long phrases from a choir's permanent repertoire begins on the word *hail*. The entrance has often been less than
satisfactory. The director trains the choir to begin a slow nose inhalation when she raises her hands to indicate they are about to start. On
the upbeat they continue the inhalation through the mouth, forming
the first vowel, [e]. As her hand moves down toward the ictus, they
release into the [h]; on the ictus, the vowel. In this case, extending the
initial, unvoiced consonant improves intelligibility.

Summary

Virtually any and all of the vocal, musical, and linguistic skills discussed
in part I can be approached and improvement effected during the warm-
up. Remain aware of the integrated nature of vocal technical skills so that
every factor contributing to a "problem spot" is addressed.

Such detailed work, costing only a few seconds if put immediately into
context, solves the problem and refines the singers' threshold of awareness. Over time your singers will have the high-grade habits you expect.
You will have trained them, one skill at a time, in the warm-up.

Keys to success in training: Understand the problem.
Understand the solution.
Isolate the skill for your singers.
Practice the skill in short increments of time.
Insert the skill immediately into the con-
text of the piece.

How to Do It: The Pre-Performance Warm-Up

Warming up for performance is quite different from warming up for regular rehearsal. Whereas the rehearsal warm-up is geared to the technical, we know that peak performance is never achieved when the mind dwells on the technical. Rehearsal warm-ups are the time for technique to be trained into the body and into muscle memory so that it becomes a habit, Robert Shaw's "high-grade habit." Performance is where, we trust along with Shaw, "song becomes spirit." Thus, performance warm-ups should get the instrument going properly, then leave it free to express.

The pre-performance mood should always, without exception, be positive. The pleasure of coming together for the special event, reveling in being dressed up, knowing that an audience awaits—all these contribute to a current of anticipation. Ensure that your comments, your demeanor, and your planning all contribute to that sense. Before the warm-up begins, congratulate your singers on the work that has brought them to this point. Only positive comments allowed.

The pre-performance pace should be relaxed and unhurried, though purposeful. Allow time to warm up the instrument more gradually. Prolong the stretching, breathing, onset phases. Spend a bit more time in the mid-range, a safe location, to ensure that legato—the phonation/respiration connection—is achieved. Allow enough time for sopranos and tenors to move carefully through the upper passaggio and to extend the range gradually. Warm them up at least a major third higher than needed in the performance repertoire. Do the same for altos and basses and give heed, as well, to extending their ranges downward if called for in the performance repertoire. Then spend a few minutes on a not-difficult full-chorus passage to bring ensemble skills to bear.

Plan time to share some of your personal thoughts regarding the concert or the music to be performed: what it means to you, a relevant story about the composer, a comment about the choir's long-term dedication to the piece, your pride in what they have accomplished, and so on. Remind the singers that they have done the work, they know the music, and now is the time to sing. Above all, stress that this is also the time to enjoy.

Then leave the chorus, allowing enough time for last-minute trips to the restroom, sips of water, checking hair and makeup, and so on, so that no one is rushed to line up for the stage. A sense of accomplishment, anticipation, and unhurried confidence should pervade.

How to Do It: The Emergency Warm-Up

Despite the best of plans, situations arise where warm-up time is minimal and under pressure. In such cases, the following four-step plan will provide the best achievable results in the shortest time possible.

1. To align and activate the instrument, establish posture and low breathing.
2. To warm up the vocal muscles safely and thoroughly, use lip-trill slides on the perfect fifth and/or octave, starting mid-range and extending the upper and lower ranges beyond the requirements of the repertoire.
3. To coordinate breath and voice, engage focused tone, and balance the sections of the choir, use Exercise 1.2, p. 29.
4. To prepare the choir to handle the situation with confidence, deal succinctly with the exigencies of the situation. Calmly explain any adjustments the singers will need to make without benefit of rehearsal. For example: "We are in an acoustic that provides very little aural feedback. Take care to rely on your own good vocal technique and trust it. You may feel as though no one else is singing. Resist the temptation to oversing. Listen with your eyes; watch me closely; trust that your technique will make this a successful performance—because it will—and sing the meaning of this music."

   Or: "The hall is quite reverberant. It will sound rich and full to you. Be prepared for me to pull quick tempos back just a bit to adjust. Consonants must be even more energetic. Watch; enunciate with skill; enjoy this beautiful music!"

How to Do It: Cooling Down

Cooling down the voice at the end of rehearsal is often overlooked, or attended only inadvertently. Athletes are trained to wind themselves down gradually, slowing the pace of physical exertion until their bodies are ready to resume normal ranges of activity. Although singers may not sweat copiously, pant with physical effort, or work up a greatly accelerated heart rate, their small muscle tissue nonetheless benefits from cooling the voice down in order to return it gradually to normal speaking function and to render it capable of another performance the next day, should that be necessary. The physical sensation that singers have of being "wide open" when the singing voice is in full use exists because the thirty-nine pairs of muscles inside the larynx, the fifteen pair outside the larynx, and the thirty-six muscles of the breathing mechanism are going full bore. At rehearsal's end they need to wind down gradually.

Cooling down is best accomplished by going from large to small in all respects:

> louder to softer dynamic levels
> longer to shorter phrases
> open/back vowels to closed/front vowels
> big singing to lip trills and humming

Cool down the chorus by closing the rehearsal with the following:

> lip trills on descending perfect fifth slides
> gently hummed four-note scales
> falsetto for the men, whistle voice for the women, with simple patterns descending five-note scales, using [ɛ] to [e] to [I] to [i], or [a] to [ɔ] to [o] to [ʊ]; soft, slow chorales on [u]

Practically speaking, most choir singers are not cooled down by the director before departing the rehearsal. Nevertheless, it is good vocal hygiene to do so. There are situations where cooling down is a real necessity:

> when the choir has had a particularly vocally rigorous rehearsal
> when the choir has several performances to do in a row, such as on a concert tour, or a string of recording sessions
> when circumstances have forced a rehearsal shortly before a performance
> when the choir serves as chorus for a run of shows

As the singers at the beginning of the rehearsal had to make the transition from voices used for general living into voices used for singing, they now do well to return their highly energized singing muscles to the low pitch of nonsinging life. Talking on a voice that has been functioning at high singing energy for a few hours is extremely dangerous. Since the talking is most typically done, as we have stated, in a range an octave below where the singing has taken place, the result of talking on the warmed-up singing voice is debilitating in the extreme. Remember that talking on that warmed-up voice is what makes singers believe they are hoarse. What they actually need is a cool-down before trying to converse in a normal speaking voice. In other words, if a soloist would cool down under comparable circumstances, so should the chorus.

5.2   Pianist and Partner

Enhancing the Choir's Training and Performance

The pianist is the conductor's partner in bringing the choir to performance-level singing. An experienced accompanist with a great ear and good musical instincts is a valuable asset. Words of insight or observation from this fellow musician may alert the director to overlooked details or possibilities. Pianists of any experience and skill level, however, can learn to accompany in ways that will aid the choir's development.

Eliminating the accompanist as note-pounder and elevating the accompanist as musician and cotrainer facilitates a "raising of the bar." Use the information below to rethink your uses of the accompanist. The pianist will appreciate this and flourish under a conductor who respects him or her as a musical partner, not a crutch. The choir will rise to the level of expectations and improve its aural and vocal skills.

At least two factors unique to the art of singing distinguish the art of choral accompanying from that of "playing the piano":

1. The vocal melodic line is dependent upon sustaining the tone with the breath.
2. The vocal melodic line is dependent upon the singer audiating the pitch (hearing it in the mind's ear) before singing it.

Too often choral directors rely upon the accompanist to "plunk out the notes" as a means of teaching parts. They may view this as necessary. In the end, however, it is counterproductive.

1. Note-pounding trains the choir to be dependent upon that practice.
2. Note-pounding impedes training and developing the choir's aural and reading skills.
3. Note-pounding models non-legato singing.

Following are several ways in which note-pounding relates to the unique characteristics of the vocal melodic line cited above.

Sustaining the Tone

Sustaining the tone with the breath is the basis of a legato singing line. The piano sustains tone only by use of the damper pedal. That fundamental difference between the two instruments, voice and piano, means that unskilled use of the piano in a choral rehearsal is more hindrance than help. Singers, amateurs especially, will invariably echo the percussive effect of the note-pounding technique. The musical line is lost to unsupported, non-legato singing. Both tone and diction suffer when consonants are carelessly tagged to the end of the preceding vowel, clipping syllables in unconscious imitation of pounded notes. The asset acquired by singing on the vowel through the entire pulse, linking final consonants to the next syllable, is lost. The musical line becomes a march as the singers pound from note to note in imitation of well-intentioned, but misguided emphatic playing.

Audiating the Pitch

The pianist produces a pitch by striking a key. The singer accurately produces a pitch only by first audiating the pitch. Audiation is to hearing what visualization is to seeing. We visualize by seeing in the mind's eye; we audiate by hearing in the mind's ear. To illustrate peer audiation, think of the times an accompanist provides starting pitches, only for it to require a second or two for the chorus to settle into those pitches. This is because some singers heard the pitch but did not audiate it before singing. (Those familiar with Robert Shaw's warm-ups can testify to his skillful use of such audiation.) The choristers' skill at audiation can be readily improved by a conductor's good rehearsal technique. Teaching parts by note-pounding reduces a choir to rote memorization at the expense of improving aural skills—not to mention reading skills.

It is a relatively easy matter to impress the importance of audiation upon the choir. First, don't accept poor entrances. Second, if it appears that poor entrances are caused by lack of skill rather than carelessness, build the skill over time with a few seconds of exercise in the warm-up. Start with random unison pitches, played briefly, then sung by the choir. Progress to a chord. Once each section is sure of its place in the chord, shift keys randomly, playing the chord briefly, then having the choir sing it. In fairly short order the choir will learn to "hear quickly," that is, to audiate automatically. The audiation/subvocalization (silent singing) activities of choral pedagogues Eric A. Johnson and Edward Klonoski that follow provide further suggestions for developing the skill of audiation.

Advanced Subvocalization/Audiation Activities

Always give students time to internalize the tonal center of a work (i.e., subvocalize do, ti, do, sol, do). Simply hearing a key-defining pattern played on a piano does not ensure that the students have actually internalized the new tonal center.

Once a tonality is established for a work, do not constantly give starting pitches to the ensemble. Encourage them to remember the tonal center in their heads. This takes time and concentration.

Make certain that singers know the tonal center for each song or section. If they aren't hearing a modulation, they have the wrong harmonic context, which means they are hearing that section in the wrong key.

Teach singers to think and hear harmonically by accompanying exercises and compositions with chords. In time, the accompaniment can be taken away and the [singers] will still be able to recall the sound of the underlying harmony. In this way, the [singers] have the correct harmonic context for the given passage. It is very difficult for an [inexperienced] singer to sing sol-re if the tonal image they have is a tonic sol-mi-do. If you teach them to hear the dominant function, sol-re will be reasonably accurate.[9]

After audiating the first pitch, singers must have the skill of knowing where the next, and the next, and the next pitches lie in the voice. They develop this level of audiation, which for singers is also sight-reading skill, in three ways. The first is intervallic sight-singing, knowing the intervals by sight and sound. The second is by recognizing the harmonic direction of the line. The third is by a singer's eventually well-honed kinesthetic sense of the pitch area. With practice, integration of the three skills becomes fluent and often intuitive, producing good readers and improved intonation. One can probably attribute the high skills of European choirs at least partially to the fact that, there, chorus pitches are not prompted by a piano but by a pitch pipe, thus increasing the audiation responsibilities of the singers.

Warm-Ups

The accompaniment for warm-ups should provide secco harmonic underpinning. Pianists sometimes feel they are offering needed support by playing every note, every chord, at a full dynamic level or sustaining as the choir sings. Not so. Singers focus more on matching the piano, less on singing well and tuning accurately. The director does not hear the voices clearly in the wash of the pedal sustaining the choir's notes. Remember that the warm-up period also provides the director a valuable opportunity to monitor individual vocal technique by listening and observing. An accompaniment thus played provides, in effect, a crutch that impedes the very skills the director is after.

A firm but not heavy touch and little or no damper pedal are the watchwords.

Spare chordal accompaniment requires that singers concentrate. For example, if the chorus sings five-note scales, the accompanist should underpin with a light, staccato I–V7–I vamping only. Intonation improves as singers learn to listen to themselves individually and in the context of the chord.

If the chorus sings five-note scales ascending by half steps, for example, the pianist should modulate during the choir's breath pause, not moving directly to the half step above. Instead of providing the next pitch, modulation allows the singers to hear harmonically where the next pitch lies. For example, the choir having completed a five-tone scale in C major, the accompanist, rather than moving directly to the D♭ (C♯) major chord in the breath pause, goes to an A♭ (G♯) dominant seventh chord. The original tonic pitch C serves as a pivot note to A♭ major, which is the dominant of D♭ major, the next key. The pitch C, formerly tonic, is now heard as a leading tone, facilitating better intonation on the coming key of D♭ (C♯).

If the warm-up is a four-part chorale, quick and light starting pitches should be given. Building and sustaining the chord on the piano is contraindicated. Pitches should be played individually, separately, and quickly. As the choir's skills improve, only the tonic pitch should be provided. The exercise should proceed without accompaniment. Remember that the piano is tuned by equal half steps. Voices are capable of closer and truer-to-function tuning (higher leading tones, for example). Only by training the choir on a cappella singing are intonation skills developed.

Rehearsals

The single most effective contribution the accompanist can make to the rehearsal of a piece—assuming correct notes and rhythms—is to play musically and artistically at all times. When playing a part is required—this practice ideally being kept to absolute minimum—it should always be played as a musical line. Even when only a short snippet is required, it should still be played with linear direction.

The written accompaniment itself should be treated for what it is, a component of the compositional whole—not a camouflage for choral blemishes. Artistic and sensitive playing brings beauty and life to the piece. It also models real music making for the singers. The accompanist now plays as a chamber musician in a trio of conductor, chorus, and piano.

An excellent accompanist is a person of high value. By virtue of skilled playing, the accompanist is the choral director's partner in training the voices, ears, and musical sensibilities of the choristers. Not every conductor is so fortunate as to work with a fine pianist. Every conductor can, however, train the available pianist to be a more effective choral accompanist.

Part II

PRESCRIPTIONS FOR SELF-DEVELOPMENT

Preparation, Development, and Execution Skills

CHAPTER 6
Some Practical Solutions to Leadership Issues

6.1 Four Stages of Group Development

Choirs often experience periods of being "settled," when they function optimally. Can these especially productive periods be prolonged? Is it possible to plan in a way that eliminates less-productive, unsteady periods?

THE COMPLAINT

Sometimes a choir seems completely out of sorts with itself. Whatever the underlying stresses, they affect the rehearsal, making it difficult to accomplish goals.

Dx, THE DIAGNOSIS

Every group experiences periods of greater and lesser productivity. The pattern is relatively predictable and, with understanding, can be managed.

Rx, THE TREATMENT PLAN

1. Learn to observe closely the conditions when the choir functions at its best and when it functions less optimally.

2. Gain an understanding of the stages of group formation in order to develop skills to work with and through—not in spite of—the various stages.

Discussion

Even a rudimentary understanding of the stages of group formation helps reduce frustration for choral directors and enables them to work productively at every stage. Groups are dynamic entities; that is, they are constantly evolving. If directors view their choirs as static and unchanging, performance will decline over time. If directors view their choirs as too changeable to meet higher expectations—for example, inconsistent in attention or attendance—potential will be underrealized. Although general traits of a choir may remain fairly constant, there is an underlying process through which all groups pass, the understanding of which enables directors to make each stage as productive as possible.

Well-established social theory holds that groups pass through four developmental stages:

forming
storming
norming
performing

Missing out on any one of the stages means that the group will underperform. Therefore, learning to recognize and manage each one is an important responsibility of the director/leader. Skillful guidance of the group from one stage to the next results in the strongest teamwork, that is, the best performance. However, the entire group may not proceed through the stages together, particularly if there are subgroups within the whole, such as the sections within a choir. Choral directors should therefore develop astute observational skills in order to guide the process wherever it is in transition.

Forming is the initial coming together of a group to accomplish a certain goal, whether it be a task goal or a social goal. This stage consists of members making their way into the group, discovering what it is like, whether or not they feel welcome. The director plays a large role in making each member feel that he or she belongs. As members shed initial reticence and begin to assert individual attitudes and habits in the group situation, some degree of conflict will inevitably arise.

Storming is the result of the uncertainty produced at this point, usually rooted in differences of personality or goals. Storming can manifest itself, for example, as a member or two whom the majority perceives as somewhat out of sync with the rest of the group, or storming can flare into argument. Many choirs find themselves perpetually stuck in this phase, whether mildly or harshly so. Skilled leaders guide their groups through storming toward norming. Glossing over or ignoring storming only results in unresolved issues that will come back to undermine performance time and again.

Norming is the stage that leads most directly to a group's optimal functioning. During this phase, group norms are established that bring the group to cohesion. Norming is the result of working out the issues of the storming phase and establishing common goals and work patterns. In simpler words, the group settles in, and individuals begin working together toward a common goal, following the accepted practices of the group. Here, the leader's skill in establishing both the common goal and the appropriate degree of conformity dictates how well the group norms. These two tasks must be approached very individually, keyed to the particular group and to the particular performance for which the group is preparing.

Performing is the culmination of the successful completion of forming, storming, and norming. During this stage, members work interdependently in a supportive and productive atmosphere. When all previous phases have been skillfully navigated, this will be the point where directors can turn their energies most fully to the musical performance at hand. This stage is, of course, where choral directors prefer to reside. Unfortunately, however, they cannot. Whenever a new person is added, whenever the task changes, whenever challenges or obstacles confront the group, big or small, short or long term, the leader should manage the change skillfully. Otherwise, havoc ensues.

Coming to terms with the dynamic nature of groups will go a long way toward alleviating some common frustrations of choral directors. Imagine the energy wasted by directors who mentally or openly strive against change in the choir. Imagine the potential left unfulfilled by directors who attempt to ignore the same changes and forge determinedly on. Understanding that the dynamic process outlined above does take place in any group—over and over again as variables change—enables directors to view their own group's anomalies objectively, rather than to take them personally or to react emotionally. Developing skills for dealing with these processes of change leads to a team sense of unity and purpose, and avoids the mire of squabble or discontent.

Continual change in any group is inevitable. The choral director who fails to deal with it does so at his or her peril. Utilizing each of these stages is absolutely necessary to high-level performance.

6.2   Effects of Group Cohesion

Many choirs have a great sense of unity, purpose, and fellowship. Is this the result of a fortuitous combination of personalities, or the charisma of the director? Does group cohesion have an effect on performance?

The Complaint

The singers are generally cooperative but lack a sense of purpose as a group. Some are eager for challenge; others must be coaxed.

Dx, The Diagnosis

Even in a choir composed of mostly dedicated and responsive members, group cohesion may be lacking. The commitment, work patterns, and habits that accompany cohesion transform a group into a team. Team members function with an increased commitment, interdependency, and specialization that enhance performance.

Rx, The Treatment Plan

1. Analyze the characteristics of the group and the norms under which it operates, beginning with such questions as

   What is the organizational structure?
   What contributions to organization and activities do members make?
   What are the patterns of communication?
   Is membership relatively stable?
   What reasons account for membership turnover?
   What traditions does the group observe?
   How important does the choir perceive them to be?

2. Gain an understanding of the basic differences between groups and teams.
3. Apply that knowledge to the analysis of the choir.
4. Develop a strategy for strengthening cohesion by reinforcing the team model.

DISCUSSION

Consider the variety of choirs and directors to be observed:

charismatic directors of successful or unsuccessful choirs
congenial groups that perform well or tend to underperform
meek or unpleasant directors whose performances are strong or
disappointing
groups of brittle collective personality that perform well or unsuccess-
fully

Questioning the whys and hows of a group's general performance level typically leads to oversimplification: the singers are excellent or weak; the director is strong or less capable. In all areas of life, pinpointing a single determining factor is usually inaccurate. Assembling a group of first-rate singers who get along famously is not enough to ensure strong performance. Neither is the strength of a director's own personal charisma. Although it is accurate to say that the traits of the group and the traits of the leader influence each other, the work (rehearsal), and the outcome (the performance), the purpose here is to determine how to make the best of the mutual influence.

Cohesion is the glue that holds a collection of people together, forming a vital group. Without cohesion, a group may continue to exist, but it will lack the unity and purpose requisite to vital performance. It will also probably lack the fellowship that is a large reward of the journey. In choirs with high levels of cohesion, singers interact with and influence each other more. Absenteeism and turnover are often lower because members have invested themselves personally in achieving the goals of the choir. When the director/leader exhibits objectivity by creating a climate of openness and by listening to suggestions or criticisms, interaction and influence are increased between director and singers.

To increase group cohesion in their choirs, wise directors look to a team model because choral groups lend themselves naturally and well to it. Although a team is a group, not all groups are teams. A team is a highly specialized group. (A choir is this already, in that it specializes in singing.) Team members experience a stronger sense of identification with the team than group members experience with groups. Team members share common goals and tasks to a stronger degree than do group members. Task interdependence and specialized roles are of greater importance to teams than to groups. These and other qualifiers that distinguish teams from groups depend heavily upon the skills and behaviors of the director/leader. Leading the choir through a metamorphosis from group to team will cultivate performance-enhancing cohesion.

6.3 The "Best" Leadership Style

Each choral situation is unique. Each choral director is unique. A prescriptive "best" leadership style would seem a delusional concept. Does any one type of leader produce a more successful choir?

THE COMPLAINT

The director's leadership style is personally well suited. There are periods, however, when the choir does not respond as well as needed. What can be done to improve these periods of frustration?

Dx, THE DIAGNOSIS

If the style of leadership is fixed and comfortable but there are repeated periods of underperformance, then the leadership style may be too static. The team leader model is most congenial for directors precisely because it is not static. With its equal emphasis on results and on people, its characteristic traits of continued learning and the application of new knowledge with a flexibility that suits the situation, the team leader model affords directors the best chance of achieving a choir's potential.

Rx, THE TREATMENT PLAN

1. Gain an understanding of leader types and evaluate where personal natural tendencies lie.
2. Analyze personal leader strengths and weaknesses with these questions as a starting point:

    What is my vision for the choir? Have I shared it with them?
    Do I communicate my expectations?
    Do I teach the skills needed to meet expectations?
    Is my technical expertise sufficient to the task?
    How often do I evaluate my own skills: musical, vocal, psychological?
    Do I monitor the choir's need for motivation?
    How effectively do I utilize rehearsal time?
    Do the singers trust me to prepare them?

3. Focus on the strengths: seek opportunities to implement them; discard or refine entrenched habits in view of the strengths.
4. Focus on the weaknesses: set goals based on areas needing improvement; develop a realistic course of action with measurable outcomes; measure progress at established intervals.

5. Study the traits of a team leader and begin to implement them at every opportunity.

DISCUSSION

Understanding basic principles of leadership is important for choral directors, for without doubt they are leaders. Most choral directors possess certain innate leadership qualities, otherwise the prospect of group leading as a career would be so daunting as to override the love of choral repertoire, a desire to perform, or other compelling factors. Certainly a strong ego, at least regarding one's own musical abilities and artistic choices, is a component of the director's personality. Indeed, are not conductors born thinking, "I'd do it differently," when sitting under another's baton? Innate skills and a strong musical ego, however, are insufficient to keep a choir performing consistently well.

Prototypical leaders (see pp. 236–37) fall into six general categories: the *command-deference* leader, the *social club* leader, the *circumspect* leader, the *benevolent* leader, the *expedient* leader, and the *team* leader. Most people naturally, by virtue of personality, fall fairly closely within one of the prototypes. Each category tends toward certain priorities, which in turn lead to tendencies of attitude and action. Any prototype might achieve positive results in a given situation. However, it is the team leader who will prove the most consistently successful choral director.

Why the team leader? Team leaders exhibit equal concern for people and results. Team leaders place a high value on motivating members to reach the highest levels of accomplishment. Team leaders also place a high value on two key traits: becoming more knowledgeable and being flexible.

Becoming More Knowledgeable

Increasing the choral director's knowledge encompasses musical, vocal-technical, and psychological arenas. Indeed, this book is plainly devoted to engendering in choral directors a thirst for continued learning. Since musical and vocal-technical issues are addressed in part I of this book, it will suffice here to repeat our credo that continued learning in these areas is a conspicuous habit of successful choral directors. The team leader concept addressed here is based upon a cross-section of the most current study and thought in the field of leadership today as we have applied it to the choral situation.

Self-awareness, an essential component of the knowledgeable leader, is the ability to assess clearly and honestly one's own strengths, weaknesses, needs, preferences, emotions, desires, and so on, as well as their effect on others. Exercised regularly, self-awareness is a musculature that will strengthen and provide the support necessary to sustain further growth. Self-assessment is the tool that exercises the self-awareness muscle, providing clarity and measurement.

Self-assessment should result in goal setting that will improve those areas found wanting or outdated. Continued and regular self-assessment will measure the effectiveness of the steps being taken to achieve the goals. The very act of making a self-assessment develops keener self-awareness. When self-awareness becomes a habit, greater effectiveness results: The leader regularly assesses his or her skills, plans, and actions in view of the current goal.

Becoming More Flexible

Insanity has been popularly defined as repeating the same action over and over again, expecting different results. How often do directors come dangerously close to the definition, hoping for different results? Team leaders exhibit flexibility in their ability to plan work processes well suited to the task at hand, to the choir, and to themselves. Flexible choral directors need high technical expertise. Expertise in the principles of leadership should also be high. Being a flexible director does not mean working to the lowest common denominator, compromising your standards, or lowering your expectations. It means mastering the art of surveying the available resources. It means drawing up, then executing plans for the desired structure—solidly and efficiently upon that particular site. This is how real performance is achieved.

Flexibility may seem an incongruous goal in the choral arena. After all, a choral director's goal is to get the members of each section to sing the same notes, at the same time, at the same dynamic level, ad infinitum. Stringent conformity is regularly required. However, a flexible approach to teaching and encouraging those matters of technical skill will improve the choir's performance in the technical areas. The more conformist and dictatorial a director, the farther down the performance will drop. The required skill is to bring singers just to the point where they must conform, and then leave it. The following diagram illustrates the dynamic nature of both conformity (compliance) and flexibility (give and take), and the importance of maintaining an appropriate balance.[1]

conformity

too little = chaos
too much = stifled performance

flexibility

too little = truculent, uncommitted performers
too much = chaos

The requirements of performance are a shared responsibility. Both directors and singers should view them as such. Leaders/directors should first communicate the ideal. If conflict exists over whether the standard is achievable, leaders should negotiate with their groups. Yet, leaders should always have a line below which they will not go. The technical and leadership skills that enable directors to work flexibly are the tools with which they ultimately bring a group up to standard.

It is important to remember, nonetheless, that although flexibility is the hallmark of team leaders/directors, it is also true that the closer the choir is to performance the more autocratic directors should become.[2] Having set a tone of openness and of shared responsibility in working with the choir, having set clear goals, and having taught the skills necessary to achieve those goals, an increasingly autocratic manner as performance approaches will not only be accepted by the choir but will also be expected. Singers will be prepared to follow because they will have confidence in where the director is leading them.

6.4 Traits That Make Exemplary Followers

The foibles of choristers can be frustrating to the director who is keenly focused on performance goals. Short of earning a degree in psychology, is it possible to understand them better?

THE COMPLAINT

Dealing with the array of personalities in the choir is consuming as much energy as the musical duties.

DX, THE DIAGNOSIS

Choir members display all the variety of human personality to be found in society at large. Recognizing patterns of how individuals tend to behave within groups enables directors to proceed objectively and advantageously.

Rx, The Treatment Plan

1. Assess the situation starting with the following questions:

   How often do facets of singers' personalities have a positive effect on the rehearsal? A negative effect?

   Which singers' personal qualities enhance the group and the work?

   Which singers require more personal attention than others? How productive is the interaction?

   Which singers appear, at least superficially, to have very little impact either positively or negatively?

   Do issues of personality generally have an impact on the director's schedule and frame of mind?

2. Gain an understanding of "followership," how individual personalities tend to function within the context of the group. Implement this knowledge to develop strategies for eliciting the best qualities from all members of the choir.

Discussion

The very definition of leadership implies the presence of followers. What is a choral director without a choir to lead? Having come to terms with common characteristics of groups, choral directors should also remember that groups are composed of individual persons. The tendencies of individual persons, when they are called upon to follow (as in a choir), will always affect the group. Understanding that there are common types of followers, and that each impacts a group differently, sharpens insight and helps directors develop strategies for working with all types of followers.

Although far less researched than leadership, the study of "followership" has yielded valuable information for leaders. Researcher Robert Kelley approached the subject from the standpoint of followers as collaborators, rather than as mere opposites of leaders.[3] Since choral singing is a collaborative effort, his approach is well suited to the needs of choral directors. Kelley categorized five styles of followers: alienated, conformist, pragmatist, passive, and exemplary.[4] Clearly, the most effective followers are those who fall under the "exemplary" style. Examining the most effective category more closely reinforces the principle of working to recognized strengths. Exemplary followers in the choir are a strength whose traits choral directors should learn to recognize and utilize.

The most salient characteristic of exemplary followers is their consistency in working toward the common good. Others view them as consistent in their attributes, which typically include being "independent, innovative, creative, and willing to stand up to superiors."[5] Their willingness to question authority is not perceived as confrontational, but rather as playing an objective devil's advocate or offering creative options. Again, their purpose is to serve group, not individual, interests.

The size of the choir plays a role in determining how directly a particular follower affects the group. In large choirs, the singers seated near an especially negative choir member, for example, will be the most directly affected. If the section leader is of the exemplary-follower type, his or her skill in working with others and positive efforts on behalf of the choir will have engendered the confidence of the section, so members are comfortable bringing the situation to his or her attention. It may then be addressed before it escalates. Such openness in communication is important to large groups, because it is possible for a problem involving personality conflict to grow to some size before gaining the director's attention. In small choirs, the impact of one singer's negativity may be more keenly felt by the entire group, including the director. Skill in dealing with such persons constructively is important for many reasons, not the least of which is that the director's authority is placed on direct or indirect display.

Exemplary followers make excellent assistants (task subleaders) to directors because of their willingness to engage leaders in constructive, alternative thinking. Their ability to get along with others in ways that benefit the group also makes them excellent social subleaders. Whether enlisted as task or social subleaders, exemplary followers are the persons most likely to bring others along positively. Although followers of the other four styles also exert influence, their methods of goal achievement may exact a toll on group cohesion. Directors do well actively to recruit persons who exhibit the traits of exemplary followers. Further, employing the considerable skills of exemplary followers as recruiters attracts like-minded prospects, increasing their number and their positive effect upon the choir.

6.5 Conflict Management

Of the four stages of group development, storming is the most problematic. How do successful director/leaders negotiate the conflict that distinguishes this stage?

THE COMPLAINT

A new tenor contributes a beautiful voice and excellent musical skills. His abilities are needed and appreciated. Unfortunately, he also exhibits a condescending attitude that detracts from his positive contribution to the group.

Dx, The Diagnosis

The storming phase of group development is one marked by conflict. While seemingly disruptive, a well-managed storming phase actually leads to the more productive performing phase. If storming goes unnoticed, ignored, or poorly handled, it may indeed bring havoc. No matter that any director would prefer to eliminate storming, it remains true that unless a group undergoes all four phases of development—storming included—it will underperform.[6] Storming is the process by which a collection of individuals become a functioning group, wherein group goals supersede individual goals. Thus successful director/leaders accustom themselves to the fact that they should not try to avoid or gloss over conflict. Furthermore, they develop strategies by which to guide the choir through the endless variations that storming presents.

The conflicts of this stage may occur among members or between the director and choir members. The nature of the conflict can stem from an array of factors that are "emotional, factual, constructive, destructive, argumentative, open, or suppressed" in nature.[7] Recognizing the underlying nature of the conflict will help to determine how the conflict should be resolved.

Among factors that influence conflict-resolution strategy are these:

How large or small is the issue?
To what extent are the parties personally invested?
Are there hidden agendas?
Does either party perceive the situation as a clear win-or-lose proposition?
Do the feuding elements view the conflict as unresolvable, in which case each will continue to view the other as the obstacle?[8]

Whatever form the conflict takes, it requires timely and dispassionate resolution at the (seen or unseen) hands of the director.

Rx, The Treatment Plan

1. View the handling of conflict with the same creative attitude that accompanies the tackling of a new and challenging composition, where bumpy efforts are expected for a time until the piece begins to sound. Some bumpy interactions are to be expected for a time until the group learns to work harmoniously together.
2. Consider the director's role in the conflict as that of a counselor or troubleshooter.

3. Keep foremost in mind the goal: a choir that works well together toward its common goal.
4. Analyze the conflict dispassionately and determine the factual issues.
5. Once the issues themselves appear resolvable, determine what emotional factors might aggravate resolution.[9]
6. Prepare to act, based upon the goal of guiding the choir through storming to performing.

DISCUSSION

The situation cited in the Complaint offers a commonplace example of conflict between one singer and an unknown number of others. If the offending tenor were a member of an athletic team, the coach would say without hesitation, "Conform to the play or you are out." A similar reprimand from a choral director, if made openly in rehearsal, would have a debilitating effect upon the chorus. The adage "Praise publicly, criticize privately" holds a measure of validity. It becomes more valuable to the conflict-managing choral director when edited slightly: Praise publicly; deal with conflict privately.

In this case, speak first and separately with several individuals. A private chat with the section and social leaders should be along the lines of, "I've noticed such and such. . . . Is there something going on? I'd hate to speak to him if there's something I should know." The conversation should yield valuable information. Some possibilities are

annoyance with the singer's comments and impatience with the director for allowing it to continue are spreading through the choir.
some singers recognize that he is overly insecure about being the only new member, and they are already planning steps to make him feel more included and relaxed.
even recognizing his insecurity, members are too annoyed by his behavior to take conciliatory measures.
someone knows that he has undue stress in another part of his life, with that pressure releasing itself inappropriately in rehearsal.

In the first case, the director must go to the individual and diplomatically state the case: that the singer's comments are causing a problem. Firm diplomacy allows room for the singer to realize the impact of his actions without such discomfort that he feels he must leave the group. While guarding against embarrassment, it firmly establishes that there is no tolerance for further behavior of such kind. An iron hand in a velvet glove allows the singer to save face and makes the point clear: The director is sure that the tenor would never deliberately choose to be a negative influence, and further makes clear the value placed on him as a person and as a member of the choir. In so doing, the tenor has room to make adjustments.

In the second case, if subleaders have the situation in hand, then an occasional friendly social remark from the director at an informal moment—during a break, before or after rehearsal—will increase his sense of belonging.

If, as in the third case, the subleaders are too annoyed by the offending personality to extend their friendship, assign the singer a social task. It should be a task that does not carry any authority, but rather allows him to do something of significance for the group. He becomes more personally involved, and the others see that, despite the unpleasant nature displayed thus far, the person has a giving side and is willing to contribute. Organizing snacks for break time or collecting turned-in music are examples of tasks he could be asked to assume.

In the final case, if the person is indeed working through one of life's more daunting situations, a brief compassionate comment from the director may be a godsend. Some words of recognition as simple as, "I really appreciate your regular attendance despite all that you are dealing with just now," could dissipate some anxiety. It may well make him feel that rehearsal is a welcoming place where he can set aside those concerns for a time.

What if the singer is completely intractable? Does there come a time when a director should ask a member to leave the choir? Yes. The ultimate responsibility is to the group. If all appropriate and reasonable measures are taken without success, it does indeed fall to the director to ask (tell, if necessary) the recalcitrant singer to leave the group. Again, firm diplomacy is required. The director need not, actually should not, ever inform others of the action taken. It will become apparent to the choir that their leader has handled the situation. Discretion will earn their respect fully as much as capable leadership will.

Note that, in the situations posited above, the suggested solutions incorporate the following steps:

place primary focus on resolving the distraction from group goals
utilize subleaders to gain information or effect resolution
effect resolution privately
treat individuals with respect and, where appropriate, compassion
instill confidence in the choir that their leader is capable of handling
   conflict diplomatically and respectfully: neither embarrassing
   members nor allowing them to disrupt the group's work
deftly guide the group through storming into performing

Wherever there is conflict, there is likely to be strong emotion. By remaining objective, solution-oriented, and fair to all involved, the director can successfully navigate a choir's path through conflict. No single approach to conflict management will be the right one all the time. The successful leader/director analyzes the variables, develops a repertoire of approaches to conflict resolution, and, over time, becomes skilled at applying the appropriate approach at the appropriate moment.

6.6 Motivation through Goal Setting

At any given time, choirs usually have several areas that need improvement. Tackling them all simultaneously may be frustrating and discouraging. By what means, then, can directors effect the greatest improvement in their choirs' ability in the shortest amount of time?

THE COMPLAINT

A choir is scheduled to perform in a district church choir festival in two months. It rehearses only seventy-five minutes each week and must also meet the requirements of weekly services. How can the director maximize the possibility of a strong festival performance given the short rehearsal time available?

Dx, THE DIAGNOSIS

A choir facing an additional challenge should prepare for it based on carefully selected goals that play to the group's strengths.

> What elements of performance does your choir already do well?
> What skills/techniques does the choir regularly exhibit and at what level?
> Exactly which skills/techniques does it lack?
> Which of those are necessary for performing the festival selection?
> How well does the choir meet its weekly performing responsibilities?

Rx, THE TREATMENT PLAN

1. Select a festival piece that the choir has already performed successfully and that showcases its strengths.
2. Apply the tool of performance profiling to identify and measure the choir's current status on the skills/techniques required for the piece.

3. Study the chart to select the two skills/techniques that will effect the greatest improvement in the available time.

4. Set rehearsal and performance goals accordingly. Measure progress by completing new performance profiles at regular intervals.

5. Explain the plan to the choir. Describe the expectations and the work plan. Provide regular feedback, calling attention in detail to the progress made.

Discussion

When asked, any director can readily recite a list of a choir's shortcomings, the awareness of which would make it possible to plan for improvement. Unless, however, awareness of shortcomings is coupled with awareness of the choir's strengths, the knowledge may work to disadvantage. In thinking that there is simply too much to be improved, a director may set too few, if any goals, perhaps limiting expectations to the sole achievement of correct rhythms and pitches. Another director may set too many goals in the zealous effort to conquer every shortcoming, inadvertently discouraging or overwhelming the choir. In neither case does a director's knowledge of the choir's shortcomings work to its benefit.

A process for streamlining the plan for improvement is found by posing the question: "How can I make the greatest impact on my choir's ability in the shortest amount of time?" Nowhere is the need to do so greater than when an under-performing choir faces a challenge. And, indeed, the same skills that produce the greatest impact in the shortest amount of time are also the skills with which a director can effect the choir's continued improvement over the long term.

Consider the sample situation from the Complaint above. In addition to regular weekly service responsibilities, which are challenge enough, the choir is two months from a festival performance. It is clear that much needs to be accomplished in a restricted amount of time. The greatest challenge is where to begin.

First, choose a festival selection that the choir has already performed successfully. This will facilitate a confident performance and free up precious rehearsal minutes for technical polishing, for exploring the meaning and interpretation of the piece, and for performance-mode practice. Selecting a new piece too close to the performance date means that most rehearsal time will be spent solely on technical skills, guaranteeing a perfunctory performance.

Next, focus efforts on the one or two skills which, at the moment, will effect the greatest improvement in the performance of that piece. Attempting too many goals leads to scattered efforts with scattered results. Attempting inappropriate goals results in frustration and little improvement. Focusing effort on one or two skills allows tangible progress to be made in the allotted time, and this progress will raise the choir's confidence as well.

With several carefully selected skills firmly under their command, the singers are free to focus on singing the music, not hindered by a laundry list of dos and don'ts. Remember that first-rate performance is not limited to those musicians of great experience and great skill. In performance we do only the things that we can do. If can-dos are performed consistently at 70 percent or higher, excellent performance can take place.

Performance profiling is a precision tool for assessing where to focus effort. It displays an objective measure of deficient skills and reveals strengths that may have been overlooked or underutilized. Chart the process on a line graph (see appendix 3 for a blank graph). This unambiguous visual representation makes it much clearer how to proceed with setting effective goals.[10]

Creating a Performance Profile

1. Identify the qualities you want to hear on this piece. Draw upon a performance of it that you especially admire—a recording or the memory of a concert—or upon how you hear it ideally in your mind's ear.
2. Use a line graph like the following sample. It will reveal exactly where the choir stands on a given piece.
3. Write down, very specifically, the performance qualities that should be consistent for the performance you seek. List them down the left side of the line graph. Now indicate on the graph a current assessment, on a scale of 1 to 10, of the choir's skill in regard to each quality. Any quality ranked below 7 indicates that improvement is needed.

The sample chart in Table 6.1 indicates that, at present, the choir's lowest level skill is phrasing, followed closely by expressivity and legato. Other qualities requiring improvement are dynamics, tone quality, agility, mental focus, and ensemble. Borderline skills are pitch accuracy, part independence, intonation, balance, posture, and breath management. At 70 percent or higher are rhythmic diction, vowels, eye contact with director, and entrances and releases.

The task now is to select no more than two skills on which to focus. Study the chart to determine which skills might influence others and compare how the choir rates in the related skills. For example, excellent eye

TABLE 6.1 Task-Specific Performance Profile

Date	Performance or Rehearsal

Quality		Assessment
		0 1 2 3 4 5 6 7 8 9 10
Score Preparation:	Pitch accuracy	=================
	Part independence	=================
	Rhythmic diction	=======================
	Vowels	======================
	Intonation	=================
	Phrasing	=======
	Dynamics	=============
	Balance	==================
	Expressivity	=========
Vocal Technique:	Posture	==================
	Breath management	=====================
	Tone Quality	==============
	Legato	=========
	Agility	==============
Ensemble Skill:	Eye contact with director	==========================
	Mental focus	==============
	Entrances and releases	===========================
	Ensemble	=========

Elements to Be Worked On

1._____   3._____
2. _____   4._____

Note: This table is adapted for choral use from Shirlee Emmons and Alma Thomas, *Power Performance for Singers* (New York: Oxford University Press, 1998), and is used by permission.

contact with the director probably influences the choir's excellent attacks and releases. Could it not also be cultivated to influence phrasing and ensemble, rated among the lowest? Examine similar relationships and choose two skills or qualities that, if improved, would reap great benefits in the two short months allotted: breath management and mental focus.

With eleven of nineteen skills in need of improvement, why these two?

Breath management is a physical skill that can be addressed effectively in every warm-up session. The foundation thus laid should be reinforced as the choir rehearses the regular service requirements, then carried over into festival preparation. Improved breath management will have a direct influence on phrasing, dynamics, legato, agility, tone quality, expressivity, and intonation. You will necessarily work on posture as a function of teaching better breath management. Remember that the physical mastery of a skill takes longer to accomplish than the mental understanding of it. In other words, proceed patiently, and be prepared to remind many times, in many ways, with good humor.

Mental focus is a component of concentration that allows the mind to zero in on a particular task. Increased mental focus improves the quality of practice and the degree of retention. Focus is also a dynamic process that affords the ability to control the performance. Given that one of the choir's strengths is eye contact with the director, it is likely that, with improved mental focus, phrasing, ensemble, and other low or borderline skills will improve.

For the two-month period, concentrate rehearsal efforts on breath management and mental focus. The clarity of purpose will be a motivating factor to the choir that will enhance progress. Having chosen goals judiciously, an improved level of performance should result. The choir can meet its weekly obligations and face its festival participation with new confidence.

CHAPTER 7
Leadership Theory for Reference

The matter of leading a group, a choral group in particular, is a multifaceted issue. It is incumbent upon directors to refine their awareness, and to develop and practice leadership skills that enable healthy group function. Those choirs that proceed through the rehearsal-to-performance cycle in a healthy, interdependent manner are the choirs that are most likely to perform consistently. The leadership skills required of directors to produce such effort are over and above their musical/vocal/technical skills. When strong leadership skills combine with high musical/vocal/technical skills, then these directors' choirs are most likely to perform consistently at a high level.

The basic organization, typology, and some material of chapter 7 have been extracted from Hughes et al., 1996, and are adapted to serve the needs of choral directors and choral singers. Additional material has been extracted from notes taken during several long conferences in March 2000 with Alma Thomas, British performance psychologist and coauthor with Shirlee Emmons of *Power Performance for Singers* (New York: Oxford University Press, 1998).

Leaders/directors need to understand not just the principles of sound leadership but also the various styles with which the principles may be effected or executed. They require the ability to discern how their own personal qualities translate into behaviors, and how to measure the effectiveness of those behaviors. A thorough understanding of the principles and techniques of motivation will aid in developing such discernment. A positive cycle results, in which motivational skills will also be more readily developed where awareness is increased.

Followers (choristers) are individual persons, not a homogenous group. Their individuality affects the group, and yet each should subordinate self in order to achieve the goals of the group (the director must do likewise). This essential interdependence is affected by a number of factors, including the size of the group, its stage of development, the roles played by subgroup leaders, and the level of cohesion achieved by the group (is it an organization? a group? a team?).

Making an additional impact upon the choir as a group are situational factors, that is, circumstances under which a group is operating. An immediate situational factor could be the task at hand, because of its power to dictate strongly. Group culture (the norms under which the choir operates) and environmental factors (rehearsal room, type of seating, lighting, quality of piano or pianist, and so on) are important. Sometimes situational factors call for the director to improve or control them. Awareness and skill are required to determine what to change, when to change it, and how to go about it.

Finally, knowledge of the interdependent roles played by leaders, followers, and situations, enable strong leader/directors to assess any given circumstance. Following evaluation, strong leadership skills enable them to develop effective plans for working with, improving, or perhaps changing the circumstance. These oft-met challenges do not occur in a vacuum, but within the rehearsal-performance cycle that is the life of a choir. Effective rehearsal techniques that implement up-to-date theories of how we best practice, how we best rehearse, and how we best practice to perform bring leader/directors' plans to fruition. Armed with knowledge, understanding, and skill in these areas of group leadership, strong leader/directors guide their choirs step by step from vision to plan to rehearsal to performance.

7.1 The Leader

Supplying an inspiring vision of the group's musical mission is perhaps the most important job of a director/leader. Second, strong directors create a specific plan that outlines what they want for their choristers. Third, they also possess mental toughness, which allows them to maintain their vision of excellence when some question their mandate. Fourth, these directors articulate the goals that will implement this vision.

In their role as mentors/teachers who give and receive feedback, directors oversee the group's development. Further, directors/leaders should know how to achieve cohesion within their sectional groups as well as the entire choir, how to deal with the emergence of task subleaders and social subleaders in each section, how to effect a shared experience for the members of their choirs, because that will produce outstanding performance. To facilitate these elements, directors should possess high-level conflict-management skills. Understanding the individuals who stand before them and knowing how groups actually function will help choral directors to be more effective leaders.

General Principles of Leadership

First, let us consider the application of general leadership principles to musical leaders. The leader of any organized group influences his or her group not only toward the achievement of his or her own goals but the group's goals as well. The achievement of these goals depends completely upon the kind of a person the leader is and the behaviors, the leader exhibits. Although the leader is critical to the process, leadership demands more interaction between the leader (director), the followers (choristers), and the situation (conditions). Each can be considered separately, but each has an impact on the other. For example, the followers' actions can be either thwarted or supported by the situation, and the leader can become more effective by changing some aspects of the situation.

What are, then, the fundamentals of leadership?

1. The leader presents a vision to the followers.
2. The leader possesses technical expertise—musical, vocal, psychological.
3. The leader is an able teacher and an articulate communicator.
4. The leader motivates his or her followers.
5. The leader is a competent time manager.
6. The leader knows how to run a productive rehearsal.
7. The leader puts personal ambitions and self-interest to the side, channeling them toward the interests of the group.
8. The leader is accessible to his or her followers.
9. The leader is patient, but resolute.
10. The leader is trustworthy.

How Followers and the Situation Affect Leadership

The leadership process is very much affected by the followers' expectations, by their personality traits, maturity levels, competence levels, and motivation levels. For example, a chorister may have a strong dedication to music or may just be interested in having fun. Such attitudes are consequential to the leaders' activities. The choristers' skills, experience, work ethic, feelings about others in their section, and trust in their leader will vary greatly. For example, those followers who form a close unit with fellow singers in their section create different opportunities or challenges for the director than do those whose section is full of contention and turmoil.

The leader/follower relationship has been affected by the trend toward decentralized authority in the world at large and by the need for an artistic organization to function with fewer resources since Congress downsized the National Endowment for the Arts some years back, thus removing financial support for musical groups. At the same time, there has been a concomitant trend toward decreased funding of school and church groups. For these reasons, making the chorus better is the task of the singers as well as the director.

Environmental variables are not the only characteristic of a situation. For example, a good director will create an environment in which the choristers' creative contributions are welcome. The choristers then feel they have a stake in shaping something new, not just maintaining the status quo. In this way, the leader/director has actively changed the situation rather than simply making the group better able to adapt.

Variables encountered by the director/leader are many. Directors may find it necessary to respond differently to various choristers in the same situation or in various situations. Choristers may respond to various directors in various ways. Choristers may respond to each other differently with another director. Two directors may have different perceptions of the same choristers or the same situations.

What Kind of Leader Are You?

A *command-deference leader* prizes results, regards people as not quite so important, maintains tight control over the organization to accomplish efficient rehearsals and good performances, and finds human relations to be less important than artistic outcomes.

A *social club leader* has a high interest in people and low interest in performance results, makes a strong effort to create a friendly rehearsal environment, even at the expense of superior vocal and musical work, and avoids taking sides by staying out of conflicts themselves.

A *circumspect leader* shows a medium concern for people and results, relies on proven criteria, and avoids taking risks. This leader's goal is to excel safely. In the event of conflict among choristers, this leader seeks compromise, perhaps at the cost of a productive solution.

A *benevolent leader* has a style defined as patriarchal, strives for high results, using reward and punishment to get his or her way. Loyalty is prized; any straying from the leader's guidelines is punished.

An *expedient leader* adapts to situations in order to gain advantage. This leader's program moves forward according to a system of quid pro quo between leader and followers.

A *team leader* shows high concern for people and results, motivates the choristers to acquire competent musical and vocal skills, and is flexible and willing to change.

Based on the kinds of leaders they want to be, most conductors and directors would appreciate an assessment of their leadership skills. To properly assess skills, leaders must look at their qualities, behaviors, and ultimately at effectiveness. They should first judge their own various leadership qualities:

charismatic potential
speaking skills
command of influence tactics
intelligence level
personality traits
experience level

Second, they should measure the impact of their behaviors. Variables such as intelligence, personality traits, values, and attitudes only indirectly influence leadership effectiveness. Leaders' behaviors are easier to measure and are more directly related to leadership success. Yet leaders with certain traits may find it easier to perform some leadership behaviors more effectively than others. (For example, leaders who are highly agreeable by nature may find it easy to show concern for followers but difficult to criticize them.)

Leadership behavior includes specific actions, such as letting the singers know when they've done a good job, setting clear expectations about choristers' performance, showing concern for singers as individuals, and making choristers feel at ease. In sum, there are two independent dimensions of the director's behavior: consideration (friendliness, support of the singers); and skill-related behavior (goal setting, motivational skills, resolving conflicts).

Third, when trying to judge their effectiveness, they must remember that, even though their followers observe their leader at every rehearsal, the followers' ratings are not always an adequate measurement. One way for leaders to improve their effectiveness is to provide themselves with feedback that describes the frequency and skill with which they perform leadership behaviors. Very valuable to the leader, this feedback offers objective measurement skills that replace a subjective approach. Yet most leaders have blind spots about their own behaviors that may prove fatal. Some of these behaviors can be a lack of confidence in their own performance; indifference to the needs of their choristers; a self-importance and conceit that interferes with common interests of leader and choristers; insufficient technical knowledge and inflexibility in adjusting to changing followers and situations.

Once leaders/directors are noted as

prone to delaying and postponing | being excessively fault-finding
having poor judgment re: | displaying excessive anxiety
   commitments | having a lack of trust in
offending choristers and personnel | colleagues
insisting upon perfectionism | being cautious and suspicious
being protective of personal | showing lack of flexibility
   methods | displaying belligerence
being a micro-manager |

then the question becomes how to change these behaviors. There are several ways. Leaders/directors can

seek insight into how they come across to others;
search out why their behavior is having negative consequences;
pursue understanding of their underlying beliefs, values, goals, and
   attitudes;
try to enlarge knowledge of tools and techniques that will accomplish
   certain strategies; and
strive to learn what specific behaviors they should use to accomplish
   these strategies.

In other words, perceptiveness, principles, tactics, and skills will do the changing.

Motivation

One of the most important qualities of good leadership is the ability to motivate others. Choir directors probably would be disheartened to learn that, under most circumstances, followers could give approximately 15–20 percent more, or even less, without the director noting the difference. Choir directors might wish to believe that better motivation would lead to higher performance from all the members of a choir, but they should realize that motivating others depends on understanding them.

"Motivation is anything that provides direction, intensity, and persistence to behavior."[1] It is not directly observable; it must be inferred from behavior. Those behaviors directed toward the organization's mission or goals define the word performance. So performance, a broader concept than motivation, is synonymous with behavior. One might logically believe that liking a specific activity would produce higher performance, but it has only an indirect effect.

Some behavior is seemingly motivated for its own sake, or by personal satisfaction at having done a good job, or by larger feelings of competence and control. This is termed *intrinsic motivation*. What intrinsically motivates one choir member may not motivate another. People with a strong need for achievement prefer tasks that provide immediate and abundant feedback and tasks that are difficult but accomplishable. This would seem to define many choristers' motivation for singing in a choir. So we see that external rewards may backfire if given to choir members who are already intrinsically motivated. Such rewards, when seen as controlling, might result in a decrease in motivation.

Leaders often assume that they already know what works in motivating their choir, but some approaches are more effective than others for producing certain outcomes. There are four broad categories of motivation:

> *Need approaches*: Singers will differ in their needs: physiological needs; security needs; needs of belonging; esteem needs; and self-actualization needs.[2] The singers will be motivated as the director meets these needs.
>
> *Individual difference approaches*: Various motives define the consistent differences between people. For example, people with a strong need for achievement like taking responsibility for solving problems and accomplishing socially acceptable endeavors, and they prefer tasks that provide immediate feedback. The leader should focus on the comparative strength of these motives belonging to his or her choristers.

Conscious and directed choice approaches:

a. *The expectancy theory*: people will achieve a motivated performance when they consciously choose to do so; people do act in response to the expectation of rewards.[3] Using the expectancy theory to motivate, the director would explain the connection between the singers' effort and the consequent performance level; discuss the rewards accruing to the effort; and convince the choristers that the advantages outweigh the effort.

b. *Goal setting* is the easiest and most familiar system of motivation. It directs attention, marshalls effort, strengthens persistence, and helps each individual singer to develop strategies for achievement and not to cease an effort until the goal is reached. The director should have valid authority, should be known to have confidence in the choristers, should have provided clear musical performance standards and goals. Followers exert the greatest effort when they receive feedback on their progress toward meeting the goals.

Situational approaches (how the situation affects motivation): Some jobs are more motivating and satisfying than others. Singing in a choir with like-minded people is high on the list because choristers honor the vocal and musical tasks, the task itself contains abundant feedback, and the task requires the use of all their musical and vocal skills. If the singer's disposition is either extremely positive or extremely negative, the leader may have more difficulty making an impact. Followers are most satisfied when they believe that what they put into their singing and what they get out of it are roughly equivalent to what others are doing. Satisfied singers are more likely to continue attending rehearsals.

7.2 The Followers

Only lately has the role of follower been studied very much. Highly effective followers contribute a great deal to the director's reputation as a good leader, but misconceptions limit our understanding of followers themselves. Successes and failures of singing organizations are often unfairly attributed to leaders when the real reason for them may be the followers. For example, when the chorus performs well, the conductor may be given all the credit for having trained them well. Just as leaders are more visible than followers, directors are more visible than the cho-

risters. Thus, the ways that leaders differ is recognized more clearly than the ways in which choristers differ.

Because attention does not often fall on followers/choristers, it is a common misjudgment to think of them as a group of homogeneous individuals. Yet each chorister's education, technical expertise, and personality traits may affect the relationship between that singer and other choristers as well as the relationship between that singer and the leader. The director's effectiveness as a leader may depend on the match between his or her personality and that of the choristers. For example, choristers who believe that they have no personal influence may prefer an organized, authoritarian type of leadership, but the director might believe in democratic leadership. Or, conversely, choristers who believe that they are masters of their own fate may prefer a democratic type of leadership, but the director might be a strong, structured leader.

Various Styles of Chorister/Follower Behavior

Estranged choristers (apt to be about 15 percent of any group) cause disturbances in their section. They enjoy pointing out all negative aspects of the choir's mission and policies. Estranged followers are sometimes former exemplary followers who were discouraged and who can be brought back into the fold when the leader reduces the level of negativity.

Compliant choristers (20 to 30 percent of choir members) carry out directions without critical evaluation and are often very active in the organization. They can be a danger to the group if the leader requests behavior that contradicts their ideas of correct musical and social deportment. Some of them are inclined to be servile and averse to conflict. The leader must assure them that the organization needs their views and their contributions.

Pragmatist choristers have learned not to disagree whether or not they are committed to the leader's goals. They tend to be middle-of-the-road performers, comprising 25 percent to 35 percent of the group. It is difficult for the leader to perceive exactly what their opinions are. Their attitude might be a coping mechanism, or they may simply be disinclined to take risks, believing the absence of failure to be more important than success.

Dispassionate choristers (5 to 10 percent) look to the leader to do their thinking, either because of their own personality type or because they believe that they must cope with a leader who expects his or her followers to behave that way.

Archetypical choristers are seen by everyone as independent, creative, courageous in standing up for themselves. They know how to get along with their fellow choristers and the leader. The best ones do not take advantage of the group or focus solely on their own rights, but rather acknowledge that they and the group have mutual responsibilities and interests. Directors should try, when feasible, to choose choristers who have these characteristics and should try to encourage such behavior.

In short, it can be useful for the director to observe his or her choristers as dominant or submissive, friendly or unfriendly, accepting or unaccepting of authority.

Choristers as a Group

Directors need to understand that choristers as a group are not just the sum total of their accumulated characteristics. A group is defined as "two or more persons who interact with one another in such a way that each person influences and is influenced by each other person."[4] Viewing a group of choristers in this way is important because it stresses the shared influence between the director and the choristers, the fact that choristers interact with and influence each other, and the fact that each chorister belongs to a number of different groups. Thus eight individuals waiting in line to get into a movie would not be a group, but eight people planning a church picnic would be. This definition also reminds us that everyone belongs to a number of different groups. People tend to identify less with organizations to which they belong than with groups to which they belong. (Thus an alto would tend to identify more with the alto section than with the whole choir.)

Choir size affects the director's behavioral style. The group size is an important issue for these reasons:

1. As groups become larger, cliques (that is, subgroups who share the same goals, values, and expectations) are more likely to develop. Directors need to identify and deal with cliques within their sections, because conflicts within sections are often a result of cliques having opposing values.

2. The size of the group can affect a director's behavioral style: leaders with a large chorus tend to pay less attention to individuals,

using more impersonal approaches than directors with a small chorus, who tend to be more considerate and to use more personal approaches with their choristers.

3. The size of the group affects the members' individual effectiveness. There will be fewer personal contributions as the group size increases—either because more people working together creates inefficiency, or due to social loafing by people when they are not held individually answerable for their efforts.

The size of the group will also determine the nature of the work. The nature and preferences of the leader in relation to the skills, strengths, and preferences of the group (amateur or professional among other characteristics) ought to be compatible. If their strengths butt up against the director's preferences, there will never be a successful group. The leader will either have to change or leave. It is the director's job to work to the strengths of his singers. If he ignores their strengths and works solely to his own preferences, only destructive emotions will be created; frustration, anger, and fear will develop. This is not the fault of the singers. This is the director's job; it cannot be avoided or ignored. He or she requires the skills to make the sections and the entire choir work.

There are four distinct stages of development to any group, especially musical groups:

Forming

Courteous interactions
Becoming acquainted with fellow members
Absence of trust
Rejection of emerging potential subleaders caused by negative characteristics

Storming

Conflicts within the sections
Elevated emotions
Changes in status as contenders for subleader struggle to find supporters

Norming

Clear choice of a subleader
Development of group norms and cohesiveness

Performing

Interdependence of group members and focus on the performance of group tasks

The director's ability to recognize the stages of group development may lead directly to the increased cohesiveness and productivity of the group.

Individual Roles within the Group

The leader's behavior is characterized in terms of two broad functions: the task role (getting the task done), and the relationship role (supporting the relationships within the group).

The individual chorister's role can be characterized by the same functions. Several types of problems can occur that will impede the performance of the groups and the organization.

Dysfunctional roles that serve selfish purposes rather than group purposes include the following:

Dominating: forcing views on others and taking group time
Blocking: hindering group work by persistent negativism
Attacking: creating an antagonistic environment by criticism and browbeating
Distracting: engaging in behaviors that distract others

Group norms govern those behaviors that the group perceives as important. These group norms are informal rules adopted by groups to regulate group member behaviors. Although seldom written down or openly discussed, they still have a strong influence on behavior because people are good at reading social cues that call attention to the norms.

What the Director/Leader Wants from His or Her Choristers/Followers

The things the director wants from his or her choristers, although many and varied (including shared goals, ability to concentrate, musical and vocal skills, positive attitude, and so on), can be summed up by the use of the word *cohesiveness*. The director wants singers to agree on the central values and the clear-cut identity of the organization. When the director wants to determine the extent of the sectional cohesiveness, there is a two-stage process. First, the director asks individuals to indicate to whom in the section they go for technical or personal advice, whom they like, with whom they spend time, and whom they avoid. Second, the director tabulates individual responses to create a chart that provides a useful way to summarize group interactions and relationships of power. (It should be noted that seating arrangements often affect the degree of mutual inter-action and reciprocal influence within groups; for example, facing for-ward rather than in circles worsens the communication. In performance, nothing can be done about this fact, but rehearsals offer a time during which experiments can be made with circular seating.)

Cohesion is the element that attracts members to the choir, promotes the desire to remain a member, and persuades members to be active within the organization. As such, it could scarcely be more important to the director.

A very cohesive group interacts within itself and influences its mem-bers greatly. It may have more stable attencance and a lower turnover (vital issues to the director), thus delivering a stronger performance. Never-theless, a highly cohesive but unskilled group is still an unskilled group that will be surpressed by a less cohesive but more skilled group. This factor relates back directly to both the musical expertise and the leader-ship ability of the director.

Sometimes members of a highly cohesive group can become so con-cerned with striving for unanimity that they suppress dissent and critical thinking. The leader should be willing to listen to criticisms of his or her own ideas and create a climate of open inquiry through his or her own impartiality and objectivity. Despite the difficulties, the development of a cohesive group is still probably better than the alternative.

Is There a Difference between a Group and a Team?

Both teams and groups exhibit mutual interaction and shared influence. Yet teams generally have a stronger sense of identity than do groups. Teams have common goals and tasks; groups may not have the same consensus about goals. Teams tend to have more task interdependence than do groups. In sum, the difference is perhaps only a matter of degree. A team could be considered a highly specialized group. Given the high recognition of common goals and tasks that a choir has, as well as the interdependence on each other that choir members have, and the strong sense of identity that sections of a choir have, a choir could easily be pre-sumed to be a team.

An effective choral team

has a clear common interest (music) and high performance standards (vocal and musical excellence);
has a high level of communication that helps members to stay focused on their goal and to minimize conflicts among themselves;

has a director who spends a large amount of time planning and organizing to make optimal use of resources, to assess the technical
skills of members, to select new members with the necessary vocal
and musical skills, and to improve the necessary technical skills of
the existing members;

is guided by a director who finds facilities and outside resources to
help his or her team.

Having looked at these four characteristics of an effective team, the
following questions may help to create a model for group effectiveness.

1. Does the chorus know what its vocal and musical tasks are? Are
   the tasks consistent with the mission? Are the tasks meaningful to
   the singers? Is the chorus given feedback about the achievement of
   the goals?
2. Is the collective membership of the chorus up to the tasks that need
   be performed? Are there too few or too many members? Are the
   members sufficiently knowledgeable and skilled to perform well? Are
   members sufficiently mature and skilled to work together and avoid
   conflicts? Are they able to communicate or relate to each other?
3. Does the group share a set of norms that will foster their working
   as a team? Have these norms been explained, instituted, and reinforced by the director? Do these norms support the overall mission of the choral organization?
4. Has the director created an atmosphere in which he or she can use
   authority in a flexible, nonrigid manner? Has the director raised
   the technical skill level to sufficient competence to allow the group
   to comply with demands of the performance conditions? Can the
   director's authority change to match the demands of a situation?

7.3 The Situation

*Not surprisingly, leadership studies have produced inconsistent results
when viewing the effectiveness of directors in varying situations. Yet the
importance of the situation cannot be overlooked. Some studies maintain
that the situation—not the director's abilities—plays the most vital role
in the leadership process. Many believe that leaders are not born to that
position, but are made by the situation.*

How Situational Factors Affect a Director's Behavior

A director's behavior may depend on his or her perceptions of several aspects of the situation:

> the principles governing his or her position
> the expectations of followers, peers, and superiors
> the nature of the director's tasks; feedback about the performance of the choristers

These demands and constraints can cause role conflict and ambiguity for the director.

Because of the variety of situations in which directors find themselves, it would be helpful for them to have an abstract scheme for conceptualizing situations. Such a scheme would be one step in knowing how to identify what might be the most critical factor in any instance: (1) the task, (2) the organization, and (3) the environment. Some researchers have assessed the strong effect that tasks have on director behaviors. Others have concluded that the external environment and the situation have an influence on the ways that directors act.

1. The labeling of tasks as boring or challenging does not reveal what aspects might have caused a particular reaction. It would be more productive for the director to move from subjective reactions to a more objective analysis. For example, choristers vary in their ability to handle structured tasks (those for which there is a known procedure) and unstructured tasks (those for which there are many possible procedures, none better than the others). Choristers with a high tolerance for stress may handle unstructured tasks easily. It is easier for a director to give instruction in structured tasks, but that is not necessarily the most helpful thing to do. Choristers need help when they do not know how to achieve the desired outcome. They may welcome being trained in their specific music and vocal skills by the director.

Singing in a chorus requires many different skills: mechanical, cognitive, and physical. Thus singing in a chorus is more enjoyable than, for example, a filing job in an office, which demands a low variety of skills. Choral singing is satisfying because it has visible and audible outcomes to the completion of the tasks, and because individuals have some control over what is done and how it is done. A chorister is content and satisfied to the degree that he or she receives feedback about how the coordinated and synchronized musical/vocal tasks were accomplished (how the performance went).

2. The way an organization's activities are coordinated and controlled represents another level of situation in which leaders and followers must cooperate. Structure is just a means for getting things done; it is not an end in itself. Choirs usually design organizational structure around their important and continuing functions—the performances. The organization's culture includes shared backgrounds, norms, values among members, and the members' subjective reactions to the organization. Directors need not just be influenced by the organization's culture; they can play an active role in changing it. They can modify their choirs' culture through their reactions to crises and by rewarding different behaviors. They can find ways to motivate the choristers to work harder or to interact differently with each other.

Why would directors want to change the culture of their choirs? One reason might be that the culture is effecting a desirable outcome but in a negative way. Directors need to be cognizant of how their own ideas may subtly affect important aspects of their organization. It is unlikely that directors in the early stages of their careers will be asked to redesign their choirs' structure. Older directors of large choirs are often unable to identify dimensions of their group's culture because they have never seen anything else. It would be wise for directors to think carefully about the possible impact of changes to the longtime culture of their organizations.

3. Environmental characteristics include technical, economic, social, and legal forces. There is conjecture that crises play such an important part in charismatic leadership that some leaders will purposely create crises to be perceived as charismatic. Followers facing strong deadlines (the concert date approaches) expect leaders to be more assertive, directive, decisive, and the leaders are less apt to use participation techniques at these crisis times.

Any director's job could be described by using the following three dimensions: demands (factors to which directors must conform, set up by deadlines, rules, or artistic policies); constraints (factors that limit the director's possible actions); and choices (the director's optional behaviors). Any approach to leadership that focuses too narrowly on one element (leader/follower/situation) will be inadequate. Clearly the leadership process differs in many situations, and the successful leader is one who quickly identifies the constraints and works to reduce them. By asking questions and listening effectively, the leader may be able to redesign his or her work.

Situational Elements as Bettered or Controlled by the Director

Several cognitive theories deal with clarifying the conscious thought processes that people use when they decide how hard to work. Leaders do well when they clarify the relationship between the level of effort and the desirable outcomes by setting goals for their followers. The so-called expectancy theory (see p. 240) presents two fundamental assumptions: first, conscious choice motivates performance; and second, people will do what they believe will provide them the highest rewards. This is a commonsense approach to understanding motivation. It says that people will be motivated to do the task (a) if they can perform the task adequately by putting forth enough effort, (b) if they will be rewarded when they put forth the effort, and (c) if they value the reward. The director using the expectancy theory to motivate his or her choristers would take three steps:

1. Make sure that the chorus understands the connection between its efforts and the completion of the project.
2. Describe to the chorus the positive outcomes if the project were completed in time.
3. Convince the choristers that the advantages of completing the project outweigh the effort demanded.

Goal Setting

Goal setting is a journey of clarification, analysis, and achievement. The director presents his or her choristers with some future goal, such as the concert in Carnegie Hall, and convinces them that they can accomplish a high performance level if they exert sufficient effort. This goal will direct the chorus's attention, mobilize their efforts, and help them to continue to exert effort until the goal is reached. Specific goals and how to achieve them, not just "do your best" goals, result in a consistently higher effort and better performance. Goals should be

specific, observable, objective, and measurable: It should be easy to see exactly what the goal is and whether it has or has not been reached.

attainable and challenging: The goals should inspire people toward doing more than they thought they could.

based on commitment and accepted by choristers: The director could allow choristers to participate in setting goals, but if the director is perceived to be competent and supportive the choristers will be committed.

designed to provide feedback about the progress toward them: Performance is always higher when the goals are accompanied by regular feedback.

When the chorus perceives that their director has legitimate authority, expresses confidence in them, provides clear standards for their performances, and accompanies the goals with constant feedback on their progress, then the director can expect high performance levels.

Conflict

In leadership as in life conflict is inescapable. When two opposing parties have interests that appear to be incompatible, such as two choir members with strong differences in beliefs or goals (vocal or musical), a lack of communication between them is probably the most important factor. The director may need to spend considerable time preparing and conducting a negotiating session in which he or she will separate the people from the problem by focusing on interests, not positions. Two aspects of conflict that can have an impact on the resolution process are the size of the issue, and viewing the conflict in either/or terms, which restricts the outcome to total satisfaction or total frustration.

Is conflict always bad? No, conflict may increase the effort of the choristers, may promote a better understanding of others as feelings get aired, may spur an impetus for change, and may encourage critical thinking. On the other hand, conflict may well increase stress, decrease cooperation between members, or lead to negative feelings and backstabbing.

There are five strategies for resolving conflicts, each approach being appropriate for different situations:

Competition (a leader-domination orientation): Best in emergencies when quick, decisive action is key, when the issues are vital to the welfare of the group, or when the leader knows he/she is in the right.

Accommodation (a strategy of appeasement): Best when cooperation must be maintained, when harmony and stability of the group are most important.

Compromising (a strategy halfway between domination and appeasement): Best for moderately satisfying both parties or when there is time pressure.

Collaboration (a strategy of effort to satisfy both parties completely): Best when both sets of concerns are too important to be diminished, or to gain commitment by making a consensus.

Avoidance (a strategy of withdrawal from any one party's interests): Best when the leader has been wrong and wants to show reasonableness, or to allow time for people to cool down, or when others can better resolve the conflict.

In negotiation the leader should anticipate the concerns, issues, attitudes, and strategies of each side, and separate the people from the problem. Active listening will help the leader to focus on interests, not positions. Winning the negotiation at the expense of another person will probably be only a short-term gain. It is better for leaders to try for win/win outcomes, which will require creative problem solving.

Diagnosing Performance Problems in Individuals and Groups

To effect an improvement to the performance level of the choir, the director must be able to diagnose the problems of both individual choristers and whole sections, thus contributing to an effective coping strategy. The problems may be in the following areas:

Abilities: Raw talent such as intelligence and musicality are characteristics that are difficult to change, even with training.

Skills: Skills—musical and vocal knowledge, a set of vocal and musical behaviors, clear standards for high level performance—are very amenable to training, which directors themselves can do.

Task understanding: When choristers lack an understanding of what they are supposed to do, directors should make sure that the messages are understood by developing their own communication and listening skills.

Choice to perform: When choristers have chosen not to perform, directors should try to learn why. Perhaps the motivation is low; perhaps the tasks appear risky. Directors can increase their singers' choice to perform well by setting better goals and/or redesigning the task.

Level of effort and persistence: The director should try to discover why the effort decreased. Perhaps the choristers ran out of steam; perhaps they needed periodic feedback. One answer is to select choristers who are already motivated by the choral tasks. Another is to set longer-term goals.

Group factors: Is the section not very cohesive, with a low performance norm? The director may need to create super goals to increase cohesiveness, thus performance. To achieve super goals the entire section must exert effort.

Environmental and organizational factors: The director needs to recognize how he or she can affect the design or structure of the organization to improve individual, section, and choir performance.

CHAPTER 8
Practice and Imagery

8.1 The Nature of Practice and Rehearsal

Long-term performance psychology research has drawn important practical conclusions about the effectiveness of practice. Does "practice make perfect"? It certainly makes permanent. Choral directors will benefit greatly from the knowledge of some proven and useful principles about the nature of practice.

Principles of Practice

Choral directors, indeed all musicians, have invested long hours of their lives practicing something, whether it be piano, voice, conducting, violin, trumpet, or all of the above. All musicians were trained in technique and repertoire. Yet how many of us were trained to practice effectively? There is no academic course in how to practice. Many of us were probably left to our own devices about how to accomplish individual mastery.

It is practice of the right kind that leads to the highest levels of skilled performance. Practicing the wrong things, the wrong techniques, or the wrong strategies actually impedes genuine progress. Choristers' ability to learn from experience and from rehearsal is of utmost importance for the director. Correct practice produces positive changes in vocal and musical performance and ensures that such gains are relatively permanent. The same psychological principles that guide effective practice apply directly to rehearsing a choir.

In-Depth Psychological Analysis of Practice

How does the choral director know what techniques, what strategies are the right ones, except by experience? Learning only by experience takes time. Adopting selected techniques from the new research on practice, which follows, will be immensely useful when one does not have years of experience.

A psychological analysis of practice methods answers salient questions: Which type of practice is most effective when performance is imminent? What type of rehearsal produces the best long-term development and retention? Which type of practice best prepares for performance? What type of practice is best for young choristers?

Random/Distributed/Variable Practice (P-RDV)

Random practice is defined as mixing a variety of techniques throughout the warm-up or practice (for example, working on three techniques in the random order 1–3–2–1–3–1 or 1–2–3–2–3–1). This replicates techniques required in a performance situation.

Distributed practice is defined as one skill being practiced in short bursts (such as a series of two-minute drills spread over the warm-up or rehearsal, as opposed to one long block), during which times the rest intervals between practice drills are more frequent than the practice itself. Distributed practice facilitates longer-term learning and retention. It is good for continuous techniques, as in the long melisma passages of *Messiah*.

Variable practice is defined as practice in which the director deliberately varies the technique he or she asks for from the singers in the execution of one particular skill, such as, the two different ways of using the consonant when making big skips to a high note.

Factors Affecting the Use of P-RDV

Progress appears to be slower, but long-term development is of higher quality, and retention and transfer are improved.

The mental difficulty can be increased by making the practices more random, more distributed, or more variable. Directors should consider their singers' levels of accomplishment. If the skill practice is too difficult, the singer may switch off. As a general rule, the older, more talented or experienced the singer, the more complex practice can be.

Use of random, distributed, and variable practice is essential at some time in training, since it offers the best preparation for an actual singing performance in public.

Blocked/Massed/Structured Practice (P-BMS)

Blocked practice is defined as the repeated practice of one skill before moving on to another (e.g., 1–1–1–1–1, 2–2–2–2–2, 3–3–3–3–3).

Massed practice is defined as doing all the practice of a particular skill in one long unit, that is, where the rest interval between practice is short or nonexistent. Massed practice produces rapid gains, although retention may not be as high. It is very useful for individual skills and techniques and gives immediate short-term gains.

Structured practice is defined as practicing a particular skill in a very controlled and identical way (such as repeating the same *pianissimo* attacks with one-beat rest between, then moving on to another note and doing the same).

Factors Affecting Use of P-BMS

P-BMS is better for producing rapid but relatively temporary improvements in skill level—a short-term effect.

Beginning and younger singers may be better served by these less mentally demanding approaches.

As there are rapid, early gains, they serve to increase the motivation of the singer, which may be of particular benefit when working with beginners or those less galvanized to rehearse seriously.

A serial random schedule (that is, where the skills are practiced in a structured rotation, 1–2–3, 1–2–3, 1–2–3) represents a halfway position between P-RDV and P-BMS and may offer the best methods for younger singers.

Overlearning (P-O)

Definition: Continued practice of a skill after it has been learned, hence overlearning.

Factors Affecting Use of P-O

Once the skill has been learned, this method is very common.

This approach "grooves" technique. As a rough guideline, overlearning up to 100 percent (that is, meaning to practice it at least as long as the singer took to learn the skill in the first place) is very beneficial, but, after that, there are diminishing returns for this method.

Use of overlearning may result in competent and skillful performance, and may dispel any negative influences from previously learned skills.

Whole or Part Practice (P-WP)

Definition: Leaving technical skills whole or breaking them down into their parts for teaching or practice.

Factors Affecting Use of P-WP

When teaching new skills that are particularly complex, a reasonable method is to break the skill into manageable parts. First, however, singers should attempt the whole skill before it is broken down.

The components of the skill should all become meaningful stages. Director and choir should agree on what is meaningful before the skill is partitioned.

However the skill is partitioned, the director should constantly stress the sequencing of the parts and how they affect each other. Furthermore, if the aim is long-term improvement, the singers should show an understanding of the sequencing and the integration of the parts before the process begins.

A Practical Example

Research has proved that there are but two quality times in a practice period—the beginning and the end. These are the moments of highest retention. Therefore choir directors should conceive of the rehearsal as a number of short practice periods, rather than as a long stretch. Dividing the rehearsal into smaller increments creates more beginnings and ends within the allotted time. In the long run, this procedure increases quality time, thus better retention.

A choir rehearsing for a performance of *Messiah* is challenged by the agility sections of "For unto Us a Child Is Born." The most productive plan is to practice the various techniques of the melismatic passages (achieving speed and clarity in the agility, and using vowel modifications for the higher notes) in small increments of time, alternated with practice of the concerted sections ("and the government shall be . . . ," "and His name shall be called . . ."). Each time the director returns to the melisma passages, and each time he or she goes back to the concerted sections, there will be another beginning and end, thus delivering more quality practice. This principle used in conjunction with distributed practice is proven to effect improvement in a shorter time than a method of spending, say, a quarter of an hour doing the melismas only.

8.2 Memorizing

Although choral singers most often perform with music in hand, there are occasions when a memorized performance is preferred or required. Memorization is expedited when the principles and strategies of memorizing are understood.

The Four Stages of Memory

The human mind remembers almost everything that happens to it, but sometimes cannot literally re-call that information. It is rare, however, that human beings forget information altogether. Remembering is not a haphazard process; efficiency of retrieval depends on the efficiency of the whole system. Your singers' memories can be enhanced when you know which learning methods suit them best.

These are the four stages of memory:

the *perception* stage, when information is received through the senses
the *encoding* stage, when singers begin trying to understand while selecting, organizing, and storing the information in short-term memory
the *storage* stage, when, understanding the information, they "groove" it into their memory paths through learning, repetition, or familiarization, and finally store it in their long-term memory
the *retrieval* stage, when your singers call forth the meaningful information that they have stored in their long-term memory

Strategies for Memorization

At the perception stage, when information is received through the senses, it is stored in four separate memories, therefore by four different learning methods: verbal, visual, motor skill, and factual. To store this information easily, the singers should be

> relaxed (when the reception of information is easier);
> intent on remembering (when the mind is set to remember); and
> focused on the information (avoiding distractions).

When rushed, tired, frustrated, angry, or feeling put upon, singers will not receive the information efficiently. Thus, new memorizing tasks should be initiated when they are beset by neither pressure nor haste.

To make encoding as efficient as possible directors should help the singers to

> be selective about how much information is needed; is all of it needed? Is some of it already lodged in the mind?
> organize the information into logical patterns, groups, links, and associations, using mnemonics, active recall, live reading and singing, live testing, and musical tapes or midi files.
> feed information in digestible quantities; divide the material into manageable pieces; be careful not to set expectations so high that they begin to believe their memory is bad.
> work on the material in short blocks; short sessions done frequently are better than a few longer sessions.

At the storage stage, information is transferred deliberately from short-term to long-term memory, so as to "groove" information into memory paths, by

> reading, singing, and familiarizing themselves with the words and music as often as possible, using all their separate memories—sight, sound, and feelings—to reinforce the grooving;
> rehearsing the meaning of the information regularly;
> reading and singing with meaning;
> using association to help them remember the information, deliberately invoking imagery to remind them of certain things in the composition; and
> getting enough sleep, and reading or singing the piece as the last act before going to sleep, which will make the memory better.

Retrieval is easier when the previous steps have been well accomplished. Other helpful methods are to

be kind to themselves while memorizing;
refrain from overtaxing the memory;
be sympathetic and positive; and
learn to relax and associate information.

Revisiting Earlier Memorizations

In some cases choirs perform parts of their repertoire from memory on a regular basis. Once memorization is accomplished, the director should take care that it remains accurate. That means allowing occasional rehearsal time for a rigorous recheck of notes, rhythms, text. A slight memory slip here or there easily becomes a mislearned—but learned nonetheless—part of the whole. The director should consistently check the choir against the score, just as a seamstress always cuts from the original pattern piece. Taking for granted that "we all know it" erodes performance over time.[1]

8.3 Performance Mode Rehearsal

Musicians have a habit of obsessing over their technical expertise, perhaps forgetting the fact that technical skills comprise only part of performance per se. Choral directors often rehearse technical musical, vocal, and linguistic skills right up to the virtual last moment. Then they devote one or two repetitions to "going straight through it." It is no exaggeration to say that this system almost always arrives too late at thinking about the performance itself. The spirit and joy of singing the beautiful music have been rehearsed right out of it, although it might be technically solid. Such a performance then often disappoints the director and the audience.

What Is Performance Mode Rehearsal?

Psychologists tell us that peak performances happen when the level of preparation has made it possible to lavish minimal attention on technicalities. When would that be? When the technical skills have been made automatic by efficient rehearsal.

The minute the technical details of the music, the vocalism, and the linguistics are under control, start performance mode rehearsal. Instruct your singers

> not to stop for any reason,
> to stay in the moment, not in the past or the future,
> not to analyze, judge, or criticize their output as they sing,
> not to grade themselves on technical details,
> to put musical inaccuracies behind them for the time being,
> not to worry about language problems,
> but . . . to sing with as much dramatic truth and personal involvement as possible.

After the first "performance," the director appraises it and, listing the good results first, speaks about what kind of spirit, musicality, and personal involvement shone through; the moments that were particularly moving, and the expression, the legato, and the tone quality that were admirable.

The director then speaks about what did not go particularly well, what was incorrect, what musical problems arose, where the singers did not follow direction, and where, specifically, the vocalism left something to be desired.

Three "performances" are done in the same fashion, after which that piece is abandoned for a time. When the director returns to the first piece, he or she explains what needs be adjusted to raise the technical standard. There are only two reasons for details to go wrong, particularly those that went wrong every time:

1. The ordinary rehearsal of the difficult spots did not sufficiently routine the skills until they were automatic.
2. The technical solution proposed and rehearsed by the director was not the best answer for the problem. There is probably a better answer.

The difficult spots are then improved either by means of a better solution or more efficient routining, until the choir executes automatically. At that time, performance mode rehearsal resumes until the choir is at ease with both technical requirements and their dedication to the performance itself.

Singers, professional or not, are loath to divert their attention from technical skills. It is difficult to accept that, once those motor skills are routined and automatic, the body executes them better if they are not the focus of the performer's attention. Motor skills, when under control, are stored in the brain as an entity, as, for example, riding a bicycle. When one first learns to ride a bicycle as a child, the process is very predictable. The father runs alongside the two-wheeler with training wheels, holding on to his child, helping to steer and balance. The child is learning three skills: pedaling, balancing, and steering. Eventually the training wheels come off, the father departs, and the child does all three things at once. In the aggregate they are called "riding a bicycle." When the child becomes an adult who has not been on a bicycle for fifteen years, it is possible to hop on and "ride," steering, balancing, and pedaling all at once without thinking about the individual skills. In the brain is lodged an entity labeled "riding a bicycle."

It is the same with musical skills, which also are motor skills. They comprise many different elements, each learned separately, but each becoming part of the whole skill that resides in the brain as one entity, such as, "singing softly," or "singing fast."

In sum, performance mode, while seldom concerned about singular skills, should be practiced and practiced a lot. In this way the technical difficulties are all but thrown away, a very difficult thing for singers to do. We all recognize the difference between a choir that sings well and one that also performs well. There is a kind of rehearsal that ensures performance skill and freedom. That is performance mode rehearsal, and it brings with it great performances.

8.4 Emotional Content

A case can be made for improving the dramatic and interpretive skills of choral singers, if the director accepts the challenge and will allow time to accomplish it. It is the privilege and task of the director, not the choristers, to make interpretive decisions. Yet the chorus is the director's instrument. When they are asked to share the interpretive vision and to be the means of implementing it, then those of their dramatic skills that are acceptable in a choral situation ought to be raised to a high level.

Music Exists in Time

What is the significance of this fact? That all interpretive elements must be executed with regard to tempos and rhythmic durations. Singers are word/body instruments whose responses must take place in specific rhythmic places defined by the music and the words. Ideas, facial expressions, perhaps body movements—all these must be allied with the musical moment. Done too early or too late, they are meaningless because they are unrecognizable to the audience.

Studying Music with Text

When music includes words, its meaning is restricted to some degree. Words limit interpretive possibilities for choral music, but they also fill out and enhance its meaning. Instrumentalists, having no text, are trained to look for musical meaning, which is unrestricted. Their music is usually fully open to interpretation unless it is clearly programmatic. When a choral text is in a foreign language, the meaning is distanced by one degree, increasing interpretive difficulty. In popular music everything can be changed by the individual performer: tempo, melody, dynamics, keys—and meaning. Serious music, on the other hand, is not so freely tampered with, except in degree: how much ritard, how fast an allegro, how soft the *piano*, and so on.

Although form and content of poetry and music exist independently, they nevertheless function concurrently. Specific musical elements of pitch, rhythm, volume, or harmony have been traditionally used by composers to "word paint" to convey emotional states and specific concepts such as direction, types of motion, light and darkness, water, and many others. Donald Ivey reminds us: "if the emotion aroused by the music is compatible with the emotion aroused by the poetry, the images have been synthesized and the expressive experience is complete."[2]

To persuade singers to pay close attention to poetry and poet, many directors mandate a separate study of the poem apart from the music, and, when performing, they present their interpretation of the text. This is admirable but omits one essential factor from consideration and from its part in the discovery of meaning. The meaning of the words is framed by the music that the composer chose to express the words. For example, it is not so important to the interpreter what Michelangelo himself meant by his words or what the interpreter thought Michelangelo meant, but what Liszt thought Michelangelo meant. That is to say, the music that Liszt composed reflected his convictions about Michelangelo's real meaning. And where are those convictions displayed? In the music, which is the true subtext of the poetry. Hugo Wolf, discovering that a poem that inspired him had been previously set by another composer, went ahead with the project only if he were convinced that the previous composer had not done the poem justice.

With regard to choral music, it is directors who must come to personal conclusions about the meaning of the choral pieces before they lead their followers to the actualization of their visions. How do directors intuit the meaning behind the text and music? The following diagram fleshes out the process by which they reach conclusions:[3]

MEANING

=

Beliefs, values (people, places, issues, objects, colors, culture, etc.)

+

Knowledge (which brings about conceptualization)

+

Responses (reactions to the beliefs and values, exploration of ways to put them to use)

+

Experience (experiments, playing with the beliefs and values until they are felt within)

+

Synthesis (planning, practice, routine until synthesized through repetition)

=

MEANING

=

PERFORMANCE

Once directors achieve a clear vision of the piece, it remains for them to give the singers the technical means by which to accomplish the vision. After the requisite technical vocal and musical skills are in place, imagery is of help in enhancing the performance. There are some meaningful variables when considering interpretive questions. One example is presented by baroque music, in which the text becomes less and less important once the exposition has concluded, at which time the basic idea begins to be examined from a musical viewpoint. The expression, as a baroque piece goes on, depends more on musical means and depends less on meaning of text. The directors' expertise at recognizing a text event, a vocal event, and a musical event will often be an important part of their interpretive creativity.

THE SCIENCE

Researcher Johann Sundberg has applied his talents to the subject of vocal expression:

"Perhaps the most important facet of perception of voice is expression. Surprisingly, we can, from listening to a voice, perceive a number of subtleties: the singer's emotional state and attitude . . . [and] whether the singer really means what the words are saying. . . . Although expression is poorly researched as an area, it is accepted that it is possible for us to hear these subtleties by identifying sound patterns. The basic perceptual qualities of the voice are timbre, including vowel and voice quality, pitch, and loudness. . . . By noting combinations of these acoustic cues, we gain information on which vowel was pronounced, the voice characteristics of the [singer], and the sound patterns, from which we deduce expression or the lack of it. These patterns reflect the movements of the different parts of the voice, which is influenced by behavioral pattern of the entire body, or body language."[4]

How to Do It: Showing the Meaning

All the understanding directors have labored to find will mean nothing unless the audience can see and hear their beliefs about the meaning. The four basic elements that transmit meaning to an audience are musical, vocal, linguistic, and dramatic. When all four elements unmistakably carry the same message (the director's interpretive decisions), then audience understanding and appreciation is heightened. Making the audience *see* meaning depends for the most part on choristers' facial responses that lead to vocal expression. These responses will be clear to the audience when the choristers have improved their imagery skills. Making listeners *hear* the director's point of view relies on tone quality, expressivity and clarity of diction, not to mention all the musical decisions: when the ritard starts, how long it lasts, when breaths are taken, the various tempos, dynamic levels, and so on. In a choral situation, the dramatic elements, which exist in addition to the musical development, often depend upon the imagery skills of the choral singers. These can be improved by imagery exercises; see p. 265.

Singers who develop strong imagery skills hold the key to performing "in the moment." Being sensitized to the experience of the music in the moment results in a physical presence that almost palpably communicates to the audience. Faces, eyes, and bodies come alive to the expressive elements of the music. Energy capable of expressing any manner of dramatic intent pours forth, carrying with it meaning and emotional content.

8.5 Imagery in Practice and Performance

Every choral director uses descriptive language to paint evocative pictures for the chorus. Imagery is practiced instinctively to inspire and to inform interpretation. Its use need not be limited, however, to the enhancement of interpretation. Imagery can also help alleviate anxieties and increase concentration. In the pre-performance period, imaging helps singers lift self-confidence and speed the actual learning of the music.

What Is Imagery?

Imagery is referred to by various names; musicians use the terms visualization, mental rehearsal, and imagery interchangeably when describing the same process. Yet they are not necessarily the same thing. *Mental rehearsal* usually describes the use of imagery to practice, refine, and make technical skills automatic. *Visualization* tends to limit imagery to the visual, for purposes of enriching interpretation, recalling past performances, rehearsing future performances, or imagining the stage situation. Imagery is not solely concerned with visualizing but rather with the use of all the senses: sight, smell, hearing, touching, feeling, and kinesthetic responses.

The two kinds of imagery used by performers are named for the senses used: external and internal. External imagery views the scene as if it were a film or video. It can be used to learn a new skill and to correct mistakes within a skill. Internal imagery views the scene from the inside out, through the singers' own eyes from their positions in the choir. With internal imagery the singers feel the muscular contractions of the movement, the inhalations, the sensation of being in the scene provided by the music. Internal imagery encourages the use of all the senses and can be adopted to practice visual kinesthetic cues required in performance. Moreover, it creates confidence through colorful imagery when that technique is practiced well.

Imagery works because the mind controls all body movements, whether fine or gross muscle movements. The mind/body connection is vital because the body itself really does not know whether the messages it receives are generated from the imagination or from the subconscious. The body simply responds to the message. When the imagery is correct and vivid, the performance will be elevated.

How to Do It: Effective Practice of Imagery

For those directors with interest and time available for expanding their singers' skills in imaging, a sample exercise is offered. Because imagery is concerned with all the senses, many are surprised to learn how vividly they use senses other than visualization, especially those singers who are unaccustomed to this kind of mental exercise.

The small amount of time devoted to imagery work (no more than two or three minutes) should commence with eyes closed and body relaxed. A goal should be set by the director, perhaps one suggested by that day's rehearsal repertoire. An example: "We are going to work on imaging a Thanksgiving dinner. The time is about two hours before dinner will be ready. The location is Grandma's house, as tradition dictates." The director should ask guiding questions that spark the imagination of the singers:

What is it you smell? Browning meat? Savory onions in the stuffing? Mince pie? The smell of the hothouse flowers you brought for Grandma?

What do you feel? Are you hungry? Are you salivating? Imagining how it will taste?

What are you thinking? Remembering your Grandma's traditional stuffing? Thinking how your plate will look with the gravy being poured over the turkey slices? Remembering the past Thanksgiving celebrations? Feeling sad and missing those who are no longer with the family?

What are you hearing? The clatter in the kitchen? The burp of the cork being extricated from the wine bottle? The noise of the football game on the television? The women's voices as they set the table?

What do you remember? The taste of mince pie, which you never liked? The feel of your knife cutting through the first slice of turkey? The crunch of the chestnut pieces in the stuffing?

What do you see? The snowy white tablecloth covered with Grandma's best dishes? The sunshine streaming in the dining room windows? All the different types of chairs around the table? Grandma looking a bit older and more tired than last year?

The feelings will be more vivid if the image is kept in the present:

Today, *now*, is Thanksgiving.
The weather today is sunny outside.
The time is almost one o'clock.
The trees are beginning to lose their leaves.
You are wearing a cozy thick sweater.
The dining room looks the same as always.
Grandma is bringing in the bird on the platter from the kitchen.
Everyone is applauding.

Let the choir members speak out to describe their response as they have success imaging.

Once the imaging skills of your singers have grown, practice the imagery based on the subject of the music you are preparing for performance soon. Guide them to the interpretation you have decided upon. Enjoy their response.

Other than the elevation of interpretative responses, imagery can be used to solidify technical skills. Using internal imagery, let your singers close their eyes and see themselves singing a certain phrase that has given trouble—modification correct (they see the mouth in the proper shape and size; they feel the tongue doing the proper vowel), appoggio in position (they image the vigorous inhalation and the chest high, ribs expanded), melody and rhythm accurate (they hear the tune).

> Imagery affects the way you function physically. Whereas verbal language simply represents the life of the senses, imagery uses the language of the body. For example, as you imagine yourself moving, the groups of muscles involved in that action will move on a subliminal level.
>
> Imagery helps accelerate your learning process. When you image a new technical skill or part of a new piece of music, the appropriate nerve impulses and pathways are used in the same way they would be used in the actual performance. The brain does not distinguish between your imaging the new skill and your actually executing it. In both activities, the information received by the brain is exactly the same! Therefore, if you combine the mental skill of imagery with the actual physical practice, you will accelerate the rate at which you learn.
>
> Imagery uses a language understood by the body. . . . Directing is a physical skill. The signals received by the body are best received in a language the body understands. Body sensations such as feeling, sight, hearing, smell, taste, distinguishing color and movement, and so forth, are the main vocabulary of this language.[5]

Mental Skills

Some readers may find it curious that a book on choral directing should include a program of building mental skills. The decision to include this material sprang from the phenomenon called peak performance. Openly or guardedly, most performers hope for a peak performance whenever they walk on stage.

9.1   Mental Skills and Peak Performance

What is a peak performance? Peak performances are exceptional; they appear to surpass the ordinary level of performance. At such a time all the performer's skills and abilities unite fully with the results of previous diligent practice. Peak performance integrates and synthesizes all the performer knows—a right-brain activity—into one complete whole. When such a performance materializes, you will conduct better than ever before, enjoying a supreme high, an experience toward which you have been working for a long time. Peak performances are rare.

Can one train for peak performance? As a choral conductor, you are no different from an elite athlete. An athlete's peak performance is the outcome of physical, technical, and mental factors, and so is yours. Mind and body cannot be separated in peak performance, which exhibits the strength of the mind-body link. In it, what one thinks is echoed by what one does. There is, of course, no substitute for complete mastery of technical skills—stick technique, an informed ear, effective leadership, and so on. However, the higher the level of physical and technical skills, the more important the mental aspects of performance become. For example, during the Olympics, every competitor has high technical and physical skills. That is why Olympic athletes readily admit that mental skills alone make the difference between the winners and losers in those contests. As Mark Spitz said in Montreal, after winning seven gold medals: "At this level of physical skill, the difference between winning and losing is 99 percent psychological." The great golfer Jack Nicklaus said, "*Mental* preparation is the single most critical element in peak performance" (emphasis added).

As a conductor, you would be wise to direct a focus to the mental side of performance that is equal to your usual concern with the physical/technical side. Eventually there comes a point in every performance when the technical and physical skills are as good as they can be, when little more can be done to improve those skills before the performance. At this level of preparation, the mental aspects of your performance will make the difference, in the rehearsal period and during the performance. One cannot order up a peak performance, but one can create a climate in which it might happen. Similarly, the mental toughness required of elite performance is not a gift; it can be learned and it requires practice. These reasons prompt the inclusion of a brief section on the most important mental skills.

The following sections discuss individual mental skills intended as guidance for choral conductors. However, as readers scrutinize the attributes of each skill and the suggestions for their practice and improvement, they should glean constructive concepts that can be passed on to their choristers, when they believe them useful for that purpose.

9.2 Relaxation Techniques

Your whole lifestyle is an important factor in nurturing your ability to deal with the pressure of performance. How you live outside performance and whether you are (physically, mentally, and emotionally) fit or out of shape directly affect your ability to focus, handle pressure, and think consistently well. As a conductor, your body must do what you want it to do. To ensure your body's help, you should communicate with it efficiently. Worry and anxiety cause your muscles to contract involuntarily and to be less effective when called upon. Because the best performances occur when mind and muscles are combined and free-flowing, you require a state of calm. The ability to relax the body and calm the mind is very important for your performing life. It is, moreover, a skill that is seldom mentioned during your training.

Self-awareness of your body is the first step toward feeling relaxed; it also sets the stage for important mental preparation. Replacing bad habits in the body with good ones is just as crucial for a choral director as for an elite athlete. Become bodily aware as you conduct your rehearsals. Gain some insight into the mind-body relationship. See what effect the body is having on your performance. Following are two exercises that will help.

EXERCISE 9.1 KINESTHETIC BODY INVENTORY

Check all your body parts. Can you distinguish one from the other? Feel one toe or finger as separate from the others. Check the front of the neck and the muscles leading down into the sternum. Switch to the back of the neck, the arms, and the shoulders. While you rehearse, begin to pay attention to the different parts of your body and how they are functioning, not forgetting the feet and legs.

EXERCISE 9.2 EYES CLOSED

Select two or three habitual conducting movements. Do each movement with your eyes open and repeat it a number of times. Now close your eyes and repeat the movement in exactly the same way. Be aware of how it feels. How well are you organizing your movements without seeing? Repeat again, eyes open, and again, eyes closed. Become aware of exactly how you do the movement, creating a kinesthetic catalog.

Relaxation through Breathing

You can acquire the ability to deal with tension in your performing life through breathing. Have you noticed what happens to your breathing when you are trying too hard, or are nervous or angry? The fast, shallow breathing is a version of the "fight or flight" syndrome. Result: You are a less effective conductor. When it occurs, the best step is to focus on your own breathing. During performance, a high-pressure time, the mind often runs ahead of the body. A deliberate return to normal breathing rhythm allows you to relax physically and mentally.

Under pressure, remember to breathe. Keep the technique as simple as possible. Focus solely on the breathing. Tune in to your own breathing pattern. Allow the breath to execute a complete cycle. Take time for a complete inhalation. Five or six mindful breaths will return your focus and control. While breathing, think positive thoughts: *I am in control. I feel good. I can take my time.*

Relaxation through Ratio Breathing

Inhale deeply through your nose to the count of 5. Exhale through the mouth to the count of 10. During the exhalation, focus on imagining yourself and your choir performing well, beginning precisely, making clean, tonally secure entrances, and so on. This type of breathing is termed *ratio*, because the length of the exhalation doubles that of the inhalation: for example, 3:6, 4:8, 5:10, 6:12. Ratio breathing combines relaxation and concentration. On the exhalation, you can focus on anything that helps you feel good and reduces any anxiety. This technique can be used effectively before and during performance.

Relaxation through Release of Tension

Another way to maintain relaxation is to scan your body for tension and then release it. First, recognize how certain areas of your body feel when they are tense. Deliberately tense your hands. Form a clenched fist. Know what that tension feels like; then allow it to melt away. Release it, then breathe carefully and deeply, fully in and out. This is the feeling you want to recognize and be able to recreate, the sensation of freedom when the muscles are relaxed.

Scan the body for the area of tension. Focus on it; release the tension; allow yourself to refocus on the freedom within the muscles. Repeat this exercise for the parts of the body that affect your conducting. When you excel at this skill, you will be able to release tension from any part of the body at will, even during performance.

Summary

Learn to relax in high-pressure situations by

learning to become aware of your body and its tensions or relaxations.
taking your time so that you are in control.
slowing down your mental and physical responses by breathing in a full cycle.
scanning your body to find the tension.
breathing easily and slowly to release all the tension.
contracting only the muscles you need, so as to save energy.
staying in the moment, focusing only on what you are doing *now*.
focusing on the pleasure of music-making, not on the importance of the outcome, which is not under your control.

9.3   Goal Setting

Judging solely by the vast number of books and articles written on this subject, one must acknowledge the importance of goal setting. Analysis of high achievers invariably reveals persons who excel at goal setting. Indeed, when one establishes goals, that process

directs attention to the important elements of the profession. *Specific goals indicate and isolate the professional skills that need upgrading—the choristers' as well as the director's.*
mobilizes one's efforts. *Even when circumstances make it difficult for director and choristers to gather their energy, stated goals provide motivating purpose.*
strengthens persistence. *When the task seems overwhelming, the setting of subgoals makes it easier to believe that long-term goals can be met.*

encourages the development of new learning skills, *thus influencing the choral director's and the choristers' confidence level and general satisfaction with their work.*

Setting Appropriate Goals

Goal setting is a path of clarification and analysis that leads to achievement. Why do some succeed at goal setting and some not? The answer lies in the questions choral directors ask themselves during the process of goal setting. The plans for achieving those goals are all-important. Such planning dictates how the thinking goes. This thinking, in turn, keeps the motivation alive, allows the drive toward success to be maintained, and guides the planning for the next stage.

The director's task is to set the right kind of goal, the type that enhances and provides direction for motivation, both personal and in the choristers. The next step is to devise a plan that will achieve the goal.

Subjective and Objective Goals

There are two types of goals: subjective and objective. A subjective goal is both personal and general, such as "to do the best that I can." Missing here is the knowledge of how good the best will be, what must be better, when it must be better, how it will be improved, and so on. An objective goal provides a clear target for which to aim, such as "to learn the Italian diction by Thursday." It is preferable to learn how to set and fulfill objective goals.

Both outcome goals and performance goals are objective, but outcome goals are those generally beyond the control of either the director or the singers. Unfulfilled outcome goals (for example, "We just must get asked back again") lead to anxiety or frustration, to a slump, and, more important, to demotivation. Performance goals are those that define what the director and the choir plan to achieve (for example, "We will sing this 7/8 piece with accurate rhythms, but also with ease and enjoyment"). Process goals define how to attain the stated objectives (for example, "At each rehearsal we will practice speaking and tapping this piece for a total of four minutes in two two-minute batches before singing, so that we can sing it accurately while making music"). These goals are firmly within the director's control and are associated with less anxiety and a higher level of performance from the singers.

To set appropriate goals directors must first define their performance objectives. They should develop, as well as reaffirm their sense of mission, vision, purpose, and direction. It is best to focus attention on specific aspects of performance that can be within the director's (and thus the singers') control: singing skills, preparation, execution, and performance routines.

Performance Profiling as an Evaluation

The starting point (and the essence of successful goal setting) is an accurate assessment of the choir's skill level at the present moment, gained by directors asking the right questions of themselves. An efficient way to do this is by performance profiling, which can particularize the choir's real strengths as well as pinpoint areas that need work. Goals are set accordingly. Once you have evaluated the choir's present level of performance, set targets and design a goal-setting program, making sure to include the choir as a partner in the plan. Table 9.1 is a linear performance profile with sample choral performance qualities entered. A similar profile, with different parameters, will be found on p. 230. Performance profiles can be done for general musicianship, vocal skills, mental skills, specific musical pieces, or all of the above. A blank profile will be found in appendix 3.

A Helpful Acronym

SMARTER is an acronym that helps sort out the process of effective goal setting. The principles allied with SMARTER have been identified from research and practice. They will remind directors of the basic principles and particularize their appreciation of whether or not the goal setting is working successfully.

S(*pecific*): Be as specific as possible when identifying goals. A vague goal provides little direction.

M(*easurable*): A successful goal can be measured objectively so that director and singers can assess improvement or its lack.

A(*cceptable*) and A(*djustable*): The choir more readily accepts goals they have helped to design. Shared decisions invite individual investment in the process—they can achieve the goals and want to do so. Goals are not written in stone. They can and should

TABLE 9.1 A Long-Range Goal Performance Profile

Date	Performance or Rehearsal

Assessment
0 1 2 3 4 5 6 7 8 9 10

Music up/eyes on conductor	=====================
Mental focus/performance mode	================
Engagement with music	====================
Appoggio posture	=================
Focused, supported tone	================
Balance	=====================
Intonation	==============
Rhythmic accuracy	=======================
Fluid jaw movement	====================
Consonants, initial, middle, final	====================

Elements to Be Worked On

1. Mental focus in performance mode	3. Appoggio posture
2. Focused, supported tone	4. Intonation

Note: This table is adapted for choral use from Shirlee Emmons and Alma Thomas, *Power Performance for Singers* (New York: Oxford University Press, 1998), and is used by permission.

be changed or adjusted when progress is faster or slower than planned.

R(*ealistic*): Goals should be realistic yet challenging. Too much challenge might lead to abandoning the goal. A goal too simple fails to provide satisfaction when achieved.

T(*ime-phased*): The progression of goals from short-term to long-term should be planned in timed phases. Target dates for each goal provide further motivation.

E(*xciting*): When goals are met, the director and the singers should feel excited by the achievement. If there is no satisfaction, the goals may have been too difficult or too easy.

R(*ecorded*): Always write down the goals with precise wording and time frames so that the details of the program are remembered.

Setting goals of many different kinds holds great importance in choir directors' quest for better performances from their choirs.

9.4 Building and Maintaining Self-Confidence

Throughout the many advisories about how to build and maintain performing confidence, one recommendation remains basic and constant. You can be only what you think you are. You are the director you believe yourself to be. A second admonition is equally important: stay in control of that over which you have control. Let go of those factors over which you have no control. Ask of each factor: Is this under my control? If the answer is no, leave it. If the answer is yes, remember it and act upon it.

Self-Talk

For every event that occurs, you experience your own personal perception of it. That perception leads to self-talk, then feelings, both of which determine behavior. Consider the following scenario.

Event: *My choir received a medium rating from judges at a recent festival.*

In my control?

The outcome—the decision of the judges—is not in my control. Leave it.

Perception: *I'm not a good enough director to bring home prizes. Others are better. My choir will never get higher ratings.*

In my control?

Yes. I can choose to view the situation objectively. I can take control of the perception. The choir has made much improvement. How did it improve? I led them. I taught them. I drew it out of them. We are a much better group now than before, thanks to my leadership and direction. Did we do the best we are capable of just now? Yes.

Self-talk: *I cannot get these singers to perform as well as other choirs. They just aren't good. They'll never get better.*

In my control?

Yes. I can choose to reframe my self-talk. I have a plan for continued improvement of this choir. We have come far, and I am proud of that. Performance will only continue to improve. We should enjoy what we've accomplished. I should recognize that my planning and work have brought about this improvement. I am good at this!

Feelings: *Frustration, insecurity, unhappiness, anger, depression, rejection.*

In my control?

Yes. I can choose to frame my emotions positively. The medium rating actually indicates progress. I could not have taken this choir to a festival two years ago. Hurray! We're on our way up!

Behavior: *I am not as enthusiastic as before. I am less interested in tackling another festival or even putting much effort into rehearsal.*

In my control?

Yes. I owe it to the choir to acknowledge that we deserve to enjoy the progress we have made in two short years. I can evaluate the judges' comments and use them to set and prioritize goals. I can say to the choir, "Look how far we have come. Now here's where we're going."

The scenario developed above represents a performance cycle. Consider how the negative and positive responses affect the cycle. Perception, self-talk, and feelings dictate behavior. Behavior directly affects the event. Negative behavior leads to poor performance, a disappointing event. Positive behavior leads to positive preparation, contributing to the likelihood of a positive event. Although I have no control over a judge's decision, I do have control over my own mental preparation—and thus the preparation of my choir—for the festival.

Making Self-Talk Positive

In order to change your usual self-talk, it is important to devise and phrase self-affirmations properly. They should always be positive, based on the positive aspects, your conducting, and yourself as a person.

Changing self-talk from negative to positive is a valuable skill. The first step is to be aware of how much negative talk you speak. Then stop to restructure it. Try to frame the source of your negativity in a positive way, as if it were a challenge to enjoy meeting rather than an obstacle to overcome. It may be difficult and awkward at first but becomes easier with practice.

Exercise 9.3

Make a list of the typically negative things you say to yourself during rehearsals and performances. Reword them in a positive form. The opening words are most important. For example, change

I can't . . . to . . . I can
If only . . . to . . . When
I find it very difficult to . . . to . . . My challenge is to
I worry about . . . to . . . I will be OK because

Practice affirmation skills so that you can replace a negative thought with a positive one before it damages your performance.

How many times has someone said to you as you prepare to step onstage and join your choir, "Enjoy!" It is, however, not easy to enjoy performance if you are worried, upset, or negative about it or some part of your personal life. Nevertheless, enjoying is a crucial part of confidence. Most of the time enjoyment and confidence go hand in hand. In fact, it is difficult to feel positive about your performance if you are not actually enjoying it. Try to enjoy your rehearsals as well. Enjoy the feeling of conducting well. Enjoy the fruits of your rehearsal labors. Walk and talk in a positive way. Enjoy the challenge of conducting even when you believe it is not going well. Practice enjoying. The more you practice, the easier it will become. Take note of how you managed to energize yourself on a day that was not so good, and use that knowledge to repeat it another time. Not every session can be splendid, but most of them can be good when you focus on enjoyment.

For further help, see the section on refocusing contained in the sections on concentration and distractions, p. 280 and p. 299.

It is within your power to increase your self-confidence, but it takes practice.

Control only the controllables.

Know what and who you are.

9.5 Anxiety Level Control

To the performance psychologist, anxiety is a complex emotional state. To the general public, anxiety is synonymous with worry, fear, and forebodings. To a musician, it is public enemy number one. When performers freeze or commit a blunder in performance, anxiety is either the root cause or the outcome. The very nature of performance places stress on performers and makes demands of their mental and physical energy. Uncertainty, insecurity, and doubt are commonplace.

Anxiety and Perception

Whenever a performance is imminent, certain thoughts race through performers' minds. How important it is. How much it means to them. What could happen as a result? They question themselves: Will I do well? Will a good performance bring something great to this organization? What if I blunder? If I don't do well, will it detract from the choir's reputation?

Anxiety, characterized by worry and tension, is a demon for many. Public performance makes many performers anxious. There are, however, others who remain free from doubt and worries. Anxiety crushes some, while others use it to increase their confidence. How performers perceive their performance, what they say to themselves about that performance— these factors trigger emotional reactions.

So . . . if anxious performers could change their thinking about what the performance means to them . . . if they could change their view of their own ability . . . if they could frame a situation positively . . . then they could transform their emotional responses. The only change is in their self-perception, and in their interpretation of the performance. In short, changing perception can be the means to free them from fear and anxiety.

Some directors manage to conduct well, stay confident, maintain their focus without too much anxiety. It is possible. It is possible because anxiety is not an evil ogre waiting onstage. Anxiety is internal. It does not exist except inside thoughts, inside the performer's own head.

Stress resulting from anxiety is not imposed by other people or by the situation. One might feel anxious about certain circumstances, but one need not become anxious. The situation may be anxious-making, but the performer can react with anxiety or not. Ultimately, anxiety is always under one's own control.

Anxiety results from performers' perceptions of an imbalance between the demands of the situation and their sense of capability to meet the demands. Example: A director views a performance as very important but at the same time does not believe that the repertoire offered is "perfect enough," or is unconvinced that the performance can reach the required level. The imbalance, the difference between the two, causes anxiety and stress. To remain in control of anxiety, performers must keep the two sides in balance—that is, they must balance their perception of the performing situation and their belief in their own ability to handle that situation. Of course, goal setting and preparation play large roles in achieving that balance.

A certain level of anxiety is actually necessary to perform well—it raises the energy level—but too much anxiety exerts a negative influence on performance. Feeling anxious is fine; being unable to manage this anxiety is not. Ideal performance arousal levels require some anxiety, just enough to feel excited and eager to perform. The ability to manage an optimal level of anxiety or arousal at each performance is a skill that makes or breaks the ideal of consistently good performance.

What Kinds of Anxiety Are There?

The relationship between performance and the performer's arousal level is the result of the interaction between two kinds of anxiety: *cognitive* (mental) anxiety and *somatic* (physical) anxiety.

Cognitive anxiety results from concerns and worries about the demands of the situation. It fosters a lack of confidence and self-belief and an inability to concentrate. As a rule, cognitive anxiety begins to manifest days or weeks before the performance.

Somatic anxiety results from the information given to the performer by the body: butterflies in the stomach, sweaty palms, muscle tension, and frequent visits to the bathroom. Somatic anxiety shows itself much closer to performance time.

The newest research concludes that control of physical anxiety level must be accomplished before the performance begins. After that, it is generally too late to exercise power over it. An eminent British psychologist, Lew Hardy, has discovered that performance depends on a complex interaction between the two levels of anxiety. Given a relatively high physical anxiety but little worry, performance declines steadily. Given a high level of both mental and physical anxiety, arousal reaches an optimal level, after which the bottom drops out, hence the use of the word *catastrophe* by Hardy. Recovery from catastrophe takes longer than recovery from a slow decline. Given optimal levels of arousal, performance energy peaks.

The term "arousal" describes the interaction between the two types of anxiety. This interaction produces either a state of emotional readiness or one of instability. At one extreme of the arousal scale the performer is highly charged and "psyched up," perhaps even aggressive. At the opposite end the performer is calm and possibly even too relaxed. There is no standard ideal level of arousal. Each performer requires a personal and specific arousal level to perform well. Managing arousal requires first that performers identify their own ideal level of arousal. Identifying the ideal level requires self-awareness, objectivity, and an understanding that the level can vary depending upon the nature of the performance.

Exercises for Controlling Your Anxiety Level

Awareness Exercises

Before applying any strategies of anxiety management, you must recognize the symptoms of both physical and mental anxiety. Use the first two exercises below to reveal your pattern of anxiety and the accompanying symptoms.

Exercise 9.4

Check the following list of symptoms to see which you exhibit. Not all somatic symptoms are negative. The number and degree of symptoms can be too high or too low, according to your own ideal arousal level. However, the presence of physical symptoms together with mental symptoms may indicate a level of arousal gone too high. Then you will need to lower the level.

Mental Symptoms	*Physical Symptoms*
indecisiveness	pounding heart
feeling overwhelmed	increased respiration
inability to concentrate	decreased blood flow to the skin
feeling out of control	increased muscle tension
narrowing of attention	dry mouth
loss of confidence	trembling and twitching
fear	nausea, loss of appetite
irritability	increased adrenaline

Exercise 9.5

Think back to an ideal performance, one in which you and the choir performed very well. *This performance represents your ideal arousal zone.* Recall how you felt and everything you did before the performance: the travel arrangements, the time of arrival, the kind of warm-up, and so on. Note all the details that can be remembered. Detailed analysis will also offer an idea of how you reached the ideal level.

Imagery Exercise

Imagery is a potent method for coping with mental anxiety.

Recall your ideal performance (as in Exercise 9.5) and watch yourself in imagination conducting as well as you can. Infuse the image with as much sensory detail as possible. This is a very effective way to reduce mental anxiety. If repeated often, it becomes a reminder of how it feels to perform really well—fuel for the performer.

Reducing mental anxiety can also be accomplished by imaging scenes that produce great calm and relaxation, such as running water, a favorite bucolic setting, and so on.

Breathing Exercises

Breathing exercises are proven anxiety reducers. They bring the physical symptoms of anxiety under control and, even more important, alleviate or calm the mental symptoms.

EXERCISE 9.7

Inhale evenly through the nose, taking several long, deep breaths. Then exhale to the same count through the mouth. While exhaling, focus on your relaxed hands. Repeat the process, but this time focus on relaxed shoulders, jaw, or neck.

EXERCISE 9.8

Ratio breathing, also found on p. 272, combines relaxation and concentration. The length of the exhalation should always be double that of the inhalation. Before performance, inhale deeply through your nose to the count of five. Exhale through the mouth to the count of ten. During exhalation direct the focus to visualizing the performance going well.

Raising Low Arousal Levels

Performers may be so accustomed to thinking "calm down" that they do not recognize when the level is too low. These exercises will stimulate low mental and physical arousal levels.

1. Do a short physical workout like running in place. This raises the heartbeat.
2. Play music that energizes you or lifts your spirit.
3. Repeat strong verbal cues to lift the energy:

   This is tough music; I love it when it is hard to handle!
   I thrive on pressure. Let's go!
   I'm ready. Let it come!

Anxiety produces unsteadiness and apprehension, but it also actually offers performers a challenge and the chance to push back their own personal boundaries, all of which can be very liberating. This powerful combination of stress and uncertainty can be villain or friend. Accepting the challenge permits it to be a friend.

9.6 The Art of Concentration

The art of concentration is virtually the most important mental skill a performer can have. In order to expand performance boundaries, to employ hard-earned professional skills, and to experience the best of your ability, you must direct and control your concentration in performance.

At the outset, several points are salient:

The skill of concentration can be learned.
Your present ability can be improved.
Concentration can be used in two ways: highly tuned for a short time, or moderately tuned and extended for longer periods.
Concentration needs to be directed at something; it also needs to be flexible and multipurpose. Only then can it deal with all the demands of different performance situations.

Intensity, Focus, Attention, and Awareness

Concentration has three components, interrelated in the process:

Intensity: Concentrating is not about trying harder; it is about the performer's adeptness at using energy in a very focused way. Intense concentration requires a focus on one thing to the exclusion of all else.

Focus: Focus allows the performer to lock concentration on the task at hand, yet it should not be so rigid that it turns into tunnel vision. The focus needs to be adaptable to the many changes going on during performance.

Attention and Awareness: Effective concentration demands an interplay between these two factors. Awareness takes in the bigger picture, while attention is paid to only one thing, one object, person, note, phrase, tempo, and so on. Conductors need to remember the specifics of their work: tempi, cues (attention), but must also be sensitive to the singers, the instrumentalists (awareness).

At its best, concentration is a dynamic process that tunes into everything around you.

Relaxed Focus

Theoretically, once you have trained your body and nervous system to conduct a piece, you should be able to find a relaxed focus at will. However, when this proves difficult, the fault usually lies in a lack of focus or a misplaced focus. Not only must you practice so that you can perform your conducting skills flawlessly without much thinking but you also have the challenge of freeing the body and mind to connect totally with what you are trying to achieve. This demands a relaxed focus; this does not indicate a lack of intensity, but a mind that is clear of irrelevant thoughts and a body that is free from the wrong kind of tension. A relaxed focus during the music feels more like *being* than *doing*.

A relaxed focus between movements or between pieces includes:

The ability to relax and to recover, however short the time. Relax your muscles, lower your heartbeat through breathing, and recover from any emotional turmoil.

The ability to become aroused and full of energy in preparation for the next piece, no matter what the situation. Generate positive energy.

The ability to image and plan what you are going to do next and how you intend to do it. Imagine what you want to do. Focus on positive information only. Recall that the body can only do what the brain is thinking. If your thoughts are negative, the body will follow through. If your thoughts are positive, the body will do those positive things. You can afford only positive thoughts.

A relaxed focus denotes a body at ease but ready, and a mind calm but focused. However widely your concentration may vary in intensity and duration, a relaxed focus keeps you alert and relaxed throughout.

Exercises for Finding a Relaxed Focus

EXERCISE 9.10

Sit quietly and allow yourself to relax. Focus on one thing in the room. Anything will do: a flower, a texture, a color, a piece of fruit, your hand. Take in all the details. Observe how unique it is. Absorb yourself in it.

EXERCISE 9.11

Sit quietly and allow yourself to relax. Become aware of the whole room, train compartment, or office in which you are sitting. Take in all the details you can see without moving your head. Now switch your focus to an object very close to you. Focus on the one object. Take in all of its details. Do this until the other objects in the background are blurred. Connect very intensely with the object you have chosen.

EXERCISE 9.12

Switch the external focus on an object to an internal focus on yourself, your thoughts, your feelings, your emotions. The ability to switch focus is a vital skill for performers; it is, in fact, crucial. Do not get bogged down in a middle zone; be focused either internally or externally and aware of what you are doing. Staying with a wrong focus (a distraction, for example) invites the performance to sink out of sight. If you can switch, it means two important skills: that you recognize the need to refocus or change focus and that you have the ability to do so. You can practice this switching skill anywhere: walking in the park, in a restaurant, even in an office.

EXERCISE 9.13

Relax. Focus your attention on a particular thought. Any will do. Let your mind and thoughts wander. Then refocus on the original thought.

EXERCISE 9.14

When you feel distracted, practice clearing the distraction from your mind by zooming in on a chosen focus. Nothing else is important.

EXERCISE 9.15

Stand quietly. Relax. Think about a particular piece you are working on. Imagine how you will cue your singers to make that very first all-important entrance. Feel it; see it in the correct sequence. Note how good it sounds. Clear your mind. Now conduct the first entrance naturally and automatically.

EXERCISE 9.16

Relax. Prepare yourself to put the past and the future out of your mind while focusing on one phrase. Then remember how you managed this focus. Practice it every day.

EXERCISE 9.17

Relax. Focus on your body. Determine where tension lies and what feels good. Switch to a particular piece and focus on conducting it very well. Switch back to your body. Check it out. Is there tension? Are there good feelings? Switch back to your piece. Practice this every day, changing the selection regularly.

EXERCISE 9.18

Use cue words or triggers to keep your focus on the task at hand. Some cue words: *slow, smooth, glide, zap*. Some triggers: clench a fist; stamp a foot; take a small step.

Enhancing Your Concentration and That of Your Singers

Consider how easy it is to lose focus between movements of a longer piece or between programmed selections. To enhance concentration in such moments, adopt some of the following suggestions while preparing yourself in rehearsal:

1. Establish a pace for yourself between pieces. This is particularly important if you are feeling angry, nervous, or attempting to gain control. (When you feel out of control, you will almost certainly do everything more quickly. Watch for this.)
2. Practice some deep breathing between pieces. This helps you to relax and feel more in control.

3. Work at some of the imagery you have planned. It could be imagery to increase self-confidence or imagery for the music itself, or imagery of you beginning the next piece exactly as you wish to.

4. Establish a ritual or routine between pieces. Rituals help you remain focused, in control, and relaxed—dealing with pressure more effectively. Well-rehearsed and well-defined rituals prevent rushing into the next piece and prevent errors. Rituals might include any of these suggestions:

   A positive physical response—relaxation, breathing, or a positive image.

   A positive preparation. Know exactly how you wish to begin the next piece. Use positive imagery and positive self-talk.

   A positive mental focus. Focus on your enjoyment of conducting, with no technical focus. Use imagery skills to rehearse mentally how you want the first two or three notes to go. No self-talk. Just do it.

Other vulnerable performance moments—when you might get off track—can be tempo changes, a sudden change in forces such as a divisi or unison section, striking dynamic changes, and so on. Prepare some refocusing plans before the performance.

1. Go over your performance pieces in detail. Ask yourself: *if I were to lose concentration in this piece, where would it be likely to occur and why?*

2. Work out a very short refocusing plan to get back on track. It might include

   key words, such as, *calm, golden, control.*

   imagery: use an image that returns you to the feelings you want. Watch and feel yourself conducting very well. Or, choose to be like another conductor whom you admire. Use the qualities of that person as a basis for your imagery.

   physical response: choose one that will make you feel good, such as breathing, scanning the body to release tension, clenching a fist, readjusting your weight.

   any combination of the preceding: for example, say *calm*; see yourself loose, smiling, full of confidence; physically, feel your weight; feel light on your feet; relax.

It is important to prepare refocusing plans and to practice them in advance. You may not need them during the performance, but if a problem should divert your focus, you will need a plan. Such detailed preparation gives a feeling of security, of confidence, and of being in control. You've got it all covered.

9.7 Dealing with Distractions

Closely allied with the concentration and focus control, along with adapting to what is happening in performance and then refocusing while under pressure, is the issue of distractions. Clearly, performers differ in their concentration style. Performances themselves differ in the demands they place on one's concentration. Concentration problems usually occur, however, because of inappropriate attentional focus, or what might be referred to as giving in to a distraction.

External and Internal Distractions

Instead of focusing on relevant cues, performers are sometimes distracted by other events, thoughts, or emotions. Anything that is irrelevant to the task in hand is a potential distraction, whether external or internal.

External Distractions	Internal Distractions
background noises in the venue	thinking about other conductors
inappropriate talk by others	thinking about past events, like an error
passing airplanes, trains, cars	thinking about future tasks later in the piece
activity in the wings or in the audience	mental rehearsal at inappropriate time
noticing other conductors in the audience	dwelling on your own expectations
noticing family, teachers, or media present	judging yourself or analyzing your skills while conducting the performance

There are always copious distractions in the performing environment to compete for your attentional focus. The list of potential external distractions is endless. Because the performer has little control over most external factors, it is all the more imperative to cope effectively through proper concentration skills.

A concentration problem that plagues some performers is their inability to forget about what happened at a previous performance or earlier in the present piece. This type of internal focus has been the downfall of many. It is also all too easy to focus on the future consequences of present actions: *What if I give a good/poor performance?* The question is irrelevant to the here and now. Worrying about what might happen acts as a pure distraction, causing anxiety, muscle tension, and tentative performance. It is vital to stay in the present. Another inappropriate attentional focus is focusing internally for too long. Getting stuck inside your head prevents attending to important cues from the environment. Both internal and external focus is needed, and, with those, the ability to switch between them.

Keeping Your Focus

What procedures will help you to remain connected to the performance and focused on what you are doing?

1. Arrive early, especially if the venue is unknown to you, or gain access to the venue at another earlier date. It is of inestimable value to become accustomed to the place, thus eliminating those kinds of distractions.
2. Build distractions into your pre-performance rehearsal time. Conduct as if the performance is actually taking place in the designated venue.
3. If rehearsal in the venue is limited, try to get as much information as possible about it from acquaintances who have performed there. If that is not possible, imagine yourself conducting well in a place where you always do well.

The key skills in dealing with distractions of any kind are

the ability to become *aware* that you are distracted;
the ability to then *relax*; and
the ability to *cope* by switching your focus away from the distraction.

Being able to switch and refocus is a lifesaver when it comes to avoiding distractions. Learn to do it and make it a priority.

1.1 Vocal Health Guidelines for Singers

General Guidelines to Vocal Misuse Issues

Most choral directors lose a significant number of singers to various vocal problems and illnesses at almost any time of year. Amateur singers shrug off vocal problems as inevitable and unavoidable. It is a good idea for you to discuss with them some basic health rules for singers. You are probably the only person in their lives who is in a position to apprise them of ways to keep their voices healthy.

After providing the general guidelines that follow below, be sure to remind your singers of specific pitfalls at appropriate times—for example, during football season, when there should be no shouting from the stands. Perhaps it will be helpful to have an assistant develop these guidelines into a handout.

Avoid throat clearing and other odd vocal noises. Throat clearing should not be done more than twice a day. Instead, try a hard swallow (two fingers on the Adam's apple, apply light pressure, and swallow hard), or drink some water. Be careful not to cough and then clear your throat. Throat clearing and yelling during sports events are vocally abusive.

Drink no more than two cups of caffeine drinks and no more than one glass of acidic juice per day. Caffeine dries the cords. Dry cords don't vibrate efficiently. Remember that chocolate has a lot of caffeine. Acidic juices also dry the cords. Using a cold-air humidifier at night is a good idea.

Drink at least eight eight-ounce glasses of water per day. The vocal cords like to be moist. They operate better that way. Drink water, not caffeine products.

Avoid smoke, smoking, and excessive use of alcohol. Alcohol dries out vocal cords. If you must drink, alternate with water to keep your cords moist.

Do not scream or yell unless it is an emergency. Walk to other parts of the house when you need to speak to someone. Get a whistle for your pet. Try to cushion all the sounds you say with a puff of air.

Avoid talking in loud settings. Use the lower end of your loudness range. In loud public places get near the person you are addressing and talk in his or her ear.

Do not talk too long without pausing to renew your breath. Air supports your voice. Breathe! Slowing down your rate of speech will help. One breath every twelve to fifteen syllables is best.

Do not hold your breath and speak. Speak on lots of air. Holding your breath while listening to someone else also overworks the voice. Breathe!

Do not punch your words or chop up your phrases. Do not whisper. Powerful punching speech is impressive but abusive to cords. Easy speech is better. Don't whisper; use a soft voice. Use a loudness level as if you were addressing one or two people standing three feet away.

Always talk while maintaining a proper sitting/standing posture. Good posture will help the lungs provide better air support.

Reduce vocal demand by speaking less. If it is your job that requires lots of talking, find ways outside the job to reduce vocal demand. Don't speak in a monotone. Use all the sounds in the range of your voice. Try to rest your voice for fifteen minutes per hour. After overuse of the voice, rest it.

Relax. Don't allow anger, tension, or frustration to fill your days. Anger, tension, and frustration will cause you to use your voice less efficiently. Learn to feel when the neck and voice area is tense. Relax this area as well.

Hormonal Problems

The facts of hormonal influence on vocalism are clear. It is a medical fact that the accumulation of fluid alters vibratory characteristics of the vocal folds during and before the menstrual period, producing loss of vocal efficiency, endurance, and range, resulting in vocal fatigue and reduced vocal control. Endocrine concerns such as thyroid dysfunction cause shifts within a person's entire life span, causing muffled sound, loss of range, and vocal sluggishness in general. As women approach menopause, vocal fatigue increases and vocal control decreases. A choral director who creates an atmosphere where vocal health is taught and respected will have choristers who monitor themselves vocally and who make an appropriate and independent decision to sing or lay out, while continuing to pay close attention.

Occupational Hazards

Most choral singers earn their living outside of the performing arts. Some of these jobs are actually injurious to the voice and vocal health. They include

> any job in an environment that is filled with cigarette smoke;
> any job in which the singer must talk over loud noise, such as being a bartender or waiter; or
> any job whose description dictates constant talking, such as being a teacher or telemarketer.

Smoking bans are felicitous for singers and others who are bothered by smoke. Restaurants and offices that are free of smoke make it possible for singers, who must depend on part-time employment of that kind, to elect table-waiting and computer temping. Occupations that require constant use of the voice remain totally debilitating and should be avoided by singers.

1.2 Illness and Medications

Singers live in a different world than other human beings. A cold is a disaster; allergies are much more than a nuisance. Even the fear that these health conditions might materialize at inopportune times is enough to trigger problems. Having some idea of how to cope with these common issues makes a big difference in singers' ever-vulnerable confidence levels. The following suggestions were advanced by the first otolaryngologist to become renowned for his research into the medical and psychological problems experienced by singers—Dr. Van Lawrence.[1] Some of these suggestions, although lacking empirical evidence, are still embraced by singers because of their need to do something about colds and allergies, their mortal enemies.

What to Do about Colds

Is this a scenario that strikes dread into your heart? It is three weeks before the big Christmas concert. You have spent the entire fall preparing an extensive program of important and difficult music. A cold passes through the choir, decimating your forces. Each rehearsal is attended by different healthy singers and missed by different singers whom the cold has laid low. No one is quite sure whether what is going around is a cold or the flu. You wonder why your singers always get a cold just when a performance is coming. You wonder whether singers with a cold should come to the rehearsal and risk infecting others. Clearly, if you could teach your singers to sidestep just one cold per winter season, your life would be much easier.

Coughs, headaches, sore throats, and runny noses are hallmarks of both colds and the flu. Colds start slowly; the flu hits all at once and is accompanied by muscle aches, chills, and a high fever. Only two or three strains of viruses cause flu each year; colds are caused by hundreds of different viruses.

Think of the cold infection as an iceberg. At the bottom is exposure but no infection because the virus is washed out of your nose. The next level is infection but no symptoms, because, although the virus is in your nose, although it replicates and infects you, although you generate antibodies, white blood cells throw it out, so you don't even know you've had a cold. The next level is mild symptoms: the virus is in the nose, but your only symptom might be a dry throat. You still don't know that you've had it. At the top of the iceberg are severe symptoms. The virus gets in the nose and the symptoms knock you out.

Most colds are picked up at home, where there is close personal contact. A cold is actually quite difficult to catch. The virus must get inside the human nose. It travels mainly by touch. Fingers become contaminated by touching communal objects, such as doorknobs, that have been touched by someone with an infection. Then it's easy to pass the virus on from fingers into your nose or into your eyes, which drain into the nose. Colds are *not* airborne.

It is suggested that severe symptoms are triggered by stress. Stress depresses the immune system. It increases the release of steroid hormones and dampens the immune responses. This is why your singers often get colds just when they do not want them. If they keep the symptoms mild, it won't matter how many colds they have.

Here are some suggestions for handling colds. Make them known to your people. It could make a difference.

> *What to do before you get a cold*: Prime your immune system into the peak of health. Take one of the substances that stimulate the immune system and increases the number of circulating white blood cells. Many singers have found that eating unsociable amounts of garlic (an antiviral) is helpful. Even if eating garlic simply makes the singer believe that it is doing some good, it might be worth it. Exercise in a nonstressful way—a daily walk is enough to send the white blood cells into circulation. As medical studies on the efficacy of herbal remedies continue, singers must keep abreast of the research results. Medical thinking changes often.
>
> *What to do when you get the first signs of a cold*: Wait until tomorrow and see how far up the iceberg the virus has climbed. Or try sucking zinc lozenges (might help; can't hurt). Forget vitamin C (see p. 297). Stay positive.
>
> *What to do tomorrow if the symptoms are severe*: Take painkillers—ibuprofen, acetaminophen, *not* aspirin—in dosages prescribed on pack. Although long-term use of nasal decongestant sprays can be addicting, for one or two days use a spray morning or evening to help relieve your swollen blood vessels. Along with it, drink copious amounts of water to ease drying of the vocal tract. Drink hot lemon and honey all day for soothing effect; it will not cure. Nor will chicken soup (although it feels good), but putting jalapeño peppers in it might promote airway secretions that will treat your sore throat and cough. Eat curry for the same reason. Do stress-free exercise. Go to work. Go to the rehearsal. Remain relentlessly positive.
>
> *What to do when your kids bring their colds home*: Treat your home like a sterile unit for a week. Wash your hands and your children's hands often. Force yourself and the children not to rub eyes or touch noses with unwashed fingers. Stay positive.
>
> *What to do when you travel by air*: Pack hand sanitizers. Use them every five minutes. To aid your effort to restrict touching your eyes

or nose, thereby passing germs along, treat the toilet door handle as though it were radioactive, also the headsets. If someone is hacking and sneezing a few rows ahead of you, remind yourself that the air on planes circulates from top to bottom of the cabin, out through the floor, not from end to end. Don't rub your tired eyes. Don't touch your nose. Stay positive.

Home Remedies

Singers are loath to go to a doctor when the malady that is beginning to show up is clearly just a mild cold. See the following sections of appendix 1.2, which are extrapolated from an article written for *The NATS Journal* (1985) by the late Van Lawrence, M.D.

Most singers are extraordinarily sensitive to the signs that some respiratory event of an infectious nature is about to take place. Following is a list of home remedies for singers to try when they feel in the early stages of some sort of trouble. Before going to the doctor, these are some professionally recommended solutions to the problem.

Early Upper Respiratory Infection

Most doctors have not seen a standard upper respiratory infection (a cold) in many years. Rather, they see an endless series of lower respiratory infections. These are more severe in terms of malaise and of time; they involve the trachea and bronchial tree. Usually this does not affect the larynx unless the patient coughs so hard that a secondary laryngitis is produced. The prevalence of lower respiratory infections would indicate that there has been a decided shift in the predominant group of viruses causing the respiratory tract infections that have been afflicting the vocal community. The early symptoms of upper respiratory infection and lower respiratory infection will be similar in most regards, as will what can be done at home.

At the first suggestion of an impending infection, the first recommendation would be that you pay close attention to the basics:

hydration
hydration
hydration

The environmental humidity should be a minimum of 40 percent. (During the initial space flights healthy astronauts invariably caught colds while they were in the capsules. When NASA increased the cabin humidity to 40 percent, virus propagation was interfered with and astronauts caught fewer colds.) In addition, monitor your body water levels by paying close attention to urine color. As long as what your kidney produces is the color of tap water, you can be certain that you are adequately hydrated.

If possible, go straight to bed. Physical rest and emotional rest are basic in early stages. Using rest properly should at least reduce the severity of the inflection, even if it does not block it completely. This is not the time to stay awake until 3:00 or 4:00 A.M.

In addition, many singers have found that keeping an upbeat frame of mind will lessen the capacity to "catch" someone else's cold. It has also become apparent that viral reproduction is inhibited by small increases in temperature. Thus, it is a good idea to induce a mild temperature elevation and sweat a bit in a sauna.

Megadoses of vitamin C are mildly antihistaminic in effect. Thus, they do dry secretions up a bit and will be helpful when allergies present. If you have not been eating well, vitamin C will improve your general physical condition. Other than this, vitamin C will do nothing for your cold.

Consider the gentle and cautious use of over-the-counter preparations. If you are genuinely in the early stages of respiratory infection and your nose is pouring hot water and your eyes are red-rimmed and weepy, the cautious and judicious use of antihistamines, four milligrams, is probably not a bad idea for controlling the messiness of these early stages of a cold. If you totally stop the flow of secretion you will prolong the duration of the infection, as you will if you decongest the nose as well.

Working out the virus as speedily as possible requires the wetness and the blockage. But congested noses are miserable to live with. Therefore, short-term use of an oral decongestant is very helpful. If you have a blood pressure problem or a tendency to be sleepless with coffee, such a medication after lunch and during the afternoon is not a good idea. Finally, the judicious and cautious use of a mild nosedrop, such as pediatric-strength Neosynephrine ($1/4$ percent) for the first few days will not do irreparable damage and may permit you to go to sleep. Remember that prolonged use—some say more than three consecutive days—of nasal decongestants can be addicting.

If you turn up a temperature elevation of more than $2/10$ or $3/10$ of a degree above the normal reading, there may be more involved than just a simple cold. Under these circumstances, help is recommended. Get to a doctor.

Awakening in the Morning with a Foggy Voice

In this scenario there will often be no other symptoms suggesting a respiratory tract infection, and the patient will not usually feel sick. The voice is simply foggy and waterlogged, refusing to respond at first breath. The culprit is often allergies, or a manifestation of an allergy with congestion of the entire respiratory tract from the nose down to the lungs. If the patient is allergic and lying horizontally, in all likelihood there will be congestion of the recumbent side of the nose at least, if not the upper side as well, and certainly there will be congestion within the larynx.

Get up; take a hot shower; move around a bit. Then begin customary vocal warm-up. If the customary time is twenty minutes, and if, after twenty minutes, the voice has not returned, chances are not good that it will return with your further efforts. You should think about seeking further help. One other early remedy is the application of local heat. Spend thirty or forty minutes in a hot, steamy environment. Keep a hot compress on the neck. An upright position helps in the draining of edema fluid. If there are other symptoms that suggest the presence of an allergy rather than a cold, one might consider the judicious employment of an antihistamine. Although they provide some relief for symptoms, antihistamines offer no help to a cold, only to allergies. If the voice has not returned after one's customary warm-up period, it is not likely to do so later on.

Sore Throat on Awakening during the Night or Early in the Morning

Being untrained medically, you must be cautious about making self-examinations and diagnoses. However, if you are accustomed to looking at the back of your throat and recognize color changes in your pharynx, then the following information might be helpful. Take a flashlight in one hand. Then, using a spoon handle or a dinner knife blade as a tongue depressor, look at your throat in the mirror. Compare the color of the back wall of the throat with the color of the soft palate and the lining of your cheeks. If the back wall is considerably redder, you are probably incubating a viral infection or a bacterial infection. Take your temperature. A temperature elevation is significant in this circumstance. It would suggest a possible need for medical attention for your impending viral or bacterial infection. Try such things as resting and hydrating yourself, and give it time.

On the other hand, if the back wall of your throat does not appear to be particularly red, it may be that an allergy is acting up again, and that you mouth-breathed, unaware, throughout the night. If so, being awake and drinking hot liquids appears to be of help to many singers, and it feels good. A recipe for a good gargle is one half teaspoon of table salt, one half teaspoon of baking soda, one half teaspoon of white Karo syrup, all mixed into eight ounces of warm water. Use liberally. Sugar or a sweet taste in the mouth promotes, for most people, salivation and an increase in mucous flow and mucous production.

Laryngeal congestion in the morning, especially with singers, is most likely to suggest reflux as opposed to allergies or an incipient cold. A discussion of reflux follows later in this appendix. Be very careful about throat lozenges or throat sprays that contain a local anesthetic. Dulling your sensory input from throat wall, tongue base, and soft palate can be bad news. If you are using or are going to use the voice for singing or acting, and your sensory input for throat wall pressure is reduced, or your awareness of the tongue base location is fuzzy, it is possible that you could overblow the instrument, or at least misuse it. Nonanesthetic sprays and lozenges are all right. If they do provoke salivary flow and mucous secretion, then they will help. Flooding the nose is helpful for very few nasal conditions, even if the solution is precisely prepared to an exact degree of salinity. You might injure the delicate cellular linings and impede the ciliary action that accomplishes the clearing of the very mucous cover that lines the entire vocal and respiratory tract.

General Malaise

"I feel bad all over." This is often the harbinger of viral illness or an infectious process of some kind. Go to bed and rest. Cancel all voluntary activities. Simply rest and wait until the story works itself out: The bad feeling disappears, or rash appears, or diarrhea and nausea begin. Do you really have a fever? Beware frequent use of aspirin. It increases capillary fragility and interferes with blood coagulation, predisposing you to vocal fold hemorrhage and its sequelae.

If you keep wet and hydrated, rested, and "up," and if you eat a good diet and regularly get eight hours of sleep, you probably won't need home remedies.

Gastroesophageal Reflux Disease (GERD)

Choral directors and nonsingers are puzzled by the seemingly sudden appearance of a "new" medical condition being blamed for all singer ills, referred to as reflux. Ten years ago an average group of people would never have heard of gastroesophageal reflux disease (GERD). In the twenty-first century, doctors have discovered that almost all singers with good breath support and almost all singers of advanced age are afflicted with the disease. GERD causes the tissue around the arytenoids to swell up. When the singer tries to put the cords together for high notes, it is not possible to do so.

Identified by its acronym, GERD is not life-threatening but it is a threat to vocal health. It is a condition in which some of the stomach acid leaks out of the stomach and into the esophagus and throat. When this acid irritates the throat, it also can irritate the vocal-cord area. This can cause the symptoms listed above, even muscle spasms in the throat. Reflux usually occurs at night when the person is sleeping. When we sleep, the stomach muscles and the esophagus relax and open slightly. This can allow some of the stomach acid to travel from the stomach to the esophagus and irritate the back of the throat where the vocal cords sit.

Although it is often mistaken for a sore throat, asthma, or a respiratory illness, the symptoms are

> burning in the laryngeal area,
> nonproductive coughing, especially in the morning,
> hoarseness, especially in the morning,
> bad taste in the mouth or bad breath,
> soreness in the laryngeal area,
> throat clearing that increases after eating,
> excessive mucous production,
> lump-in-the-throat feeling, and
> reddening of the vocal cords, swollen tissue near the back of the cords.

Reflux is sometimes caused by hiatal hernia. To test for a hiatal hernia, do the following:

1. Drink a pint of liquid.
2. Lie flat on your back immediately and stay there for forty-five seconds.
3. Turn on your right side and stay there for forty-five seconds.
4. Now stand up and bend over as far as you can to touch your toes. Hold that position for forty-five seconds. If you regurgitate or feel the liquid rising into your chest or mouth, the esophageal sphincter is open, permitting an esophageal reflux. See a doctor.

If you do have a hiatal hernia, do not eat at any time close to going to bed.

However, it is not necessary to have a hiatal hernia to develop reflux. Because singers perform at night, they like to eat afterward and then go to bed. If your stomach is full and you lie down, you will get reflux. Gas and stomach acid will seep back up onto the vocal cords, and you will feel as if you are choking and you may have a bitter taste in your mouth. This is because the cords or the arytenoids are in spasm.

Helpful Remedies

1. Physicians prescribe the use of medicines like Axid, Prilosec, Pepcid, and Zantac. (Some counsel against the use of Tagamet.) Over-the-counter antacids like Tums, Rolaids, Maalox, or Mylanta are also useful; taking two tablespoons of Maalox or Mylanta before bed-time can be helpful.
2. Changing the diet is a must.

   Learn to eat more, smaller meals during the day, rather than one or two big meals.
   Do not eat during the two hours before going to bed or lying down.
   Avoid smoking or tobacco, caffeine, and alcohol.
   Avoid chocolate, mints, nuts.
   Avoid ice cream, because it is fatty.
   Carbohydrates are fine because they can be digested rapidly.
   Limit dairy product consumption, especially late at night.
   Limit spicy, fried, or high-acid foods, especially late at night.
   Drink at least eight eight-ounce glasses of water each day.
   Avoid foods that cause heartburn or indigestion, such as tomatoes.

3. Changing behavior and environment has a major effect.

   Sleep with the head elevated.
   Place blocks under the head of your bed or purchase a wedge pil-low. Most people experience a reduction of symptoms if the bed is elevated six to twelve inches, or if a foam wedge is sub-stituted for a pillow. The larynx must be higher than stomach level.
   Don't sleep on your right side. That favors reflux and causes symptoms.
   Do not wear clothing that is tight around the waist. This encour-ages reflux.
   Do not eat two or three hours before going to bed at night.
   Reduce stress. Exercise regularly.
   Do not exercise or lift heavy items immediately after eating.

The newest prescribed regimen for sufferers of GERD is in constant fluctuation. A visit to a medical professional is a must when no relief ar-rives after following the general admonitions above.

1.3 Pharmacological Recommendations

Please consult with a medical professional before deciding to take any medication, in order to make sure that it would be right for you and to find out about possible side effects and complications. The following section provides only recommendations.

Medicines for Allergies and Colds

Any sort of inflammatory condition affects the mucosal lining. (Mucosa: the wet covering of sinus and nose linings, mouth, middle ear, all the way down to the lungs and out to the alveolae.) All these surfaces are covered with mucosa lining, which contains mucous and goblet cells. Mucous cells and goblet cells are fluid-secreting. Most medications taken for symptomatic relief of colds, allergies, or other inflammatory conditions will alter the mucous secretions of the muscosa.

> If the cells secrete more, there will be a wetter vocal tract.
> If the cells secrete less, there will be a drier vocal tract.

Medications can increase mucous production, decrease inflammation or pain. All these effects will influence vocalization.

Antihistamines

In mucosal surfaces there are cells that mediate infectious and traumatic inflammation (even that caused by smoking). When a person has such an inflammation, the body releases certain chemicals, one of which is histamine, an inflammatory chemical, which is an acute response. Once histamine is released, it cannot be stopped, but antihistamines prevent its effects by blocking the body's receptors. There are other chemicals released, as well, but they are slower acting. The slower-acting chemicals respond better to steroids than to antihistamines.

Antihistamines are best taken orally, and early on, because histamine's effects come early in illness. Antihistamines' usual properties include sedation, although now some are available that do not sedate.

- Those with sedating potential include Benadryl, Atarax, Tavist, Chlortrimaton, and Trenalyn.
- Those with nonsedating potential include Hismanal (slow and sustained), Claritin, and Allegra.

The advantage of taking antihistamines is that they will give relief if the patient has allergies and hypersecretions (copious amounts of drainage) and thus irritation. The drawback to taking antihistamines is that they are drying agents, and therefore they thicken the mucous. The vocal cords will be afflicted, and the singer will have a harder time clearing mucous from the cords. Singers should double their intake of water when taking antihistamines.

Decongestants

The primary purpose of decongestants is to decrease swelling in the nasal area, but decongestants will affect other areas as well.

- Decongestants include Entex, Sudafed, and Zephrex.

All three of these drugs have adrenalinlike properties. Their side effects include dryness, tremor, or rapid heartbeat.

Decongestant/Antihistamine Combinations

- These drugs include Dimetapp, Actifed, and Tavis.
- Rutas is a combination drug that is very powerful and is not recommended for singers.

Corticosteroids

The vocal cords have a poor lymphatic supply, and the fluids in body tissues are governed by the lymphatics. Thus if one gets fluid in the spaces between the muscle fibers of the vocal cords it is hard to remove. Steroids help to get rid of some of the proteins that bind the fluid there; this gets fluid out of your cords and your nose. Diuretics will not do this job. The best bet is a topical or systemic corticosteroid.

If the cords are sore and inflamed, steroids will make them feel better, but there are disadvantages to their use as well. After taking steroids, a singer's voice does not seem normal, even though singing is exceedingly comfortable and easy.

Steroids affect the entire body. They are normally produced by the adrenal glands, which secrete more steroids in the daytime (when you need them) than at night. This is part of the reason why patients complain of more discomfort at night. If the patient takes steroids from outside, such as pills, the body knows that it contains too many steroids and shuts down the adrenal glands. Then the body is living on outside steroids, which is called steroid dependence. The results can include arthritis and joint pain; efforts to stop dependence can lead to water-weight gain and withdrawal symptoms. Because of the danger of steroid dependence, steroids should not be taken more than once every three months

There are topical steroids and systemic steroids, each of which has its advantages and disadvantages.

Topical Corticosteroids

- Vanceril, Beclovent, Vancenase, Beconase, Asthmacort, Rhinocort, and Nasacort are used for asthma and laryngitis (nose and lungs). Once inhaled, they go into the vocal tract, onto the vocal cords, and into the lungs. They help to reduce inflammation and help with lingual tonsilitis.
- Some of these drugs, such as Nasalide, are suspended in an irritating liquid.
- Vasoconstrictors like Neosynepherine and Afrin can become habit-forming; when they are used excessively, the nasal membranes become tired of constricting and give up. However, if the singer limits use to two sprays three times a day, it can be used long-term. They are not absorbed systemically.
- Becanade and Masenade are not habit-forming. They are used in the nose to prevent allergic rhinitis. They reduce inflammation in the turbinate membranes without causing sedation, and they prevent chronic inflammatory factors from producing prolonged swelling.

Systemic Corticosteroids

Systemic steroids have an effect on the entire body. They reduce edemal fluid and can be used for arthritis, hoarseness, rhinitis, or any type of swelling. Systemic steroids affect not just the cords themselves but also address inflammation and edema fluid in the intrinsic muscles of the larynx, which control the cord and arytenoid movements.

- Medrol, Aristocort, and Prednisone knock out inflammation. As long as the problem is allergic, traumatic, or irritant, these drugs are fine. Just be sure they are not masking another disease.

These drugs are good for a quick bailout, never for a chronic vocal-cord problem. They can be used as a last-ditch helper if a big performance is coming up, although the singing range might be lower even though the patient is on the medication, because the cords have edema.

When to use systemic steroids, then? During the fall weed season you may have an acute allergy reaction. You will release histamine, so there is a need for an antihistamine. If inflammation builds up, take a steroid briefly to get rid of it.

Topical Vasoconstrictors

- These include Afrin and Neosynephrine, which are all right for most people, even singers. All give very quick relief from nasal congestion, but use must be short-term (not for more than three days).

After three days there will be a rebound effect: The blood vessels get tired and just stop constricting. The rebound will last for three or four days. You may have a hemorrhage of the vocal cords, because the vocal cords have poor lymphatics. A hemorrhage can create scar tissue, which will interfere with adduction of the cords. The rebound effect could also affect one cord, giving aperiodical vibration.

It is possible to use steroid spray and elevate the bed at night so that there is no fluid in the head that swells the nasal passages, then use a decongestant during the day.

Adrenergenics (Stimulants)

- Epinephrine, Proventil, Ventolin, Broncaid, and Primatene are sympathetic nervous system stimulants, mostly for asthmatics. These drugs open up bronchial airways to give better breathing. However, they tend to reduce mucous production of the lungs.
- During acute, severe allergic attacks (such as bee stings, asthma, or angioedema of the tongue, lips, or vocal cords), adrenalin can be used. The narrowest part of the vocal cord is in a subglottic area and can swell.

Mucolytics

Mucolytics act to break down or lower the viscosity of mucous. They include the following:

- Water!!!!! Drink eight eight-ounce glasses of water daily.
- Guifenasin, sold under the brand names Humibid and Guaifid. Humibid will thin mucous and works well with water. It will not

make the patient nervous or jittery. The latest research maintains that guifenasin will exacerbate reflux problems.

- Phenylephrine, sold as Entex, is an expectorant and a vasoconstrictor. For most patients, these two functions are well balanced and little drying occurs. Use when both expectorant and decongestant functions are needed. Entex also thins and increases secretions. It is therefore good for those who complain of thick secretions, frequent throat clearing, or postnasal drip. Other mucolytics include

Organidin (organified iodine)
Moistur 10 (artificial saliva)

Miscellaneous Drugs That Affect the Vocal Tract

- Diuretics: Lasix, Hydrodiuril, and Dyazide. All three dry the vocal cords.
- Beta blockers: Inderal and Tenormin. Beta blockers block the effects of the sympathetic system, and can be positive for singers at times: for example, stage fright with tremor can be helped.
- Nonsteroid Anti-inflammatory Drugs (NSAIDs): Ibuprofen, Aspirin, Ansaid, and Feldene, etc. These drugs thin the blood; one aspirin will thin the blood for a week. If the patient is singing hard while taking these drugs, he or she could risk a vocal-cord hemorrhage.

The "Aspirin Triad" consists of sensitivity to aspirin, nasal polyps, and asthma. A patient with any of these three conditions cannot take any of these drugs.
Tylenol will reduce fever and reduce pain but is not anti-inflammatory.

- Cough preparations: Opiates, Dextromethorphan, and Tessalon.

Codeine dampens the cough reflex. A cough traumatizes the cords. Suppress that cough!
Tessalon and Xylocaine are used in surgery to knock out cough reflex. This is generally worth doing for a singer, since coughing does such damage to the cords.
You can also use an expectorant.

- Cromolyn Sodium: Intal and Nasalcrom. These drugs are inhaled and are used for allergies. They keep the tissues from releasing histamine.

Appendix 2
Stemple's Vocal Function Exercises

The goals of physiologic vocal therapy are to modify and improve laryngeal muscle strength, tone, balance, and stamina. The practitioners seek to improve the balance among these processes: (1) laryngeal muscle effort, (2) respiratory effort and control, (3) supraglottic modification of laryngeal tone, and (4) attention to the health of mucus membranes, that is, in terms of hydration and reflux disease. Of the various orientations of vocal therapy, physiologic therapy in these exercises is the only one based on knowledge of vocal function evaluated through objective voice assessment including acoustic, aerodynamic, and stroboscopic analyses.

Question: of what use could such exercises be to choral conductors? Answer: they can encourage their singers to do them daily, since completion of these exercises takes such a short time. They will improve the vocalism of untrained singers because they actually improve vocal function. They are also useful to directors who seek to improve and maintain their own vocal function. Directors do a great deal of speaking, sometimes over the full sound of the choir, a vocally debilitating practice. Bear in mind, however, that the results will come over a long term, not swiftly. Although devised some time ago by a speech therapist, they are now widely put to use by otolaryngologists. They can also be used for cooling the system down after rehearsals or performances.

Vocal Function Exercises are a series of systematic voice manipulations, similar to physical therapy for the vocal folds. They were designed to strengthen and balance the laryngeal musculature, balancing airflow to muscular effort. The advantage of direct exercise is the coordination of many laryngeal muscle activities with respiration as a series of related actions. The exercises also address indirectly problems such as tone focus, onset of vocal-fold vibration, and laryngeal area tension.

Normal voicing is dependent upon a balance between three subsystems: respiration, phonation, and resonance. Whenever one system is disturbed, other systems will adjust to accommodate the disturbance. Adjustments tend to unbalance the vocal system, the result being inappropriate voice production. Whole body health is necessary for good vocal health.

On all the exercises the tone should be monitored for voice breaks, wavering, and breathiness. All exercises should be done as softly as possible. Because it is more difficult to produce soft tones, the vocal subsystems will receive a better workout than if louder tones were sung. Extreme care should be taken to sing a forward tone that lacks laryngeal tension, using just the efficiency of the cord vibrations. Vowels should be postured before inhalation. An easy, not breathy, onset should be encouraged.

Maximum phonation time increases as efficiency of vocal-fold vibration improves. The time does not increase because of supposedly improved "lung capacity." Even aerobic exercise does not improve lung capacity. It is, rather, the efficiency of oxygen exchange with the circulatory system that increases the time, thus giving the singer a sense of "more air."

Singers are encouraged to make a graph on which to mark times from each exercise and the progress attained. Because of normal daily variability, singers should not compare today with tomorrow, and so on. Weekly comparisons are better. The estimated time of completion for the program is six to eight weeks.

Each exercise is to be done two times in a row, the series done two times per day. No artistry is required, just bare function; for example, one does not have to sing low pitches to work on muscles that permit a singer to access low notes.

EXERCISE A.1 WARM-UP EXERCISE

Sustain an [i] vowel as long as possible on F above middle C for females and F below middle C for males. Placement of the tone should be extremely forward, almost but not quite nasal. Production should be as soft as possible, but not breathy, in order to engage the vocal subsystems.

The goal of Exercise A.1 is based on reaching 100 ml/sec of airflow volume. If the volume is equal to 4,000 ml, then the goal is 40 seconds. When an airflow measure with the proper machinery is not available, the goal can be equal to the longest [s] the singer is able to sustain.

EXERCISE A.2 STRETCHING EXERCISE

Glide (or slide) from the lowest possible note that phonates to the highest note possible, on the word *knoll*. The goal is to have no breaks. A very forward placement of tone is necessary. When breaks occur, the glide should be continued without hesitation. If the voice breaks at the top of the range, even though the singer believes himself or herself to have more range, the glide may be continued without voice. The folds will continue to stretch. Do not lateralize the lips. Go up to the highest note and stop.

Gliding forces the use of all the laryngeal muscles, stretches the vocal folds, encourages systematic, slow engagement of the cricothyroid muscles. Glides improve muscular control and flexibility.

EXERCISE A.3 CONTRACTING EXERCISE

Glide from the highest note to the lowest note on the word *knoll*. The goal is to have no breaks. Institute a feeling of more space in the throat on the way down. A downward slide encourages a slow, systematic engagement of the thyroarytenoid muscle.

EXERCISE A.4 POWER EXERCISE

Sustain C, D, E, F, and G for as long as possible on the vowel [o]: C4 for women; C3 for men. The goal is the same as for Exercise A.1. As the singer begins to run out of air, the large vertical abdominal muscle [rectus abdominus] should be pushed, not the throat. Permit the vocal cords to do the job.

Some singers experience minor laryngeal aching for the first day or two of the program. It is similar to a muscle ache that might occur with any new muscular exercise. It will soon subside. Singers are encouraged to continue the program through the discomfort.

APPENDIX 3
Performance Profile Chart

Date	Performance or Rehearsal

Quality	Assessment
	0 1 2 3 4 5 6 7 8 9 10

_____

_____

_____

_____

_____

_____

_____

_____

_____

_____

_____

_____

Elements to Be Worked On

1. _____   3. _____
2. _____   4. _____

Note: This table is adapted for choral use from Shirlee Emmons and Alma Thomas, *Power Performance for Singers* (New York: Oxford University Press, 1998), and is used by permission.

APPENDIX 4

"*Choral Tessituras*" (*A Statement of the American Academy of Teachers of Singing*)

Problems of Tessitura in Relation to Choral Music

It is common knowledge that a great many teachers of singing hesitate to permit their pupils to participate in choral singing because experience has proven that, due to the unusually high *tessitura* dominating the arrangements of many choral works, harm is done to the voice.

The subject of *tessitura* involves certain basic facts pertaining to the safe use of the singing voice. These, in the opinion of many teachers, have been and continue to be widely misunderstood and frequently disregarded by composers, arrangers and publishers. In order to clarify the basic principles involved and their practical application as well, the American Academy of Teachers of Singing presents the following beliefs, which have been reached through prolonged investigation and study and confirmed by experience.[1]

In this connection, the designation *tessitura*, or "heart of the range," is used in accordance with the definition given by Grove's dictionary as "the prevailing or *average* position of the notes in relation to the compass of the voice, whether high, low, or medium," and is not to be confused with the word *range*. In the following tabulations the vocal limits allocated to the various voices of choral music only are those of the *average amateur singer*, not the professional artist.

We believe

1. that a general tendency exists among composers and arrangers to write voice parts in a dangerously high *tessitura*, and that continued singing in this high *tessitura* is apt to strain and even permanently injure young and adolescent voices, and to prevent normal development of the vocal apparatus.

2. that the safest and best *range* and the safest and best *tessitura*[2] for the various voices are as follows:

FIGURE A4.1

3. That although group singing tends to reduce the mental hazard, no singer can be expected to sing in ensemble a high tone he cannot sing reasonably well in solo singing. For example, the tenor section as a unit cannot be expected to negotiate high B♭ if members of the group cannot sing it individually.

4. That the easiest volume for singers in the upper half of the range is best vocalized *mezzo forte*, and that successful *piano* and *pianissimo* singing are more difficult and require training and guidance.

It must be repeated—and emphasized—that the above beliefs refer to choral singing by amateurs. Directors will find in the groups individual voices of greater *range* than the ones cited above, but such individual cases cannot be considered as the standard in estimating the safe *range* and *tessitura* for the average voice.

General Observations and Suggestions

Published music should provide some indication of *tessitura* as well as range. The range of a song may be conservative and yet the *tessitura* so high as to constitute a strain on amateur voices.

Voice teachers and choral directors should avoid cataloguing voices, particularly male voices, with any degree of finality if the student is less than twenty-two years old. The young voice, especially the untrained one, may not reveal its adult caliber in the earlier years.

Chorus directors should assume the task of keeping in touch with the progress of individual voices, and, because this involves frequent voice trials and the willingness to shift a singer from one part to another, it is frequently neglected. There is the endless temptation to encourage young people to sing certain parts not because their voices are ready for this particular *tessitura*, but because the chorus needs more voices on that part. The choral director should restrain his ambition to produce a perfectly balanced ensemble and to perform overambitious musical programs at the expense of the vocal welfare of his individual singers. This effort on his part would be minimized if composers and arrangers would consider carefully this important matter of *tessitura* and confine their writings within the safe compass of the average young voice.

Appendix 5

"Early Music and the Absence of Vibrato" (A Statement of the American Academy of Teachers of Singing)

Healthy Vocal Technique and the Performance of Early Music

It is a cause for serious concern to the voice teaching profession when conductors, either choral or instrumental, require qualities of vocal tone that may contradict the principles of healthy voice production. Although singers must bear the ultimate responsibility for maintaining the health of their own voices, conductors and collegium directors can and do have enormous influence—in the professional world as a source of income and opportunity, and in the academic world because of ensemble performance requirements.

Today, the Early Music Movement is "big business," not only on campus but also in commerce. The literature recorded by "authentic" organizations grew to astonishing proportions in the 80s and early 90s. More and more untrained singers and singers-in-training are drawn or compelled to the movement as it burgeons in schools and colleges. What was once identified as "music before 1750" has expanded to incorporate Haydn, Mozart, Beethoven, Schubert, and beyond. Understandably, the question is often asked: how early is Early Music?

The so-called Early Music Movement is not as recent a phenomenon as some might believe. For more than a century musicologists have been engaged in editing and publishing the works of outstanding composers from all historical periods. Others have been identifying and characterizing performance conditions and practices, thereby enabling conductors to know the stylistic requirements needed in recreating music from the past. Today's scholars continue to debate the notion of "authentic" performance and challenge the fine points raised by opponents and proponents of the very concept of authenticity. Meanwhile, singers (whether amateurs in school and church choirs, or career-bound vocal majors in colleges, chamber choirs, and the like) are increasingly caught up in the controversy and challenged to meet what could be unreasonable vocal demands—demands often made by conductors without a working knowledge of untrained or developing voices, who seek to impose their understanding

317

of appropriate musical style or simply their own idiosyncratic musical tastes. In this statement, The American Academy of Teachers of Singing turns to what are considered by some to be the special vocal demands of Early Music.[1]

Members of the Academy are troubled by the increasing complaints of colleagues. Their students are being asked to apply purportedly historical vocal techniques in the performance of Renaissance and Baroque music before they are able to perform the much simpler vocal tasks relevant to the basic development of their voices. The problem is compounded when the aesthetic choices of vocally ill-informed or unaware directors extend to questions of vocal vibrato and timbre. Certainly, the uses of wide vibrato, rapid-fire flutter, or wavering tremolo have no place in any singing repertory. The *natural* vibrato that every healthy voice develops is something else entirely. Vocal authorities of today and in years past are generally in agreement that demands for so-called "straight tone" singing for extended periods, or the deliberate alteration of a natural characteristic and healthy vibrato (one that does not call attention to itself as too fast or too slow) can be injurious to the vocal health and natural progress of young voice students.

The timbral characteristic which accompanies the demand for straight tone is the "white" voice (It., *la voce bianca*; Fr., *la voix blanche*). This and other timbral choices, some of which can easily degenerate into pressed phonation or its opposite, breathy production, pose advanced technical and interpretive problems, and are not to be undertaken too early in the developing singer's experience. Certainly the conductor of an Early Music group or the choral director who espouses authentic performance practice, whatever that might currently be (and it is constantly changing), has the right to choose the voices for his or her ensemble. There are enough vibratoless, "white" voices in the world at large to make up groups of such singers to satisfy the conductor whose taste runs in that direction. Asking aspiring young singers to produce sound qualities that are potentially damaging, however, is tantamount to vocal abuse.

Professional singers and singers with advanced technical training may have at their command a greater palette of vocal colors suitable to meeting the demands of those Early Music conductors who are enamored of a particular sound quality. However, even here individual voices vary greatly, and the professional singer must monitor his vocal health closely. The voice teacher should be the primary resource for the development of specific timbral vocal techniques. If these techniques cannot be developed in a healthy fashion, the professional singer should reconsider any prolonged participation in Early Music (especially when such participation brings with it arbitrary vocalization) just as he would reconsider an inappropriate operatic role or musical theater assignment. As it happens, much can be found in the early music repertory that is ideally suited to the aspiring young singer, and, if it is permitted to be sung with healthy, natural tone production, it should be a near perfect learning vehicle. One would be hard pressed, for example, to find better English language repertory than the combination of poetry and music found in the Elizabethan lute song and madrigal for the integrated development of the voice, interpretive resources, taste, and general musicianship of the vocal student whose native language is English.

Part of our responsibility as teachers—a large part from the ethical point of view—is the protection of gifted individuals who show great promise and, if properly nurtured, may contribute to the promulgation of the vocal art of the future. Surely it is time to bring to bear our inter-disciplinary influence—pedagogical, therapeutic, scientific, and medical—upon those instances of Early Music study and performance that are observed to contain unacceptable levels of risk or manifestations of vocal abuse. The individual private voice teacher may have only one avenue of approach—advice to the pupil. Teachers on school faculties may have enough access to conductors to be helpful. Those teachers who have access to the pages of publications for conductors might also serve a useful purpose by discussing dispassionately the pros and cons of what is perceived by some as appropriate period tone, both to its nature as evidenced by contemporary writings and to its relation to vocal health. Organizations of singing teachers might help to support the individual teacher with articles on the subject, which can be offered to students to demonstrate that the risks are perceived by the profession at large and are not simply the result of the individual teacher's personal viewpoint.

Finally, it behooves us as teachers to become better informed on the nature of Early Music and the expectations of its creators, first executants, and modern interpreters.

> Did early writers describe in unmistakable terms the sounds they admired and those they disliked?
> Did the ranges used preclude or promote the use of any particular type of tone?
> Was a distinction made between a soloist and an ensemble singer?
> Do we have any reliable information on the vocal longevity of the singers of the period?
> Did they go on singing well into their later years, as some of our recent and present singers do?

The historical paper trail, recordings that reach toward authenticity, and such local organizations as impinge on our consciousness and may represent the effort of respected and esteemed colleagues—all these are sources for expanded awareness and reasoned response by members of our profession.

Certain it is that across the centuries the human larynx has not undergone any radical transformation. Enterprising modern singers, their mentors, and their collaborators have blown the accumulated dust off seven hundred years of superb vocal music and illuminated the more remote corners of a glorious and gratifying repertory. The health of the voice should always be paramount in our thoughts as well as our ears. Any theory or practice of questionable validity should be explained carefully and challenged. As we familiarize ourselves with the unknown, we must increasingly be aware of insistent demands for inappropriate vocalism. The assertion of questionable tonal preferences, rehearsal procedures, or performance practices which compromise a singer's vocal health and natural function are our mutual concern.

NOTES

INTRODUCTION

1. Emmons and Thomas, 1998, pp. 161–176. In *Power Performance for Singers*, coauthors voice teacher Shirlee Emmons and performance enhancement consultant Alma Thomas apply this research to the singer's art. Adapted from their work, the same concepts may be applied to the choral director's art.

2. Miller, 1987a, p. 17.

CHAPTER 1

1. Sundberg, 1993.

2. Miller, 2000b, p. 38.

3. Miller, 2000b, p. 32.

4. Quotes in the final paragraph have been excerpted from the original manuscript of Miller, *Training Soprano Voices*. They were deleted prior to publication.

5. Sundberg, 1993, pp. 6–7.

6. Griffin et al., 1995, p. 50. Reprinted with permission from The Voice Foundation.

7. Adapted for choral use from McKinney, 1994, pp. 78–79.

8. Adapted for choral use from Miller, 1986, pp. 4–11.

9. Adapted for choral use from Appelman, 1967, pp. 13–23.

10. Adapted for choral use from Sundberg, 1987, pp. 35–48, 57–63.

11. A lip trill is executed by blowing air through vibrating, protruded lips while singing accurate pitches. Except for the pitch frequency, the sound is very like that of little boys playing with their toy cars and making engine noises. Singers who find it difficult to lip trill at first may try the following aids: (1) inhale through the mouth; exhale a short burst of air through loose lips, imitating a horse whinnying; (2) lick the lips before commencing the trill; (3) with teeth and lips shut, place index fingers at the corners of the lips and push against the teeth while blowing air. If these fail, tongue trills sometimes suffice.

12. Miller, 2000a, pp. 27–28.

13. "Vocal fry is the lowest phonational register, occupying the frequency range below the modal or normal register. It has a characteristic popping, frying, or rattling sound which is capable of very little variation of timbre. Its main use is to supply very low notes which are not available in the modal voice. . . . Excessive use of the fry can result in vocal problems." McKinney, 1994, p. 95.

14. Sundberg, 1993, pp. 4, 7.

CHAPTER 2

1. Miller, 1992, p. 20.

2. Morrow, 1988, p. 24.

3. Morrow, 1988, p. 24.

4. Miller, 1992, p. 20.

5. Coffin, 1987, p. 4.

6. Coffin, 1987, p. 56.

7. Vennard, 1967, pp. 163–167.

8. Vennard, 1967, pp. 163–167.

9. Titze, 1982, p. 37.

10. Miller, 1992, p. 20.

CHAPTER 3

1. Hanson, 1987, p. 10.
2. Coffin, 1980, pp. 115, 117.
3. *Cover* is a term colloquially used to describe the contained (nonbellowed) sound of male high notes in and above the upper passaggio, when men go into sufficient head resonance in their upper ranges. Miller (1989, p. 14) gives us a more meticulous definition: "Cover is best described as a process of conscious equalization of the ascending scale through vowel modification so as to *diminish* register demarcations, not to *exaggerate* them."
4. Coffin, 1980, p. xi.
5. Miller, 1989, p. 17.
6. Brown, 1996, p. 109.
7. Brown, 1996, p. 109.
8. Sundberg, 1988.
9. Coffin, 1987, p. 50.
10. Miller, 1991, p. 27.
11. Miller, 1991, p. 28.
12. Haasemann and Jordan (1991) suggest that, for this vowel, the singer encourage the tongue to push forward almost to an [l] consonant to find the correct position. This suggestion appears to work effectively for young singers.
13. Moore, 1990, p. 3.
14. Kiesgen, 1997, p. 29.
15. Bunch, 1993, p. 75.
16. Metfessel, 1932, p. 18.
17. Brodnitz, 1953, p. 84.
18. Sirbaugh, 2004, p. 299.
19. Moens-Haenen, 2003.
20. Seashore, 1938, p. 12.
21. Seashore, 1938, pp. 10–13, 30–52.
22. Appelman, 1967, p. 25.
23. Bunch, 1993, p. 54.
24. Appelman, 1967, p. 23.
25. Titze, 1994, p. 291.
26. Raynes, 1999.

CHAPTER 4

1. Boone, 1997, p. 161. Reproduced with permission from The Voice Foundation.
2. Harvey, 1997, p. 150. Reproduced with permission from The Voice Foundation.
3. Extracted from Harvey, 1997, p. 145. Reproduced with permission from The Voice Foundation.
4. Extracted from Gregg, 1997, p. 166. Reproduced with permission from The Voice Foundation.
5. Extracted from Gregg, 1997, p. 168. Reproduced with permission from The Voice Foundation.
6. Sataloff et al., 1997, pp. 156–158. Reproduced with permission from The Voice Foundation.
7. Sabol et al., 1995, p. 35. Reproduced with permission from The Voice Foundation.
8. Wormhoudt, 1993, p. 111.
9. Miller, 2000b, p. 29.
10. Miller, 2000b, p. 30.

11. Spiegel et al, 1997, pp. 138–139. Reproduced with permission from The Voice Foundation.

12. McKinney, 1994, p. 115.

13. McKinney, 1994, p. 82.

14. McKinney, 1994, p. 89.

CHAPTER 5

1. It is not uncommon for singers to mistake the warmed-up condition of their voices for hoarseness. If the "hoarseness" goes away after thirty minutes, then the problem is that they sang for a long time in a range much higher than their speaking range. As soon as the cords relax—a warm drink will help—they will see that they were not hoarse; they just could not phonate easily in a range lower than that in which they were singing. Thus this symptom affects sopranos and tenors more than the lower voices.

2. Robert Shaw, personal communication to the Collegiate Chorale, April 6, 1948.

3. White, 1978, p. 39.

4. Alma Thomas, personal communication to Constance Chase, May 14, 2000.

5. Personal communication from Robert Shaw to Shirlee Emmons, October 8, 1946.

6. These exercises are borrowed from Stemple's Vocal Function Exercises, appendix 2.

7. A caution: nasal consonants (e.g., ng [ŋ] or humming) can be detrimental when overused. Lip trills or tongue trills provide a useful alternative when trying to promote sensations of "forward" placement. Extended humming of vocalise patterns can cause inefficient muscular habits such as tongue retraction, unless proper placement of tongue is deployed by the director. Lip trills and tongue trills can help establish a steady airflow rate and a balance between air flow and pressure while encouraging forward placement and ease.

8. Johnson and Klonoski, 2003, p. 38. Permission to reprint granted by *Choral Journal*.

9. Johnson and Klonoski, 2003, p. 37. Permission to reprint granted by *Choral Journal*.

CHAPTER 6

1. Private communication with Alma Thomas.

2. Private communication with Alma Thomas.

3. Hughes et al., 1996, pp. 321–326.

4. Hughes et al., 1996, pp. 324–325.

5. Hughes et al., 1996, p. 325.

6. Private communication with Alma Thomas.

7. Heller, 1998, p. 35. Reproduced by permission of Penguin Books, Ltd.

8. Private communication with Alma Thomas.

9. Heller, 1999, p. 37.

10. Adapted for choral use from Emmons and Thomas, 1998, pp. 81–88.

CHAPTER 7

1. Kanfer, 1990, p. 76.

2. Maslow, 1954.

3. Tolman, 1932.

4. Shaw, 1981.

CHAPTER 8

1. This material has been extracted from *Power Performance for Singers* by Shirlee Emmons and Alma Thomas (New York: Oxford University Press, 1998), and is used by permission.

2. Ivey quoted in Friedberg, 1984, p. 16.

3. Emmons and Thomas, 1998, pp. 198–199.

4. Extracted from Sundberg, 1994, pp. 120, 121. Reprinted with permission from The Voice Foundation.

5. Drawn from Emmons and Thomas, 1998, p. 162.

APPENDIX 1

1. Lawrence, 1985. Reprinted with permission from *NATS Journal*.

APPENDIX 4

1. The American Academy of Teachers of Singing was established in 1922, its original goal being to establish much-needed ethical rules of conduct for voice teachers. The first cadre of members was comprised of the most able and principled members of the profession at that time. Since then, the Academy and its forty members has continued to uphold the standards on which it was originally founded. At the present time, its influence can be measured in the existence of the National Association of Teachers of Singing, a large and inclusive body, whose earliest presidents were founding Academy members. NATS, with the Academy, now stands guard over the ethics and ever-expanding research knowledge of the profession. The Academy publishes its own papers on its Web site: www.americanacademyofteachersofsinging.org, and they are available to interested parties upon writing to the Publications Officer, Robert Gartside, at 20 Loring Rd., Lexington, MA 024211–6945. As each new paper, written and approved by the entire membership, is completed, it is published in the *Journal of Singing*, a publication of the NATS organization.

2. The *tessitura* limitations do not prohibit the composer or arranger from writing for the full range of the voice. If composers and arrangers will keep within the suggested range and favor the recommended *tessitura*, voices will be protected, and the choral music will be more effectively performed.

APPENDIX 5

1. On the American Academy of Teachers of Singing, see note 1 to appendix 4. This Academy statement was first published in *The NATS Journal* in 1994 and is reproduced with their permission.

Annotated Bibliography

Apfelstadt, Hilary, Loretta Robinson, and Marc Taylor. 2003. "Building Bridges between Choral Conductors, Voice Teachers, and Students." *Choral Journal* 44:2, pp. 25–32.

Appelman, D. Ralph. 1967. *The Science of Vocal Pedagogy.* Bloomington: Indiana University Press.

An exceedingly thorough text of the vocal mechanism and science of singing. The chapter on phonation defines the action of the laryngeal structure, cartilage, and muscle, in detail and, importantly, in clear, understandable language. In chapter 9, Appelman advances a theory of basic vowels (formants are charted) and "quality alternates" (a modification in which frequency and intensity are not controlled). This articulated theory is the forerunner of much research that continues today. The text is well balanced upon the concept that "scholarly knowledge or great performance skills alone are not enough" (p. 8).

Baken, R. J., and Robert F. Orlikoff. 1987. "The Effect of Articulation on Fundamental Frequency in Singing and Speakers." *Journal of Voice* 1:1, pp. 68–76.

Boone, Daniel R. 1997. "The Singing/Acting Voice in the Mature Adult." *Journal of Voice* 11:2, pp. 161–164.

Brodnitz, Friedrich S. 1953. *Keep Your Voice Healthy.* New York: Harper Row.

Brown, Oren. 1996. *Discover Your Voice.* San Diego: Singular Publishing Group.

Bunch, Meribeth. 1993. *Dynamics of the Singing Voice.* 2nd ed. Vienna: Springer-Verlag.

Dr. Bunch has long been known for her command of vocal science, and her book reflects that broad knowledge in her highly condensed, pragmatic discussions of posture and breathing, phonation, resonation and vocal quality, and articulation. Other chapters in this physically slim but intellectually thorough book reflect also her strong interest in artistry, the psychological aspects of teaching and learning, coordination between the skills demanded of a singer, and "the singer of the future." She notes the great advances in vocal science, and, to professionals in the field, she makes a strong argument in favor of steering a course between attempts "to describe something sensory by the use of imagery and sign-language" alone and the use of "obscure terminology [favored by] medical science" to describe such a sensory skill.

Chase, Constance. 2004. "Using the Warm-up to Improve Choral Tone and Breath Management: Exercises for Balanced Onset." Unpublished paper.

Coffin, Berton. 1980. *Overtones of Bel Canto.* Metuchen, N.J.: Scarecrow Press.

———. 1987. *Coffin's Sounds of Singing: Principles and Applications of Vocal Techniques with Chromatic Vowel Chart.* 5th rev. ed. Metuchen, N.J.: Scarecrow Press.

Dr. Coffin explains the results of research in the field of acoustic phonetics and how the research applies to singing. He thoroughly addresses registers, agility, diction, and breath, stating first the traditional approach, then presenting the results of research that either confirm, discard, or expand on tradition.

Stated perhaps too simply: the fundamental issues of breath, resonance, and phonation may be addressed concurrently from an acoustical standpoint. Coffin has translated formant frequencies into musical notation, jaw openings, and phonetics. Because vowels—which form the changing shape of the vocal tract by movement of tongue, jaw, and lips—have measurable pitch, it is possible, via harmonic pronunciation, to bring the laws of vibration and resonance into concord. When that occurs, breath management is also enhanced.

Dehning, William. 2003. *Chorus Confidential: Decoding the Secrets of the Choral Art.* France: Pavane.

Dickau, David C., and Allan Robert Petker. 1990. *Choral Questions and Answers.* Vol. 3. Cheshire, U.K.: Intrada.

Emmons, Shirlee, and Alma Thomas. 1998. *Power Performance for Singers.* New York: Oxford University Press.

> *Dr. Emmons, a voice teacher, and Dr. Thomas, a performance psychologist, have described how to achieve concrete, demonstrable performing excellence, teaching the reader superior management of the cognitive part of the performing equation. Each of the required mental skills is discussed in depth. The proven psychological tenets of performance itself, the ideal performance state, pre-performance preparation, and post-performance evaluation are presented in highly pragmatic detail.*

Friedberg, Ruth. 1984. *American Art Song and American Poetry.* Vol. 1. Metuchen, N.J.: Scarecrow Press.

Garretson, Robert L. 1993. *Conducting Choral Music.* 8th ed. Englewood Cliffs, N.J.: Prentice Hall.

Gregg, Jean Westerman. 1997. "The Singing/Acting Mature Adult—Singing Instruction Perspective." *Journal of Voice* 11:2, pp. 165–170.

Griffin, Barbara, Peak Woo, Raymond Colton, Janina Jasper, and David Brewer. 1995. "Physiological Characteristics of the Supported Singing Voice, A Preliminary Study." *Journal of Voice* 9:1, pp. 45–56.

Haaseman, Frauke, and James M. Jordan. 1991. *Group Vocal Techniques.* Chapel Hill, N.C.: Hinshaw.

> *This excellent and well-organized text presents a very good accommodation for amateur singers. It shares our opinions on several points: (1) amateurs need some education by the director; (2) amateurs need real vocal answers and not a lot of theory; (3) vocal technical skills are best learned by amateurs when they relate to repertoire. Their "Foundational Method List" of vocal techniques to be taught to choirs organizes the material, which includes many exercises, planning guides, and less in-depth information.*

Hanson, Lloyd W. 1987. "A Survey of Research on Vocal Falsetto." *NATS Journal,* January/February, pp. 9–13.

Harvey, Pamela Lynn. 1997. "The Young Adult Patient." *Journal of Voice* 11:2, pp. 144–152.

Heller, Robert. 1998. *Managing Teams.* New York: DK Publishing.

———. 1999. *Learning to Lead.* New York: DK Publishing.

Hirano, M., Y. Yoshida, T. Yoshida, and O. Tateishi. 1985. "Strobofiberscopic video recording of vocal fold vibration." *Annual Otolaryngological and Rhinological Laryngology,* 94, pp. 588–590.

Hixon, Thomas. 1987. *Respiratory Function in Speech and Song.* London: Taylor and Francis.

Horii, Yoshiyuki. 1989. "Acoustic Analysis of Vocal Vibrato: A Theoretical Interpretation of Data." *Journal of Voice,* 3:1, pp. 36–43.

Hughes, Richard L., Robert C. Ginnet, and Gordon J. Curphy. 1996. *Leadership: Enhancing the Lessons of Experience.* Chicago: Irwin.

Indik, Lawrence R. 2001. "Consonant Feedback in Singing." *Journal of Singing* 57:4 March/April, pp. 15–19.

Johnson, Eric A., and Edward Klonoski. 2003. "Connecting the Inner Ear and the Voice." *Choral Journal* 3:44, pp. 35–40.

Jordan, James. 1996. *Evoking Sound: Fundamentals of Choral Conducting and Rehearsing.* Chicago: GIA Publications.

Kanfer, R. 1990. "Motivation Theory in Industrial and Organizational Psychology." In *Handbook of Industrial and Organizational Psychology,* ed. M. D. Dunnette and L. M. Hough. Vol. 1. Palo Alto, Calif.: Consulting Psychologists Press, pp. 75–170.

Kelly, Terence. 1995. "The Authenticity of Continuous Vocal Vibrato: An Empirical and Historical Examination." *Journal of Singing*, 51, pp. 3–14.

Kiesgen, Paul. 1997. "Warning! Soft Singing May Be Harmful to Your Health." *Choral Journal*, August, pp. 29–31.

Kriegel, R. J., and Marilyn Harris Kriegel. 1984. *The C Zone. Peak Performance under Pressure.* New York: Anchor Press/Doubleday.

Lamb, Gordon H. 1993. *Choral Techniques.* 3rd ed. New York: McGraw-Hill.

Large, J., and S. Iwata. 1971. "Aerodynamic Study of Vibrato and Voluntary 'Straight Tone' Pairs in singing." *Folia Phoniatric* 23, pp. 50–65.

Lawrence, Van M.D. 1985. "Laryngoscope." *NATS Journal*, November/December, pp. 32–35.

Maslow, A. H. 1954. *Motivation and Personality.* New York: Harper and Company.

McKinney, James C. 1994. *The Diagnosis and Correction of Vocal Faults.* Rev. ed. Nashville, Tenn.: Genevox Music Group.

> *Dr. McKinney's handbook is a welcome addition to the literature and a useful tool. His descriptions of anatomical functions are concise, accurate, and they explain the salient points with clarity. He often supplies an exercise to demonstrate the principle at hand. The diagnostic and correctional portions are equally well organized, valuable in content, and very practical in nature.*

Metfessel, Milton. 1932. "The Vibrato in Artistic Voices." *University of Iowa Studies in the Psychology of Music.* Iowa City: University of Iowa Press.

Miller, Richard. 1982. "Diction and Vocal Technique." *NATS Bulletin*, January/February, p. 43.

——. 1986. *The Structure of Singing: System and Art in Vocal Technique.* New York: Schirmer.

> *This text represents the most integrative presentation to be found among in-depth pedagogical sources. As the title indicates, the interrelationship between technical and artistic components is rigorously advanced. Plentiful charts, diagrams, and exercises add to its value as a vocal pedagogy resource.*

——. 1987a. "The Flat Earth School of Vocal Pedagogy." *NATS Journal*, November/December, pp. 17–18.

——. 1987b. "Taming the Terrible Triplets of the Vocal Tract." *NATS Journal*, May/June, pp. 33–35, 42.

——. 1989. "'Covering' in the Singing Voice." *NATS Journal*, November/December, pp. 14–17.

——. 1991. "Thinking Phonetically." *NATS Journal*, January/February, pp. 27–28.

——. 1992. "How Singing Is Not Like Speaking." *NATS Journal*, May/June, p. 20.

——. 2000a. "Sensation Associated with Melismatic Movement." *Journal of Singing* 56:5, pp. 27–30.

——. 2000b. *Training Soprano Voices.* New York: Oxford.

> *Professor Miller, internationally preeminent in his field, gives us here an exhaustive discussion of efficient methods for training sopranos, coupling the latest scientific information on the subject with the results of much practical experience in the field and a broad knowledge of the methods used by master teachers from the past. Excellent diagrams and charts flesh out the science, and well-chosen examples from the soprano repertoire provide a series of exercises, each pertinent to a vocal skill.*

Moens-Haenen, G. 2003. "Vibrato." *The New Grove Dictionary of Music Online*, edited by L. Macy. http://www.grovemusic.com.

Moore, Dale. 1990. "A Plea for Dialogue." *NATS Journal*, January/February, p. 3.

Morrow, Virginia. 1988. "The Significance of Recognititon of the Vowel Core in the Teaching of Singing and in Voice Rehabilitation." *NATS Journal*, January/February, pp. 24–30.

Proctor, D. 1980. *Breathing, Speech, and Song.* New York: Springer Verlag.

Raynes, Christopher. 1999. "Blend." Unpublished paper.

Robinson, Russell, and Jay Althouse. 1995. *The Complete Choral Warm-up Book: A Sourcebook for Choral Conductors.* VanNuys, Cal.: Alfred.

Sabol, Julianna Wrycza, Linda Lee, and Joseph C. Stemple. 1995. "The Value of Vocal Function Exercises in the Practice Regimen of Singers." *Journal of Voice*, 9:1, pp. 27–36.

Sataloff, Robert T., Deborah Caputo Rosen, Mary Hawkshaw, and Joseph R. Spiegel. 1997. "The Aging Adult Voice," *Journal of Voice* 11:2, pp. 156–160.

Seashore, Carl. 1938. *Psychology of Music.* New York: McGraw-Hill.

Shaw, M. 1981. *Group Dynamics: The Psychology of Small Group Dynamics*, 3rd ed. New York: McGraw-Hill.

Simonson, Donald. 1992. "Harmonic Relationships between Sung Pitch, the First Vowel Formant and the Singing Formant: A Study in Enhancing Acoustical Efficiency in Singing," *Voice* (London: British Voice Association) 1, pp. 103–124.

Sirbaugh, Nora. 2004. "The Vocal Print." *Journal of Singing* 60:3, January/February, pp. 297–300.

Skelton, Kevin D. 2001. "Vibrato and Voice: The Choral Singer," *Choral Journal* 44:7, pp. 47–54.

Smith, Brenda, and Robert Thayer Sataloff. 1999. *Choral Pedagogy.* San Diego: Singular.

Brenda Smith conveys here many of the tenets put forth in Group Vocal Techniques *in addition to her own insights and exercises. Having worked closely with Wilhelm Ehmann and Frauke Haasemann for many years, her knowledge of their work is extensive. Dr. Sataloff contributes chapters on anatomy and physiology, medical care of voice disorders, and performing arts medicine. Included is Richard Miller's "Historical Overview of Vocal Pedagogy," an excellent summary.*

Spiegel, Joseph R., Robert Thayer Sataloff, and Kate A. Emerich. 1997. "The Young Adult Voice." *Journal of Voice* 11:2, pp. 138–143.

Sundberg, Johan. 1987. *The Science of the Singing Voice.* DeKalb: Northern Illinois University Press.

Sundberg's contribution to the vocal science literature brings together for discussion research from wide-ranging fields of scientific endeavor. The anatomy and functioning of the human voice is fully explored. The chapter "The Choral Voice" presents the subject from the technical-scientific perspective, addressing such topics as the similarity of phonation frequencies among choral singers. The chapters "Speech, Song, and Emotion" and "A Rhapsody on Perception" are of interest because they report objective scientific data relative to topics that nonscientists customarily discuss from a subjective point of view.

———. 1988. "Vocal Tract Resonance in Singing." *NATS Journal*, March/April, pp. 11–19, 31.

———. 1993. "Breathing Behavior during Singing," *NATS Journal*, January/February, pp. 4–9, 49–51.

———. 1994. "Perceptual Aspects of Singing." *Journal of Voice* 8:2, pp. 106–122.

Syer, John, and Christopher Connolly. 1984. *Sporting Body, Sporting Mind.* London: Cambridge University Press.

Titze, Ingo R. 1982. "Why Is the Verbal Message Less Intelligible in Singing than in Speech?" *NATS Bulletin*, January/February, p. 37.

———. 1994. *Principles of Voice Production.* Englewood Cliffs: Prentice-Hall.

A complex text from a leading current voice scientist. Dr. Titze's own preface states, "The first six chapters are formidable" (p. xiv). A threefold approach to making the concepts understandable is adopted: the written word, scientific or mathematical formula, and graphic illustration. Sample chapters include "Biomechanics of Laryngeal Tissue" and "Vocal Fold Oscillation." Written as a text for the study of voice science or speech-language pathology, it is also of use to professionals in any field related to the mechanisms of voice and speech production.

Tolman, E. C. 1932. *Purposeful Behavior in Animals and Man.* New York: Appleton-Century-Crofts.

Vennard, William. 1967. *Singing: The Mechanism and the Technic.* Rev. ed. New York: Carl Fischer.

Vennard's book is a classic vocal pedagogy source. Chapter topics include acoustics, breathing, attack, registration, resonance, vowels, articulation, and coordination. The chapter on breathing is particularly helpful due to its clarity and comprehensiveness. Each paragraph is numbered for easy access, making for an exceptionally useful index. A thirty-page thesaurus presents terminology used in general science, acoustics, vibration, properties of tone, essentials of a musical instrument, musical instruments, resonance, physiology of breathing and of the larynx, and of resonance, registration, resonance imagery, phonetics, neurology, psychology, pedagogy, research, and voice classification.

Vennard, W., and M. Hirano. 1971. "Varieties of Voice Production." *NATS Bulletin* 27, pp. 26–30.

Webb, Guy B. 1993. *Up Front! Becoming the Complete Choral Conductor.* Boston: E. C. Schirmer.

White, Robert C., Jr. 1978. "Stop Voice Abuse!" *Music Educator's Journal* 63:2, pp. 38–42.

Wormhoudt, Pearl Shinn. 1993. *Building the Voice as an Instrument.* Oscaloosa, Iowa: Micro-Media Services.

INDEX

Consonants (*continued*)
  high notes, defusing consonants for,
    88–90
  initial consonants, 84
  Italian double consonants, 87
  jaw openings and, 83
  middle consonants, 84–87
  schwa, the, 85–86
  singing versus speech, 62
  stopped [t], 81
  as vowels, 87
Cool-down, vocal, 204–205
"Corners," 122
Cover, 114, 322
Crescendo. See *Messa di voce*

Decrescendo. See *Messa di voce*
Diction. *See also* Consonants,
    International Phonetic Alphabet
    (IPA), Tongue, Vowels
  diphthongs, 65, 73
  intelligibility, 66–68, 87–88, 90–91
  as less important, 76, 90
  as "natural," 77
  tone and, 75–79
  tone versus text, 76–77
  vowel modification and, 65
Diphthongs, 65, 73

Falsetto
  exercises to access, 112–113
  training modal voice by means of,
    113–114
  use of in mature males, 111–112
  various types of, 110–111
Fioratura singing. *See* Melisma
Followers
  situations and, 236
  study of, 240–241
  traits of exemplary, 221–223
  types of, 240–242, 244
Forte singing
  breath and, 55
  training, 132
  vowel modification and, 130–132
Front vowels
  how to execute, 72

Glides, 190–191. *See also* Slides
Goal setting, 227–231, 249–250, 273–
    276. *See also* Motivation

Groups
  cohesion in, 216–217
  definition of, 242
  individuals within a group, 244. *See
    also* Followers
  size of, 242–243
  stages of group development, 214–216,
    243–244
  team model, the, 217, 245–246

High pitches, singing
  beauty and, 197
  breath and, 53–54, 107
  defusing consonants for, 88–90
  falsetto, 110–114
  modification of vowels and, 46, 54
Hoarseness, 184, 323
Humming, 191, 323

Imagery
  definition of, 265
  effective practice of, 265–267
  technical skill and, 7–8
  training appoggio and, 21–22
Individual instruction, 168–171
  when to refer, 174–175
International Phonetic Alphabet (IPA)
  advantages of learning, 96–97, 122, 124
  how to mark scores, 97–100
  how to teach, 122–124
Interpretive decisions, 261–264
IPA Consonant Chart, 92–95
IPA Vowel Chart, 69

Leadership
  as affected by followers and situation,
    236
  assessing leadership skills, 237–238
  leadership theory, 234–251
  principles of, 235
  solutions to common problems, 213–231
  team leader, 218–221, 237
  types of leaders, 219, 236–238
Legato
  breath and, 30–36
  definition of, 31
  how to execute, 33–34
  importance of, 31–32
  other musical connections and, 32
  training of, 33–36
Lip-rounding. *See* "Corners"